HINDU KINGSHIP, ETHNIC REVIVAL, AND MAOIST REBELLION IN NEPAL

HINDU KINGSHIP, ETHNIC REVIVAL, AND MAOIST REBELLION IN NEPAL

Marie Lecomte-Tilouine

OXFORD
UNIVERSITY PRESS

OXFORD
UNIVERSITY PRESS

Oxford University Press is a department of the University of Oxford.
It furthers the University's objective of excellence in research, scholarship,
and education by publishing worldwide. Oxford is a registered trademark of
Oxford University Press in the UK and in certain other countries

Published in India by
Oxford University Press
22 Workspace, 2nd Floor, 1/22 Asaf Ali Road, New Delhi 110002

© Oxford University Press 2009

The moral rights of the author have been asserted

First Edition published in 2009
Oxford India Paperbacks 2011
10th impression 2026

ISBN-13: 978-0-19-807225-6
ISBN-10: 0-19-807225-2

Typeset in ITC Legacy Serif Std 10.5/13
by Sai Graphic Design, New Delhi 110 055
Printed in India by Manipal Technologies Limited, Manipal

for Angélique Héron de Villefosse

Contents

Photographs and Map

PHOTOGRAPHS

Acknowledgements

All the chapters have been revised to varying extents. I would like to thank Boyd Michailovsky for his suggestions on the Introduction and Chapter 1, Mary Des Chenes who edited Chapter 3, Michael Hutt and David Gellner for Chapter 5, Declan Quigley for Chapter 6, Michael Roberts for Chapter 8, and David Gellner, who translated Chapter 7 from the French. I also wish to express my gratitude to Mahes Raj Pant for his interesting remarks on Chapters 3 and 6, as well as to Chitre Bahadur Gharti Magar and Krishna Rana Magar who collected some information for me.

Finally, I thank Bernadette Sellers who revised the language of the whole volume.

Publisher's Acknowledgements

The publisher acknowledges the following for permission to include articles in this volume.

Bulletin de l'Ecole Française d'Extrême-Orient, for 'Spirits, Shamans, and Englishmen: Perception of the Others in *Vir Caritra*, a Nineteenth-Century Nepalese Novel'; originally published as 'Les Mondes à part. Représentation des esprits à travers un roman népalais de la fin du XIXe siècle', vol. 89, Paris, 2002: 107–26.

Diogène, for 'Hindu Power in a Tribal Territory: The Cult of Bhume among the Magars'; originally published as 'Le culte de la Déesse-Terre chez les Magar du Népal', vol. 174, 1996: 24–39.

Archives de Sciences Sociales des Religions, for 'The Enigmatic Pig: On Magar Participation in the State Rituals of Nepal'; originally published as 'Entre orthodoxie hindoue et cultes tribaux', vol. 99, 1997: 9–32. Translated and revised as 'The Enigmatic Pig: On Magar Participation in the State Rituals of Nepal', and published in *Studies in Nepali History and Society*, vol. 5, no. 1, 2000: 3–41.

École des Hautes Études en Sciences Sociales (EHESS), for 'Desanskritization of the Magars: Ethno-History of a Group with No History'; originally published as 'La désanskritisation des Magar, ethno-histoire d'un groupe sans histoire', in 'Tribus et basses castes', in M. Carrin and C. Jaffrelot (eds), *Purushartha*, vol. 23, Paris, 2002: 297–327.

Social Science Press, for 'The History of the Messianic and Rebel King Lakhan Thapa: Utopia and Ideology among the Magars', in

D. Gellner (ed.), *Resistance and the State: Nepalese Experiences*, New Delhi, 2003: 244–78; reprinted in 2008.

Berg Publishers, for 'The Transgressive Nature of Hindu Kingship in Nepal'; originally published as 'The Transgressive Nature of Kingship in Caste Organization: Monstrous Royal Doubles in Nepal', in D. Quigley (ed.), *The Character of Kingship*, Oxford, 2005: 101–22.

Centre National de la Recherche Scientifique, for 'Regicide and Maoist Revolutionary Warfare in Nepal: Modern Incarnations of a Warrior Kingdom'; originally published as 'Massacre royal et révolution au Népal', in B. Steinmann (ed.), *Le Maoïsme au Népal. Lectures d'une révolution*, Paris, 2006: 113–45. Translated by David N. Gellner (ed.) as 'The Modern Incarnations of a Warrior Kingdom: Regicide and Maoist Revolutionary Warfare in Nepal', *Anthropology Today*, vol. 20, no. 1, 2004.

Social Analysis, for '"Kill one, he becomes one hundred": Martyrdom as Generative Sacrifice in the Nepal People's War', Special issue on 'Noble Death', Michael Roberts (ed.), vol. 50, no. 1, 2006: 51–72.

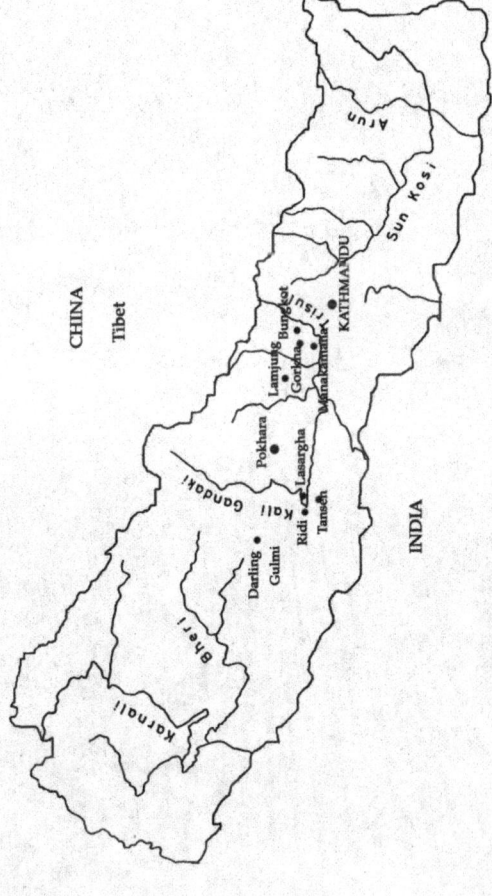

Map of the Main Sites Mentioned in the Text

Note: Map not to scale.
Source: M. Lecomte-Tilouine.

1: A Hanging Bridge over the Kali Gandaki (Photo: M. Lecomte-Tilouine).

Introduction
Stereotypes, Alterocentrism, and Alterization in Nepal

For a long time, Nepal was presented as a model of harmony and tolerance. Its highly composite population maintained apparently peaceful relations, and therefore few studies focused on group interaction. With the 1990s, two successive, yet interrelated, contestatory movements emerged: ethnic revivalism, which transformed the society while itself emerging from that transformation; and the Maoist rebellion, which attracted worldwide attention both for its bloody aftermath and its anachronism. I lived for some months in central Nepal before the emergence of these movements, studying a multi-caste and multi-ethnic village community, where group interaction determined identity, behaviour, and village politics. In such a context, isolating one specific group from its neighbours was simply impossible. This first experience of fieldwork formed my own conception of Nepalese culture, gave shape to the Nepali language I spoke, and decided my future interests. This collection of essays reflects the approach I then adopted—that of basing my analysis of identity and interactions on both written sources and oral conversations, a combination that makes it possible to consider the diachronic dimension of the various groups' relationships. The volume follows two main threads, those of tribal identity and Maoist rebellion, confronted with Hindu kingship and caste organization.

Nowhere more than in the hills of central Nepal has the Hindu caste organization come in close contact with the tribal world. It is believed that Hindu kingdoms were established there only in the fifteenth century because of the alliances that Hindu rulers contracted with the local population, especially tribal chiefs. The indigenous people, or *janajātis*, still form a third of the country's total population. Among them, the Magars, the main autochthonous population of central Nepal and the focus of this volume, represent the largest janajāti group of present-day Nepal, with over one and a half million individuals. They form the Nepalese janajāti group which in the past had developed the closest relationship with Hinduism, Hindu kingship and caste organization, and which countered it most radically recently. In this volume we shall explore the strategies adopted by the Magars in the course of their relations with their high-caste neighbours, from sanskritization and ritual integration to contestation, de-sanskritization, and revolution (Chapters 2–5). These strategies are of course not unilateral, and should be understood within the scope of action allowed to this group by Hindu ideology, and instrumentalization of the latter within the state organization (Chapters 3 and 6). For this reason, they can only be comprehended in their historical context. However, the lack of information on most of the regions which, two centuries ago, had become the kingdom of Nepal, led us to use all the means available to us. Various data thus bring grist to our mill: fiction (novels and poetry), inscriptions, chronicles, myths and rituals, social behaviour, and contemporary accounts, as well as academic or polemical publications.

Our investigation begins and ends with fiction, leading the reader into two quite distinct symbolic universes: first, on a journey with a young Brahmin into the world of spirits, tribal shamans, and English gentlemen (Chapter 1), and finally on another journey, this time in the company of soldiers offering themselves in sacrifice on the bloody path of the Maoist revolution (Chapter 8). Through these two journeys, made one century apart, we will explore the relations with Otherness, be it the result of old classifications as in the first case, or of a new ongoing construction, as in the second. They serve as a framework for underlining some features of Nepalese society and its evolution. The first fiction, a shamanic journey, depicts a travel into alterity, into various worlds existing apart, yet co-existing and interacting with the human, Hindu space. In many respects, the Hindu-tribal relation depicted in this work appears not only as a conquest, but also as a special way of treating Others, which relies on one's ability to view oneself from someone else's perspective, a way that we call alterocentrism. In this book I try to show how alterocentrism has evolved into its complementary face, that is, alterization, parallel to an increasingly negative evaluation of several Hindu fundamental principles. Whereas alterocentrism seems to be a corollary of the social complexity and holistic nature[1] of caste society, alterization emerges with dualist conceptions of society and political opposition. We will return to these two notions later. The last journey into Nepalese fiction is an illustration of how this evolution, whose roots can apparently be traced to tribal revivalism, in turn nourished the Maoist revolution and contributed to the formation of its universe, which is characterized by bilateralism and asymmetry. The Maoist ideology in Nepal thus converges with the tribal movement in the sense that both have led, via different paths, to a conception of society that is composed of two moieties, the oppressors and the oppressed for the first, the Aryans and the Mongols for the second. Both models were constructed in opposition to the caste organization and Hindu monarchy, and in many respects overlap each other.

We have chosen a narrative and fictional framework for this study, considering, like Michel Foucault, that '...discourse is not only what translates struggles or systems of domination, but also what one struggles for, and the means by which one struggles'.[2] Focusing on the case of Pierre Rivière,[3] who killed 'his father, mother, brother and sister', Foucault highlighted the real 'battle' of discourses, which took place between doctors, representatives of the law, villagers, and the murderer himself, that surround the fate of an individual.

[1] The caste system was defined as holistic by Louis Dumont (1966). Such a system cannot be explained by its component parts alone, rather the system as a whole determines how the parts behave.

[2] '...le discours n'est pas simplement ce qui traduit les luttes ou les systèmes de domination, mais ce pour quoi, ce par quoi on lutte...' (Foucault, *L'ordre du discours*, p. 12).

[3] Foucault (ed.), *Moi Pierre Rivière*.

The social dialogue in Nepal recalls this multi-sided narrative dynamism. It evokes a permanent construction game in which the same elements are placed in different orders by different players to make up an edifice that is more or less fragile.[4] In such a context, social anthropology cannot remain the study of a single group, region, or time. Against the backdrop of the diversity characterizing the geographical environment, status, language and religion of Nepalese society, and the communal and political trends of these last decades, identity has been constructed through a relational game between groups in perpetual motion, where each is defined with respect to the Other. However, this chronic instability does not mean an absence of functioning rules. These, we would argue, shape the way the Other is treated, and are followed by everyone. Their study thus represents, rather than that of the changing social regroupings they regulate, an effective way in which to understand Nepalese and, more generally, Hindu society.

Nepalese society has long been structured by the caste system, that is, a social organization founded on internal alterity. Though this type of social organization was clearly imposed on a large section of the population, notably the indigenous peoples, over the course of a few centuries identity and alterity, as we show later, present reflective (or retroprojective) features rather than projective ones.

When dealing with identity and alterity, the anthropologist cannot dissociate him/herself from the study, for s/he is also representative of Otherness in the society studied. The problem is how to take oneself into account, or how to carry out an embryonic auto-epistemology, without being ensnared into a purely subjective narrative.

A position now common in anthropology takes the view that since objectivity is a utopian goal, it is preferable to adopt a clearly committed attitude and delight in subjectivity. In Nepal, for instance, this trend is advocated in the field of history by Pratyoush Onta, who 'suggests that historians abandon the disciplinary virtues as "objectivity" along with the state-centric view of Nepali history',

---

[4] For a closer look at the way the terms 'communalist' or 'sectarist' have been used by various groups in competition, see Chapter 4.

and 'produce passionate poly-centric histories...'.[5] A multiplicity of subjective accounts would thus allow one to solve the problem of the free exercise of research and of the links between 'objectivity' and the 'official viewpoint'. However, to borrow Plato's allegory, this would amount to painting with a single colour the shadows which are all that men chained in a cave can perceive of the outside world, arguing that a reproduction of their exact colours is impossible. The multiplicity of such paintings in monochrome would not provide a better understanding of the world, but would at least have the advantage of troubling the men in the cave, who would realize that there are as many realities as there are painters.[6] I should add that the chained men would not get a more accurate understanding of the outside world were the artists to begin by explaining their choices of using a particular colour, following the precept of the subjectivists who often suggest that the 'subject' (that is the scholar) defines his own position at the outset.[7]

LONG-LASTING AND EPHEMERAL STEREOTYPES

Leaving aside the issue of objectification in anthropological study, the objectification through which inter-personal or inter-group relations are constructed *within* the society studied is likely to be erased by an over-reliance on a subjective viewpoint. This objectification is manifest in the stereotypes that regulate, among other things, political and social relations in Nepal, and play a fundamental role in group identity. A short excerpt of a chat posted on *sajha.com* provides an illustration of the strength of old Hindu stereotypes in contemporary Nepalese society:

Superior Nepali (Pandit): All newars are stupid 'JYAPU'. They live in great cultivate land but they dig every land with using 1000 century's old tool.... Anyway, we are Bahun and we are superior in Nepal. You Mongols follow us....

---

[5] Quoted in Kraemer, 'Requiring a Social History: Must Nepali History be Re-written?'

[6] In this sentence, it is not clear whether the passionate polycentric accounts ought to be written down by the same person or by several. The result, however, would not be clear in either case.

[7] We shall note in passing that this initial effort is contradictory, since it assumes that objectivity regarding the subject is possible.

Great Newar: ... Are you trying to say that Newar [are] also corrupted thief people as you...?

Chettri-desh raxhak ['the protector of the country']: ...Bahun ra Newar...ja bhagera hamro deshbata [Bahuns and Newars, go away from our country].

Discussions of this type finds an echo in large-scale political relations. For instance, when the first prime minister after the advent of democracy was asked by Indian journalists as to why the Teraiwasis (inhabitants of the Terai) had not enlisted in the Nepalese army, he replied: 'It is because they are cowards'.[8] While 'the superior Pandit' and 'the protector Chetri'[9] are old ideas, stereotypes also fluctuate with political situations and ideologies. The Magars of the Gulmi region, for instance, adopted a new image for their group in the 1990s. They were and are still divided into two categories: the Twelve clans and the Eighteen clans. In the 1980s, the Twelve clans were said to be 'higher' because they employed Hindu priests and ate pure food; however, the members of the latter group now claim that the Eighteen clans are 'the pure Magars' and conceive of themselves as a mixed group 'of Thakuri blood and Magar milk'. In the case of the indigenous peoples of Nepal, 'authenticity' has thus emerged as a new criterion for prestige, counter-balancing previous evaluations in terms of Hindu orthodoxy.

Stereotyping is a banal corollary of social clustering, but one consequence of the castes' holistic functioning is that any point of view is relative and determined by the group stereotype. All perceptions are viewed as having been modified by the position of the subject (as a member of a specific group) within society. It seems that the caste structure thus relies not only on acknowledging the difference of each group within it, as stated by Louis Dumont,[10] but

[8] *The Nepal Digest*, 14 August 1998.

[9] The name of this caste deriving from Kshatriya, is spelled as Chetri, Chhetri, Ksetri, Kshetri, Ksatri, and Kshatri. I have retained the various spellings found in citations, but otherwise use Chetri in this book.

[10] As Louis Dumont (*Homo Hierarchicus*, p. 242) had already noted long ago: '*La différence reconnue d'un groupe, qui l'oppose à d'autres, devient dans le schéma hiérarchique le principe même de son intégration dans la société*' (In the hierarchical scheme a group's acknowledged differentness whereby it is contrasted with other groups becomes the very principle whereby it is integrated in society) (English translation: Dumont, *Homo Hierarchicus*, p. 191).

also on emphasizing and *mastering* these differences. The emphasis on the castes' alterity reaches a point where social groupings are not distinguished from animal species, either in language (for both are termed the same, *jāt* or *jāti*), or in the way they are conceived. Indeed, social groupings are often described as made up of peoples having the same distinctive physiological features.[11]

What I have called the 'mastering' of the various values specific to different castes or groups refers not only to their knowledge, but also to the ability to use them, particularly to evaluate one's own values. In addition, this 'mastering' was shaped and controlled by the State in Nepal. Indeed, group specificities were acceptable only if shared by all members of the same jāt (caste or ethnic group), and up until the 1960s the Nepalese State always exercised control over jāt-specific practices and values to ensure this principle.[12]

Though a global hierarchy based on status purity characterizes the whole social organization, which was legally controlled until 1963, nothing is considered absolute by any group.[13] This can be seen, for instance, in the range of criteria used by different groups inhabiting the same locality to claim a superior position. In central Nepal, for instance, three groups are in competition: the Brahmins argue that they represent 'the first human beings beneath the gods', the Kshatriyas that they are of royal descent, and the Magars that they are the first inhabitants of the region and its only legitimate masters. Being holistic does not prevent the society from recognizing the legitimacy of each of these points of view, which are taken into account by the entire population depending on the

---

[11] The colour of the skin and the form of the nose are important criteria of group distinctiveness, but the physical distinction can go as far as believing that the low castes have one pair of ribs less than the high castes (personal communication, K. Lundstrom-Baudais, about the region of Jumla, western Nepal).

[12] On this subject, see M. Lecomte-Tilouine, 'The Ruling of the Social Groups: From Species to Nation'.

[13] In contrast, the class-related variations in tastes or opinions in a country like France are not usually known on a global level, and individuals perceive their own choices as 'natural', if not universal. Their class base forms an unformalized reality, which is revealed in all its complexity in sociological studies such as Bourdieu's *La distinction, critique sociale du jugement*.

context (as demonstrated in Chapter 2 regarding autochthony). One consequence of the knowledge cultivated of the Other's distinctiveness and unique perception of the self, which stems from their belonging to a particular group—and which also highlights the relative nature of one's own values and perceptions—is the attitude of alterocentrism, as stated above.

THE OTHER AS THE SELF'S REFERENCE POINT: ALTEROCENTRISM

The reflexivity of inter-personal relationships struck me at once when I began my fieldwork in central Nepal. I had the feeling that the individual, when facing the Other, projected onto himself or herself a vision of his/her own person or culture as seen by the Other (or at least from what was culturally constructed as this particular Other's point of view, that is his stereotypic point of view).

To clarify what I mean by alterocentrism, let me give a simple and clear example. In the hills of Nepal, several people, on meeting me for the first time, told me by way of introduction: 'for you, we are black people', whereas I felt that it would have appeared more natural for them to remark that compared to them, I am white. The villagers at once adopted my supposed perception of themselves, rather than the reverse. The idea was sometimes developed further: 'for you, we are *all* black people', which conveyed the idea that compared to you, our distinctions in terms of skin colour are so insignificant that we must all be ranked in the same low category. The Other's supposed point of view thus modifies not only one's perception of the self, but also that of the group, and even of society at large. This is how a hierarchy based on variations in skin colour is suddenly rendered meaningless when faced with someone of a radically different hue and her supposed perceptions.

The paradigm of skin colour was often correlated with or replaced by that of wildness. Once, for instance, when I met a man in a remote village in Pyuthan district and asked him who he was, he replied: 'Well, I am a Thakuri, but does it really matter? For you, we are all savages, *jangali*'. As with skin colour, the 'civilized' aspect of the radical Other had the faculty of abrogating at once the internal hierarchical ranking of groups, which were merged into a single category opposed to the new one in a spontaneous construction made on the basis of the Other's supposed point of view.

This attitude is, of course, striking for the anthropologist, who thus clearly perceives that his/her presence itself modifies the society studied by creating an undifferentiated group of 'us' through his/her stereotypic point of view. It also reveals that the anthropologist, in his or her own relationships with and influence on the society observed, should be understood not only as a subject but also as a particularly objectified subject (that is, as a member of a defined category of Others with whom precise types of relationships are socially and culturally determined).[14]

In this context, alterocentrism is primarily social and thus differs from Jean-Paul Sartre's concept of reflexive conscience, in which the Other's gaze reveals that the self-subject is also an object from a moral point of view. However, both concepts have in common their reflexiveness, since alterocentrism is constructed by lending to the Other a stereotyped vision of oneself as a member of a defined category (be it social or racial). Alterocentrism (like the reflexive conscience) is a retroprojection. It is thus a complex or indirect form of ethnocentrism, a social construction of a self-definition retroprojected through the intermediary of another group, to whom this view is assigned.

The extent to which different points of view on values and practices form part of the villagers' common experience and knowledge probably expresses one of the functioning principles of the caste organization. Contrary to communalist societies, where autonomous groups cohabit with little knowledge of their neighbours' practices and views—or without taking them into consideration—which leads to culturalism, caste, being holistic, fosters attitudes of relativism and reflectivism. Interestingly, however, this relativism is not universal; it finds its limits within the boundaries of the Hindu kingdom, which includes categories of beings treated in different ways. On the other hand, Hindu relativism is unique in that it incorporates non-human beings, such

---

[14] And this remains true even after a long stay. I have often seen my closest friends worrying about whether they appear black, wild, or even ape-like in my eyes.

as animals and spirits. The latter are viewed as alter egos, while the excluded human groups may be said to embody strangeness rather than Otherness.

HIERARCHY AND ALTEROCENTRISM

Even if the anthropologist's alterity follows him/her like a shadow, s/he is not the only person to embody Otherness within the groups that make up Nepalese society. S/he may therefore get the opportunity to observe relations between these indigenous Others. Let us again take a short example. One night, after returning from a successful hunting expedition with a group of people including three Magars and one Brahmin, we were invited to eat our pheasants at the house of one of the Magars. A glass of alcohol was placed before each of us, except the Brahmin, who then protested: 'and what about me'? In response to his apparent wish to drink, all the Magars laughed and ignored this unacceptable proposition, thus collectively upholding his 'normal' position in the social hierarchy. The Magars had separated the 'drinkers', or *matwālī* (a category that included myself), from this Other. In this instance, perhaps influenced by my own presence, objectification (of the Brahmins by the Magars) was clearly stronger than subjectivization (the will of this particular Brahmin under those particular circumstances). Such instances are frequently observed among untouchable groups in their relations with individuals perceived as pure, including the barbarous anthropologist. In my own experience, it was simply impossible to obtain water or cooked food from them, even if I asked.[15] Of course, in these two cases, taking the other's alterity into account is certainly based on the fact that until the 1950s, individuals from lower castes were severely punished if they 'polluted' people from upper castes by offering them any 'cooked' food,[16] water or alcohol. However, the necessity of not polluting the Other seems to form only one aspect of a more general principle, which has more to do with respecting

[15] In the village where I had been conducting studies since the 1980s, in 2006, with the local Maoist government, commensality rules evolved, but were still very restricted since the only food that could be received from 'impure' castes was tea.

[16] 'Cooked food' includes milk and any food that has been transformed, such as a sliced cucumber or a peeled banana.

the Other's otherness and not imposing or projecting on him one's selfness, since the same phenomenon takes place even when there is no question of purity.

The acknowledgment, maintenance, or even reinforcement of the Other's alterity thus appears as important as hierarchization based on the criteria of pure and impure. It is true that under exceptional circumstances, such as collective meals, the former criterion does not rule out the latter, and is subordinated to it. Thus, the Nepalese, like other Hindus, believe that what is valid for the highest group is acceptable for all others. However, the food considered proper for Brahmins is not viewed as 'good' or even 'appropriate' *by* others *for* themselves (and even *for* others *by* Brahmins). The high content of sugar and butter in the Brahmins' food, for instance, disgusts the Magars. The latter repeatedly define themselves as those who do not like sweetness, as opposed to their high-caste neighbours. This difference in taste as a marker of identity is so strong that the Brahmins' festive food, which consists of bananas and yoghurt or rice pudding, became the object of collective protest by the Magars of Darling (Gulmi district) when the Magar village headman, who thought it would be easier to offer the same things to everybody, tried to impose it on them at the Dasain festival instead of the meat and alcohol he had to serve them traditionally. The headman subsequently had to resort to the previous custom of offering a specific meal to each of the groups inhabiting the village he was responsible for.

Furthermore, if social hierarchization results in a tendency on the part of the highest groups to impose their diet on others in the case of collective meals for reasons of convenience, instances abound when they also recognize the specificity of their own diet and take into account that of the others. This may reach a point where an individual offers another person not only something that he dislikes, but even something strictly forbidden for himself. For instance, the Brahmins of Karikot, Syangja, buy beer and pork for their Magar guests when they invite them to a wedding. This food is then prepared and served separately by the latter, since it is highly polluting for the former. The Brahmin host explained, 'just as chickens eat grain, and cows grass, Bahuns eat rice pudding and bananas, and Magars pork and alcohol', again revealing how the various human groups are similar to animal species and requiring specific treatment. Of course, it may be argued that it is more often Magars who are seen running downhill to find bananas for their Brahmin domestic priests when they come to perform a ritual and have to be fed at their home than a Brahmin buying pork and beer for Magar guests. But the principle is shared by all, and appears clearly in the ritual context where the divine beings receive the food appropriate to their identity—milk, goat, sheep, buffalo, chicken, and even pigs—whatever be the devotee's diet. In this last instance, the general hierarchization of society presents an anomaly, since the class of gods, collectively ranked above men, is internally divided into different categories based on their diet, yet are not degraded by it relative to human beings. They, in fact, form a kind of parallel, superior society.

The idea that each group has a specific diet that only suits its members is repeatedly demonstrated to the foreign anthropologist who asks to stay in unfamiliar places. The first answer is usually 'No, you can't stay here because we don't know what you eat and we can't feed you properly', regardless of whatever caste the host belongs to. Upon insisting that any food would be fine, shelter is indeed offered, but villagers keep worrying that the foreigner would waste away from being fed the local food.

The same holds true of many other registers. During my stay in a village in the Gulmi district, people made almost no comment about my European clothes and behaviour, except on two points: walking barefoot outside (even over very short distances),[17] and going out with my hair loose. Although a great many villagers had no shoes themselves, walking barefoot was incompatible with the 'civilized' status they had projected on me, and was the object of much reprobation. In the same vein, going out with my hair loose was incompatible with my stereotype, since it was an attribute of witches,

---

[17] In fact, the Magars suggested several times that I keep my shoes on when entering their houses although this is considered polluting, explaining that 'it is long and boring to remove sports shoes'. And I could never figure out if it was a matter of simple politeness—if they thought that their rules were not to be imposed upon a foreigner—or if they had decided to ignore their purity rules with someone who was transgressing them anyway by not respecting the menstrual taboos imposed on women.

wild men, forest spirits, and people in mourning for the recently dead. On the other hand, within these limits of the acceptable for my 'stereotype', any eccentricity perceived as 'ultra-modern' or 'ultra-civilized' (like sleeping in a bag, watching the moon or birds with binoculars, wearing male clothes, and listening to music with headphones) was not only accepted, but much appreciated, because it was seen as normal for my jāt, species. My person was so closely linked with modernity that whenever a helicopter was seen in the sky, people thought it was going to land and take me away. They were somehow disappointed to see me finally leaving their village on foot, as they themselves would. In this context, integration is thus not about behaving like the others, but of being representative of a distinct, definite, and stereotyped group, while remaining within the limits of the locally socially acceptable.

DIALOGUE WITH OTHERS:
'TRIBAL PEOPLE' AND ANIMALS

The Hindu-tribal dialogue is based on alterocentrism, because the 'tribal people' embody something more than alterity for high-caste Hindus; they express or induce relativity, highlighting the arbitrariness of social rules and values. Both parties' different practices indeed reflect their specific values and ideologies. An example of this phenomenon can be found in the play *Śilanyās*. (The play has recently been severely criticized by the Nepal Magar Association, which asked for its removal from the school curriculum for its offensive portrayal of their group.[18]) Written by a Nepalese Brahmin and published in 1964, the play depicts the kingdom of Gorkha at a time when the king was a Magar, before its conquest by the Hindu king Drabya Shah in 1560. The words placed in the mouth of the Magar king by the Brahmin author are quite remarkable for their reflexive relativism. In one episode, the Magar king reminds his high-caste courtiers that all people are made of the same flesh and blood, and are thus fundamentally identical. He

---

[18] In another similar case, in the novel *Sumnima* written by B.P. Koirala, the Brahmin hero revalues his own culture by comparing it to the imagined Kirant one. The book was rejected and burnt by the Kirant recently (see Hutt, 'Reading Sumnima').

then goes on to explain that both Brahmins and Magars eat 'rotten food': the Brahmins appreciate spoiled milk (that is, yoghurt) the same way as the Magars do their fermented beer. The Magar king ends his discourse by demonstrating that the persons who emerged from Brahma's mouth, that is, the Brahmins, cannot be anything but impure since only impure things may come out of the mouth, whereas the Magars, who emerged from Brahma's feet, are the purest creatures since people bow at the feet of others, and worship this part of the body.

The criteria on which purity and impurity are based are thus not absolute in Hindu society since the exercise of relativizing or contesting them is undertaken very frequently, and seems easy for a Brahmin when placing these arguments at the doorstep of an imaginary Magar character.[19]

The customs of a group, such as the Magars, lead their Hindu neighbours to re-evaluate their own values in relation to (what they believe to be) Magar values (=alterocentrism) as is seen in the play Śilanyās, and at the same time to reject this group in the most radical alterity, where human beings are associated with malevolent spirits and the wilderness (=alterization), as appears clearly in the novel Vīr caritra (Chapter 1). The equilibrium of these two complementary aspects seems affected by the context, notably the context of enunciation, but also by the general context and its specific political situation, which creates new categories of alterized beings. As though they were taking upon themselves the alterity of the previously alterized Others, their emergence induces an incorporation of the latter as relative Others. Such seems to be the case of the Maoists.

Contrary to the various categories distinguished in the past, on the basis of their caste status, religious practices, languages, etc., the most recently constructed category of beings, the Maoists, has no social, religious, linguistic, or racial roots, but is entirely constructed on the basis of opinion and commitment. Their ideology, however, has led them to follow specific practices, which are considered

---

[19] These extracts are quoted by Tek B. Pun (2060 VS/2003), who recalls his experience as a Magar student when studying this text, which contains many derogatory passages about his group.

anti-Hindu. Both Maoists and their opponents view each other as dehumanized beings, as sanguinary and transgressive creatures, and the Maoists, as shown in Chapter 7, have probably contributed to the construction of this new social order by challenging and reversing the ancient Hindu institutions of war and sovereignty. Once this reversal takes place, all values are inverted: the 'great men' of the past become the exploiters, the king a butcher; happiness is sorrow, life is death and death brings life (Chapter 8). This emergence of a new political power operated through transgression is far from being a revolution in itself, as transgression is central to the monarchic institution as well (Chapter 6). What is more revolutionary, perhaps, is the absence of relativism towards the Maoists and within the Maoist discourse, in their relations with the enemy. It may be suggested that this is temporary, and/or due to the fact that materialist dialectics provides the Maoists with a self-sufficient ideology by exploring several aspects or points of view simultaneously.

In contrast to their attitude towards those alterized human beings, the Nepalese (at least in the region of central Nepal with which I am familiar) often relativize their worldview vis-à-vis animals. Adopting the latter's point of view, they frequently present themselves as demons, for instance: 'we are Rakshas (anthropophagous demons) for animals'. This relativism sometimes goes even further when the very nature of the self is revealed from some animals' point of view. Thus, parrots are said to distinguish witches from ordinary people and to sometimes disclose this by saying it out loud, crows know one's hidden feelings, etc. However, the relationship is sometimes more intimate. On one occasion, for instance, a villager told me that men moult regularly. And when I asked how he knew that, he explained that sloughed human skins are only perceived by snakes, who fear them, believing them to be real men. In the same vein, he went on to say that only men see the frightening sloughed skins of snakes, which are unaware that they actually are moulting. In this case, each member of a couple of alter egos possesses knowledge about the Other's real nature. Man deduces his real nature from his perception of the Other (the snake's frightening sloughed skins and its unexplained fear, which is attributed to the sight of sloughed human skins). This reasoning comes close to Descartes' analogy about the thinking subject: 'I think, therefore I am', and so I can apply this principle to the Other and consider that since he thinks as I do, he is thus as I am. The point of reference in the reasoning, however, is not the self but rather the Other: the snake is moulting and I can see it. It frightens me. On the other hand, the snake is sometimes frightened for no apparent reason; it may be that I also moult and it can see me. Now, I do not see my sloughed skin, so the snake does not see its own either.

BAD SPIRITS, MUSLIMS, AND WESTERNERS: THE REVERSED OTHERS

Relativism is also applied, though in a much more developed way, vis-à-vis wild spirits. One could even say that this principle is at the root of their conception, through mirror-inversion.[20] The forest spirits are a kind of 'reversed' humans. On the physical register, their feet are turned backwards, their hair, though long, stands up straight on their heads, they eat from the tops of their hands, and some have hollow backs. Their perception and one's perception of them is equally reversed and/or relative. They can be standing behind you when you see them in front of you. A single grain of rice offered by them may feed an entire human family but if they touch the villagers' grain when it is drying, whatever the size of the heap, it will not be sufficient for the family. They live in the jungle, wild beasts are their domestic animals, and they hunt the villagers' domestic animals as if they were wild beasts. They awaken when men are asleep and they see in the dark. The point of view of these anti-human beings, clearly the product of self-alterization, is nevertheless often taken into consideration by villagers, whatever their caste, to relativize their own values. First, the harm that the forest spirits cause men is said to be reciprocal. The spirits provoke disease in men just as men do in them, through a permanent bilateral game of fear. They steal the villagers' produce as do the latter in their wild realm, and men believe they harm the wild beings as much as the latter harm them. This predatory mirror game regulates the unexplained and brings meaning to unforeseen events. In addition, the ideas and

---

[20] On this construction, see Lecomte-Tilouine, 'Hommes/divinités de la forêt'.

values attributed to these antinomic beings are also often taken into consideration. Thus an old Magar once told me, 'Cowdung, for us, is very pure, but for the forest spirits, it is shit.' The old man continued with this train of thought: 'The forest spirits hate all products of the cow, but they eat its meat. In fact, the cow only eats grass, it is thus very pure, why not eat its flesh? But they do not eat fish, because fish eat corpses.' In his opinion, the forest spirits had different ideas of purity and impurity, with which he somehow agreed in theory because they seemed more logical than his own: shit is shit and the flesh of pure animals should be eatable; but his doubts concerning the soundness of his own values did not affect his practices, which defined him as a human being as opposed to wild beings.

The forest spirits played the same role for this old Magar as the Magar king had for the Brahmins in the play *Silanyās*: as a category of beings sharing the same universe, but with a distinct point of view of their own, determined by their specific position within the universe and its attached values. Distinctive features are thus attributed to invisible beings who play the same role as other categories of alterized human beings, showing that alterocentrism relies primarily on attributing values and practices to the various categories of beings (that is, to stereotypes), rather than on observing their practices. In times of sickness, a villager offers a domestic animal, or what he conceives as legitimately belonging to the human sphere, to the wild spirits. In the conception of a world ruled by competition between two antagonistic universes, the domesticated and the wild, this offering is both a substitution (of the sick person by one living being belonging to the human realm) and a compensation (for the destruction and theft that humans carry out in the forest). As shown in Chapter 2, this compensation often takes the form of restoring something to the wild world: a chicken is sent to the forest, alive, so that it can become wild 'again' and thus regain the spirits' property. Within this framework, it is normal for wild spirits to offer men their own domestic animals, that is, wild pheasants, when humans pass diseases on to them.[21] The meaning of one group's practices

---

[21] The glance of wild spirits makes humans sick, and the screams of villagers who graze their cattle in the forest have the same effect on the spirits.

and values is thus relative, and makes sense only in relation to the Other's supposed values and actions.

In central Nepal, along with forest spirits, witches (*boksī*) and Muslims are also considered 'reversed' or 'negative', *ulṭo*, and not simply—hierarchically—different, that is, high or low (*ṭhulo/sāno* or *uccā/nīc*), pure or 'spoiled' (*choko, biṭulo*). Both these categories are described as 'reversed' on the basis of their practices, but are not treated the same. In the case of witches, villagers adopt an alterocentric view when referring to their 'reversed activities'. Thus, they say that they should not wash on certain days of the week or sew on others because it would be *ulṭo kām* or 'reversed activities'. On such days, it is the witches who perform these activities. The point of reference, again, is the Other, whose practices negatively affect those of the self. This idea—witches wash on this day, so if I washed, I too would be a witch—shows once again that identity relies not only on pure and impure activities, but on the observance of behaviour deemed proper to each category of being. In this case, it is not even the activity itself that is negatively or positively connoted, but its time schedule.

The precautions against assimilation into another category of being form an important component of children's education. They are taught to separate the wild and the civilized, the masculine and the feminine, right and reversed (*sulṭo* and *ulṭo*), the pure and the impure, for all these categories may be confused, and have to be internalized during childhood. Identity construction and maintenance are thus fruits of a verbal or prescriptive education, whereas learning skills rely above all on children's observation of adults.[22] Children are viewed as wild creatures who need to be refined or domesticated. When their parents prepare food, they often steal small pieces of raw meat and pop it in their mouths unless prevented by a gentle rap. Reprimands remind them to not behave like wild animals. When they start eating corn on the cob with their teeth, they are told to take the grains off by hand before eating, as they would turn into monkeys otherwise; girls are forbidden to play the flute lest they grow moustaches, etc.

---

[22] Sagant, 'Traditions enfantines: l'apprentissage des techniques au Népal oriental'.

The other category of 'reversed' human being, the Muslims, is depicted as being negative in a manner more absolute than the witches. The ways in which they wash their faces or sacrifice their animals (by cutting the throat instead of decapitating it), for instance, are said to be 'reversed', as is their religious prescription to wear a beard while Hindus are exhorted to keep some hair on the top of their heads (the *tupī*), etc.[23] These reversed practices are not likely to be adopted by others, and neither are they used by Hindus to relativize the validity of their own practices and values. Furthermore, interrelations with this category of negative Others are said to produce negative results. The reaction against Muslims' actions is a factor often mentioned as being a driving force behind the major historical transformations of Hindu society, or, more precisely, of what among their practices is today negatively perceived by the Hindus. These practices are now considered medieval innovations to protect Hindus from the Muslims. Such is the case of child marriages, the custom of Sati, and even the caste system itself, which are often depicted as protective measures that emerged as a reaction to the Muslim invasion of India.[24] The Muslims, as a unique negative category, thus play a major role in Hindu society as those who allow the rejection of some social practices and values into the sphere of strangeness once they became negatively connoted.

However, this specific treatment of Muslims does not rule out a disposition for alterocentrism, well illustrated by the following joke that praises some practical advantages of Muslim monotheism over Hindu polytheism, which a Brahmin boy[25] in Isma, Gulmi, told me:

---

[23] Muslims are even said to put their shoes on 'backwards', that is, the left one first (personal communication, G. Maskarinec).

[24] This is an idea I heard mentioned several times in Nepal, but one that I have never seen written down. It is, on the other hand, one of the main ideas among Indian Hindu fundamentalists as this short excerpt taken from www.hindutva.org shows: 'Sati, along with Child Marriage, the conducting of Wedding ceremonies (among Punjabis) in the dead of the night after midnight, and the practice of women covering the face veil (Ghungat) [sic] were the result of the oppressive conditions prevailing during the dark days of Muslim tyranny during the middle ages in India.'

[25] Jivan Kumar Pantha.

One day a Hindu and a Muslim were quarrelling. About what? The Hindu was saying that he was the greatest and the Muslim was saying that he was the greatest. So the Muslim told the Hindu: 'All right, let us jump into this pond and let the one who is taken out from there first be the greatest.'

The Hindu agreed and both of them jumped into the pond.

The Muslim called: 'Hare Allah'[26] and the god Allah arrived immediately and took him out of the water. As for the Hindu, he first said: 'Hare Shiva', but while Shiva was arriving, running, he said again: 'Hare Vishnu' and Shiva went back. Then Vishnu arrived in turn, but he said once again: 'Hare Ram' and Vishnu went away, considering that he was calling Ram. Again, while Ram was on his way, he called 'Sita', and Ram went away, noticing that it was Sita who was being called. In this way, the Hindu died in the pond.

Chapter 1 shows how Westerners ('the white people'), like the Muslims with whom they were often associated in the past under the broad category of 'beef-eaters', are also somehow perceived as reversed people, and assimilated with the malevolent and shamanic spirits a century ago. But their status evolved during the first half of the twentieth century, at least in Kathmandu Valley and the tourist regions of Nepal, and alterocentrism ensued. This evolution is visible in the way that descriptions of the country, especially anthropological writings about Nepal, which were mainly produced by Westerners until 1990, were received.

IDENTITY AND ANTHROPOLOGY

As several authors have noted, foreigners' discourses were viewed as the truth in Nepal, and never discussed or challenged until (roughly speaking) 1990. Their views were adopted by local groups such as the Tibeto-Burman population, which defines itself as Mongols from the Mongoloid class to which they were assigned by British scholars. Scholars on both sides have highlighted this uncritical reception of Western scholars' discourse. Seira Tamang qualifies it as an 'uncritical adulation', and John Whelpton as 'excessive deference'. However, as noted by the same author, '...there seems a tendency now in some quarters to go to the opposite extreme and react with indignation when outsiders express any definite opinion on Nepali'.[27] This new trend is clearly linked to the development

---

[26] Some ethnocentrism is nevertheless obvious in the story, which is told in a district where no Muslims live.

[27] *The Nepal Digest*, 15 July 1999.

of political liberalization (and consciousness) and the possibility of openly expressing a feeling of domination.

One of the criticisms directed against foreign anthropologists by Nepalese scholars is that the former offer a biased reading of Nepalese society, or of one group within it. In written form, one of the first examples of this type of criticism can be found in Dilli R. Dahal's 'The Fallout of Deviant Anthropology'.[28] (Perhaps forgetting his own occupation as a social scientist) Dahal defines Nepal as 'the classic case of a society, without social scientists of its own, defined on the basis of someone who is from without'. To him, 'The honest social scientist must, first and foremost, protect and honour the persons who are the subjects of his/her necessarily intrusive study. All too often, research can jeopardise the very community which has helped advance the career of the scholar.' Dahal shows how a Western anthropologist passed judgement on the communities he was studying: 'The Limbu are characterised as an innocent and naive people, in stark contrast to the Brahmins who are portrayed as cheats or otherwise dishonest in their dealings.' This example concerns two Brahmins, who are described by both a Western author and his Nepalese critic as 'crooks'. However, the critic also shows that these Brahmins have even cheated other Brahmins, and that powerful Gurungs also behave in a similar fashion. So the Western anthropologist is said to have been selective in his use of the information available, and the critic concludes: 'this selection was based on his desire to prove a hypothesis he brought with him into the field site'.[29] The critic does not take into consideration the possibility that this was a bias held by the main group studied by the anthropologist rather than (or as much as) one he held himself, and therefore stemmed from an involuntary or unconscious dimension of anthropological writing, that is, the uncritical adoption of local stereotypes to describe reality.

We cannot but agree with Dahal when he states that local stereotypes should not be indulged in or constructed by anthropologists. They should not be ignored or left aside either because of

[28] *Himal*, May 1996.
[29] Let us note in passing that this criticism is a good example of how anthropological discourse calls for a response, even if it has to wait twenty-five years for it, as was the case with this last dialogue.

the moral reprobation they universally arouse, but must be analysed for what they are, as stereotypic characterizations, caricatures, even images used in the rhetorical representations of identity and social relations. The portrayal of Brahmins as crooks and 'tribal groups' as honest people has certainly not been offered solely by foreign social scientists,[30] and D.R. Dahal's criticism should serve as a warning to those who still promote such statements as 'truths' rather than stereotypes. A recent example has been provided by 'five responsible professionals', who collaborated to publish 'four truths' about the Tharus.[31] One of them, 'a local Tharu chronicler and a historian',[32] depicts the Tharus as 'naive but otherwise brave', 'peaceful and indigenous' and 'trustworthy', in contrast to the Brahmins who are said to be 'unable to farm and to fill the Nepal royal coffer', 'sycophantic', and fulfilling 'their self-interests at the whole world's and their spouse's expense'. This author nonetheless concludes his article with these words: 'If the documents obtained by Tharu... are studied..., this will certainly help demeaning stereotypes of the Tharu and present them as they really are.'[33]

This mixture of scholarly exercise and abuse is nowadays frequently found in the writings of 'indigenous' writers. It represents, of course, an answer to an erstwhile political and academic situation, with scholars of high status initiating the process. The list of humiliating considerations put forward about tribal people by high-caste Hindu scholars is too long to quote, and two examples relating to statements made about the Magar group by eminent Nepalese scholars will have to suffice. The first concerns the treatment of Lakhan Thapa, a nineteenth-century Magar rebel, who is described as 'ridiculous' by the Brahmin historian Balcandra Sharma in his classic book on the history of Nepal. In fact, this Magar rebel's name had become synonymous with 'ridiculous person' in the Nepali language till his story and actions were re-discovered in the

[30] Yet there is an ancient Orientalist tradition of Western scholars mocking the Brahmins. In the context of Nepal, see M. Lecomte-Tilouine, 'On Francis Buchanan Hamilton's Account of the Kingdom of Nepal'.

[31] Krauskopff and Duel Meyer (eds), *The Kings of Nepal and the Tharu of the Tarai*.

[32] The three quotations above are from K. Meyer, Introduction.

[33] Quotations taken from Panjiar, 'In My Own Words', pp. 51–5.

1990s by Magar intellectuals. Following the demand presented to the government by the Nepal Magar Association, he was recently named the official martyr of Nepal (Chapter 5).

The second example is taken from the famous historian Baburam Acarya, whose answer to the question 'Have the Magars any connection with the Licchavi period?' reads:

Magars reared pigs during the Licchavi period. On the other hand, the Licchavis were ritually pure. Some of them were Buddhists too. *Therefore, they could have vanquished the Magars had they so wanted.*[34] But they did not establish any relationship with the Magars. Licchavis regarded Magars as untouchable.[35]

This assertion, which merits a long psychoanalytical study on the association of purity (and Buddhism) with military superiority, is not based on any written testimony. Interestingly, it begins with the main reason behind the disgust expressed today by the high castes vis-à-vis the Magars: their association with the pig (see Chapter 3). Baburam Acharya's statement is clearly based on this recent construction and not on historical documents, since the oldest inscription mentioning the pig shows that it had no negative connotations in ancient Nepal.[36]

Nepal, a rare example of a country that was not colonized by Westerners, presents a particularly interesting case. If we accept the point of view of the janajātis, which is now shared by most Nepalese, the country was rather dominated by Indian Hindu groups. Imperialism in Nepal thus comes from India, and what the Indians call British colonialism is labelled the 'Anglo-Brahmin Empire'.[37] We believe that the janajātis transpose the accusations levelled against Westerners in India or the Middle East on the Hindu high castes in Nepal. The janajātis feel that the Hindu high castes have tarnished their reputation, subjugated them politically and intellectually, or omitted them from their writings. They have called

[34] My emphasis.

[35] *Regmi Research Series*, 5 (11), 1973: 212.

[36] An inscription from the Licchavi king Amsuvarma (first half of the seventh century) reads: 'know that we are pleased with you as you have nursed to care fowls, pigs and infant deer and fishes...'; D.R. Regmi, 1983, Vol. 2, p. 43, Inscr. LXVIII.

[37] Niresh Tamang, 'The Brahmin Stranglehold over Nepal'.

for a new branch of social and historical science that would bring them justice. In the words of Mahendra Lawoti (2001):

With the 'unification' of Nepal, Hinduization was promoted actively by the state under lands brought under its control....The Indigenous Peoples term this phenomenon as internal colonisation....The Indigenous Peoples face cultural imperialism because the state and society promote the Parbatiya culture.... Another form of imperialism is demeaning stereotyping of the Indigenous Peoples. They are considered dumb and illiterate and their backwardness is attributed to alcoholism, laziness and so on.

Niresh Tamang (1999) takes the process of feminization of the Other, denounced in the Western-Oriental relationship by Edward Said, as an illustration of the way indigenous people were treated by high-caste Hindus. He claims that the Indian subcontinent's film industry somehow emasculates Mongol men through their exclusion from love affairs, whereas their women are depicted as being involved with men from other castes or with Caucasoid partners. Interestingly, this observation, which may be interpreted as manifesting the well-known inferior position women occupy—through their participation in inter-group relations, or in the depiction of the supposed sexual freedom of tribal women—is viewed by the author as a political project of genocide. It is, in his eyes, a Brahmin plot to pollute the indigenous Nepalese blood in order to completely destroy the Mongoloid race. This reveals the strong fear of being 'erased'—by inter-marriage or other means—often expressed by janajāti groups in Nepal (see Chapter 4). This fear is obviously related to an endogamous ideal, but also seems to be linked to the political dimension that is conferred on the notion of distinct human categories. Indeed, despite the fact that the formation of political parties along religious or ethnic lines was forbidden by Nepalese law, the janajātis have succeeded in organizing themselves into powerful ethnic associations and proving their subjection through statistics that have been available since the 1990 census, which brought out the ethnic and caste composition of the population. In this context, diluting the notion of distinct peoples would ruin both their present organization and their capacity to claim group recognition and representation.[38]

[38] This may partially explain B.K. Rana's reaction to D. Gellner's description

The scheme of intellectual domination is thus neither bipolar nor unidirectional in Nepal: the most common agonistic 'social' writings are currently from 'tribal' or 'Dalit' scholars, and are directed against their 'high Hindu caste oppressors'. Western scholars are not spared either, and in the words of a Nepalese writer, 'like other hallmarks of the Western world, social sciences too carry an air of superiority'.[39] Social sciences in general thus seem to represent a form of 'intellectual feudalism' because of their inaccessibility. The process whereby the accusation of domination is transferred, which generates negative effect within the group, is thus endless: while Nepalese tribal groups or Dalits suffered at the hands of Bahun-Chetris, the latter were in turn subjugated by Indian imperialism[40] and Western domination. The Indian Oriental, on their part, suffers from Western neo-colonialism. Within this long chain of domination, various dual oppositions are emphasized, depending on the context.

Social anthropology is indeed, as these examples seem to show, an illustration of the fact that discourse (as defined by Foucault) not only translates struggles but also what for, and the means by which one struggles, but domination may also be one of its objects of study. Thus, one of the tools used by upper castes to dominate the janajātis of Nepal is said to have resulted in introducing social hierarchy among them. This hierarchy is today vehemently criticized

---

of Nepalese society as a hybrid one, and his suggestion that this component be recognized: 'Hybridity offers no meaning when you are seeking to establish your fundamental rights based on equity. Contrarily, Gellner provides indirect support to the elites and nothing to the commoners' (*The Himalayan Times*, 2 May 2003). B.K. Rana, on the other hand, thinks in terms of group and not individual equity. This dialogue between a Western and a Nepalese scholar evokes the characteristics of their respective societies and their correlated ideologies. Hybridity exists everywhere, but is negatively connoted and kept in the background in caste or tribal organizations, while it is emphasized in modern Western countries through the myth of individual equality. Rana asserts: 'We should not accept what others tell us about ourselves.'

[39] Prakriti K.C., 'Feudalism: A Beginner's Interpretation'.

[40] See, for instance, D.B. Bista (*Fatalism and Development*), who claims that all social ills prevalent in Nepal came from India, and everything indigenous is good by definition.

by the Nepalese janajātis, who claim that this practice, imposed on them by force, has never been adopted internally. While the origin of internal hierarchization among janajāti groups is not known, several anthropologists have attested to its existence in the 1960s.[41] Pignède's depiction of this phenomenon among the Gurungs, in particular, was recently contested by Gurung activists, who went as far as burning his book in public. However, a section of the Nepalese code of 1927 shows that claims of social superiority within this group were not unknown in the past (see Chapter 4):

> Throughout the dominions of Gorkha, there is only one Gurung name and *jāt* all members of which can take cooked rice from each other, even if alliances are made with girls or widows. In case, therefore, any Gurung claims to be of a higher caste status than others, or ostracizes another Gurung in respect to cooked rice, he shall be punished with fines....[42]

From this, we can deduce that though some form of internal hierarchization did exist in the past among the Nepalese janajātis, it is no longer part of their recent opposing political strategies. In this context, anthropology appears as a disturbing witness to past social practices,[43] the existence of which is simply denied because they contradict the new dominant ideology, and seem to invalidate it. In a context where the janajātis present themselves as guardians of very ancient pre-Hindu customs and institutions that are opposed to caste ideology, there is no room for such a past. However, an attempt to understand the various social strategies adopted by janajātis in the course of their history and within their local contexts may allow for new thoughts on the Hindu-tribal relationship. It

---

[41] See Pignède (1966) on the Gurungs, and Fürer-Haimendorf (1964) on the Sherpas.

[42] *Regmi Research Series*, 20 (8), 1988: 148.

[43] Now, it is publications using Bernard Pignède's study on the Gurungs that are burned. Thus *www.yetizone.com*, 21 November 2005, announces: 'In what may be a first for any web site, YetiZone is to be ceremonially burned in a "book burning" on 30 December 2005 by Gurung politically correct activists....they do not like the works of the French surrender-monkey anthropologist Bernard Pignede and have decided to burn all his books, and anything that uses his material. As YetiZone's culture page about the Gurungs was based on Pignede's politically incorrect research, YetiZone is to be printed out and burned.'

may provide answers to fundamental questions such as: how and under what circumstances did the caste system develop on the Indian subcontinent with such strength that the Nepalese State had to set a limit on its proliferation[44] among 'tribal' groups? And why is this past now so unacceptable—in theory, at least—that even referring openly to caste is often considered indecent? Exploring these questions may contribute to a better understanding of the way domination functions, and thus give shape to a potential tool for emancipation.

[44] For more documents on this subject, see M. Lecomte-Tilouine, 'The Ruling of the Social Groups: From Species to Nation'.

2: Tamang Shamans in the City of Patan (Photo: M. Lecomte-Tilouine).

1

Spirits, Shamans, and Englishmen
Perception of the Others in *Vīr Caritra*,
A Nineteenth-Century Nepalese Novel[*]

Few Himalayan texts mention or describe spirits.[1] They are almost non-existent in historical documents and ritual handbooks. However, these supernatural beings form a group that is closely related to human beings, and whose influence on everyday life is considered crucial. Girishavallabha Joshi's (1867–1923) text appears to be an exceptional document, as it brings some historical depth to our knowledge of the Himalayan religions.

In 1899, this high-caste Ayurvedic doctor composed a long text titled *Vīr caritra*.[2] The title, which can be translated as 'Adventures of a hero', is probably a pun, since *Vīr* also designates a category of spirits depicted in the novel. Below the title, the author or editor has specified in brackets that it is a 'novel', *upanyās*, and in effect the text may be viewed as an adventure novel. It represents the first novel written in Nepali, a language hitherto considered not literary (but usable for administrative purposes[3]). While the first part of

---

[*] Originally published as 'Les Mondes à part. Représentation des esprits à travers un roman népalais de la fin du XIXe siècle', *BEFEO*, 89, 2002: 107–26.

[1] In this text I use the term 'spirit' to mean supernatural beings, but it goes without saying that they are not denied their corporeality.

[2] All the orthographies are those that have been employed in the novel.

[3] The Nepali language began to be used in inscriptions as early as the fourteenth century. Nepali was used for administrative purpose only, while

the text appeared in 1903, it was only published in its entirety in 1965. The reason for this very long delay between publications is not known.[4]

Vir caritra clearly reflects the specific context of late nineteenth-century Nepal during the reign of the Rana Prime Ministers, when the Court was under the influence of luxurious British fashions while the people were isolated from all external influences. The Nepalese could only dream of an imagined Occident or Far East, based on what they could see of their Court.

Vir caritra was apparently written to entertain the women of the Rana harem. The author, who was disabled, was carried to the harem daily in a palanquin to read a new episode. This context certainly influenced the text, which was obviously written to please the Rana. Thus, for obvious diplomatic reasons, the story takes place in the Kali Gandaki region of central Nepal, far from the court and kingdoms of Gorkha, Lamjung, and Kaski, which were linked to the then Shah and Rana rulers. Expensive costumes, palaces and gardens, topics dear to the aristocracy in Nepal and elsewhere, are described in abundance. Lastly, and perhaps in order to flatter the Rana's pretensions, the author attributed to Nepal all kinds of technical innovations which had actually just been brought to India by the British.

It is difficult to judge the impression this novel must have made on its Nepalese readers, but to the contemporary Western reader the narrative appears endless, muddled, and frankly mind-boggling. This strange impression reflects a special conception of the world, notably one linked to the presence of the spirits.

The structure of the narrative in *Vir caritra* is akin to those found in Indian, Persian or Arabic literature. In particular, this novel,

---

Sanskrit was used in literature, religious texts, etc. During the nineteenth century, some Nepali translations were made of Sanskrit texts and poetry.

[4] The first part of this novel, approximately 120 pages long, was published in 1960 VS/1903 by Pashupat Press, Kathmandu. According to Kamal Diksit, the author of the introduction to the first complete edition of the novel (1965), this first part enjoyed great success among the public. Youngsters, forbidden by their elders to read literary works in any language other than Sanskrit, used to hide and read it. The first complete edition of the novel (511 pages), however, appeared only in 2022 VS/1965, Jagadamba Prakashan, Lalitpur.

qualified by K. Pradhan[5] as 'gothic', presents strong analogies with the Indian folktale, *kathā*. In fact, the story of Agnidatta borrows many elements from Book V of the *Kathāsaritsāgara* anthology, which, according to legend, was itself written with the blood of *Pisāca* spirits and in their language.[6] More specifically, following the structure of the story of the ten princes, *Vīr caritra* is a kind of *digvijaya* or 'conquest of the regions'.

The story is complex and difficult to summarize, as each adventure has many sub-plots woven into the thread of the narrative, which leaves the Western reader feeling dizzy. If we do not take into account the numerous bifurcations, the thread of the narrative is relatively simple. A Brahmin and his wife distribute their goods to their next of kin during a food shortage and leave their village, accompanied by their two sons, for the holy confluence of Ridi, where they plan to live as ascetics. On the way, one of their sons becomes a *Rākṣas* demon[7] and takes over the kingdom of the *Masān* (death spirits).[8] Their other son, Agnidatta, along with his parents, enters the kingdom of Ban Jhankri,[9] the shaman-spirit of the forest, and his spouse Nidhini. He puts an end to Ban Jhankri's reign, then ends that of Suna Jhankri, 'the golden shaman', that of Ritthe Jhankri, 'the shaman with a necklace of *ritthā* pearls',[10] and that of Tukuca Prasad Danava, a cannibal demon. In each enemy kingdom, he establishes his allies and 'spiritual children', and finally enters into three matrimonial alliances himself, one with a snake-girl, Nāg kanyā, another with a demoness, Rākṣasanī, and the third with the daughter of the king of Palpa. The son born of his union with the

---

[5] Pradhan, *A History of Nepali Literature*, p. 168.

[6] Verschaeve, *La cité d'or et autres contes*, p. 8.

[7] The names of the various spirits are transliterated at their first occurrence, then Anglicized. The term Rakshas is generally translated as demon. These spirits are man-eaters, and are said to possess the ability to fly.

[8] Masan designates the cremation ground and the category of anthropophagous spirits that haunt them.

[9] This term is sometimes spelt this way, and sometimes without a nasal inflection (*jhākrī*) in the novel.

[10] This translation was given to me by a villager from central Nepal. However, *ritthā* also means 'very black', referring to the colour of the *Sapindus mukerossi* seed, called *ritthā*.

demoness becomes the king of the Masān ghouls, succeeding his uncle, Agnidatta's brother, who recovers his human appearance. The two brothers then continue on their way to Ridi to meet their parents as if nothing had happened in the meantime.

Jean-Pierre Vernant (1999) specifies the interest narratives hold for the anthropologist by stating that they present a vision of the world in a subjacent way. We shall add that beyond their actual content, the form of the narratives can also reveal a particular vision of the world. Thus *Vir caritra*, like *A Thousand and One Nights*, displays a very peculiar form that we may qualify as arborescent: the course of a story leads, with as many ramifications, to several other sub-plots connected by fine threads to the main plot. In the text studied here, however, a logic underlies the apparently random events, for the world in which the hero evolves presents a structure that is similar to that underlying the narrative. The form and content mutually reinforce each other, as if a story could hide other stories just as the world hides other worlds.

Contrary to the Indian tale, which F. Lacôte[11] defines as: '... account put into the mouth of a hero...who tells his own story or reports the accounts made by some other characters, which contain, in their turn, those that the latter have heard from various persons, and so on'; or contrary to *A Thousand and One Nights*, where the heroes can also be defined as 'narrative-men',[12] *Vir caritra* does not present embedded narratives so much as embedded adventures, which take place in embedded worlds. However, in both the embedded adventures contained within the main adventure and in the additional stories contained within the story, there exists a common proliferous structure.[13] In this context, the art of the narrator apparently consists in confusing the listener or reader by

---

[11] Lacôte, *L'histoire romanesque d'Udayana, roi de vatsa*, p. 13.

[12] According to the expression given by T. Todorov, *Poétique de la prose*, p. 37, 'hommes-récits'.

[13] One cannot be satisfied with qualifying the additional accounts of Indian folktales as useless, 'inutiles' (Lacôte, *L'histoire romanesque d'Udayana*, p. 18), or by considering that it is only through a 'taste for variety' that '...the course of the account was decorated by tales having no direct link with the subject and placed there more or less artificially...' (Verschaeve, *La cité d'or et autres contes*, p. 9).

fitting the episodes together in a way that requires a real effort of memory to recall them. The reader (or listener) is likely to lose the thread and then be carried away, with no mooring or landmark, by the tumultuous flood of the narrative, in which phantasmagorical images unravel at a dizzying pace, recalling the visions of Rimbaud's drunken boat after the boat-haulers were killed.

During ordinary journeys, the characters are attracted to separate worlds connected to the human world through secret passages. Their capacity for attraction evokes the black holes in the cosmos that absorb matter. In these anti-worlds, tricks and disguises are the only means of fighting perdition. Through a controlled and reasoned adoption of Otherness, the hero finds a possibility of escaping and reaching his initial destination. The concomitance of the narrative structure and that of the world is thus not fortuitous: it underlines a proliferating form of thought in which closed accounts are nevertheless connected by thin bridges to others in manner similar to that of the universe, closed, yet dangerously pierced by narrow passages giving on to anti-worlds.

If we recall the way Raymond Roussel explored the possibilities of language in his novels, by developing all possible meanings of the terms of an initial sentence in order to reconstitute it at the end of an extravagant story, the account in *Vir caritra* seems to explore the infinite possibilities of journeys in worlds grafted onto the phenomenal world like strange blisters during the course of routine travel, where arrival and departure respectively open and close the account. As in Roussel's novels, where the apparently arbitrary sequence of events in fact obeys a carefully elaborated logic (to follow the meanings of the words included in the first sentence by approximate homophonies), it seems that here, the arbitrariness of the adventures is founded on a subjacent logic, which is that of the spirits.

These unsuspected 'worlds apart' are separated from the human world to which they are connected through concealed ways, and maintained by secret mechanisms or insurmountable walls. By evoking J. Lacan's 'points de capiton' (quilting points[14]), which link the One to the Other, these passages separating and connecting the worlds of the spirits and men are of cardinal importance in

[14] And not 'caption points' as they are sometimes translated into English.

the constitution of human identity in the Nepalese context. The discourse on the Other and Otherness is expressed in relation to the spirits and their numerous separate worlds.

The novel develops a pattern of thought that is still widespread in Nepal. Thus, the idea that our familiar universe is dangerously strewn with openings through which one slips into monstrous repetitions of the world is not a romantic invention: in the Nepalese hills, for instance, children warn newcomers of small holes in the rocks, which are said to lead to the immense palaces of Bhut spirits. There, humans are fed a kind of anti-food composed of worms and sand using anti-manners (since the food is given on the back of the hand) by anti-beings: who are very black or very white, very tall or very small; some have their feet turned backwards, while others have no heads or long hair standing up straight on their heads. From various details, it is obvious that fiction in *Vir caritra* has more to do with the incongruous layout of representations from various groups than with idiosyncratic designs. The marvellous takes the shape of a journey to the worlds of Others': shamanic tribal spirits and English gentlemen, who occupy spaces outside the world and whose customs and habits, described at length, are to be fought, diverted or thwarted by the hero. People can penetrate these parallel worlds inadvertently, in which case they are either eaten, or remain enslaved forever. Others, chosen by the spirits, are summoned to these worlds.

THE CALL OF THE SPIRITS

The spirits select the two young heroes of the novel in a way that recalls the 'shamanic crisis'. Vishnudatta, the younger brother, faints at the top of a tree which he had climbed to cut wood. He falls. Later at night, he awakes feverish and shivering from the cold. He then convinces his father to accompany him so he can warm himself by the crematory fires he sees in the distance. There, they both witness a terrible scene, that of ghouls feasting on the flesh of corpses and quarrelling for food. But the young man displays extraordinary determination, as if he had been possessed. He walks fearlessly and warms himself by a burning pyre. Suddenly the skull of the corpse burning on that pyre bursts, projecting brain tissue. Some liquid matter reaches the lips of the famished young man, who swallows it. Immediately the goddess of the dead spirits (Masān) rises from the ground. She informs the boy that she has seen how courageous he is and that the general of the Rakshas had recently passed away: '... by my Tantric power, I made you sick and, having led you up here, I've made you eat the food of the demons'. She then offers him a sabre, a skull and a necklace, the title of general, and names him Demon-of-the-broken-head. Lastly, the goddess declares that he will soon become king, and then disappears. Vishnudatta looks at his body:

Four white fangs one cubit long, protruded from his mouth. Black hair similar to a billy goat's had grown around his eyes, and his mouth was as red as Lakhe's.[15] He was very surprised to see his hair black as ink and standing straight up on his head.

The boy then rushes at his father to devour him, but the Goddess reappears to stop him in his haste. Suddenly, the entire scene (the crematory field, demons and ghouls) vanishes from the sight of the amazed father, who is now left alone.

The strange behaviour of the young man, his disease, his sudden and pressing attraction for crematory fires, and even the unexpected explosion of the skull thus did not happen by mere chance, but were caused by the will of a supernatural being in order to reaffirm the fundamental principle that orders and gives meaning to the phenomenal world: arbitrariness in the human world is causality in the world of the spirits.

The consumption of human flesh instantaneously transforms the young man into a Rakshas, because in Hindu society, one is defined overall by what one eats. We will reconsider the portrayal of the spirits as cannibals, and the impact of this representation from the point of view of their prey, that is, human beings. Another striking feature of this episode is the total loss of any memory pertaining to his past, as displayed by the boy immediately following his metamorphosis, indicating that this is not a mere physical change, but an essential transformation.[16]

---

[15] The most terrifying Newar demon.

[16] In the same way that mediums forget what happened when they were possessed.

It is difficult to say how the world of the Rakshas and Masān spirits is organized in relation to the human one. A little like the goddess who rules over it, it seems to emerge only for the situation being played out, disappearing immediately after, perhaps from/into the ground as she does. In this episode, the call of the spirits is strengthened by the materialization of their world, set up as the framework for the hero's initiation, which is marked by the consumption of that most taboo matter for man, his own flesh, and, more specifically, the quintessence of this substance, the brain. The cremation field belongs to the supernatural: an inversion occurs there, through which the sacrificers are transformed into the sacrificial victims of the evil spirits, thereby demonstrating another perspective on sacrifice. The cremation field is also part of the supernatural because it is illusory or temporary, a fact that invites the reader into the complex logic of Nepalese accounts relating to the hereafter, where it is never clear what occurs to man after death. Devoured by ghouls, the dead person joins their troops, although he is also said to start a journey, at the end of which he becomes an ancestor. It is rather as if two principles coexisted in each of us: an animal and physical one which is fed by the flesh of animals when alive and eaten in its turn in the tomb, or when cooked on cremation fires. There, it remains thereafter to eat other men. The other principle, which is spiritual, ensures the perpetuity of the human lineage by becoming an ancestor. Like a threshold, death leads man into the spirits' world and activates a displacement in perspective, where man, once emptied of vital and spiritual principles, is nothing more than meat, and becomes the food for his monstrous alter egos.

After Vishnudatta is elected King of the Rakshas, his brother Agnidatta is in his turn called to another world. With his parents, he has settled in a cave to spend the night, when a block of rock falls from the back of the cave and gives access to a second room in which the three of them are forced to take refuge once a tiger makes an appearance at the entrance to the cave. At the back of this second room, they discover an iron gate. Unlocking its strange snake-shaped mechanism, they enter an extraordinary garden where an old woman waits to take them to her mistress. One then understands that all the apparently fortuitous events that have just taken place had been planned and instigated by a spirit. The young man is then led along a complicated path and by many monstrous assistants up to Nidhini, the mistress of the place. She declares (p. 16):

O Pandit, the night before yesterday, you were resting under a pipal tree and I was enjoying the fresh air as I flew through the sky. I was charmed when I saw you and thus led you here, causing you many difficulties! ...I wish that we could experience the pleasures of love and life together. Here you will be king on my throne, think about it....

Nidhini's summons thus follow another logic: it is not about the selection of an exceptional man, but the ravishing of a sexual partner. In fact, the hero, as well as the reader, soon learns how Nidhini unceasingly attracts new lovers from the human world, of whom she tires extremely quickly, and who are then turned to stone statues that decorate her immense garden. Agnidatta brings four of these statues back to life, after which they recount their misadventures. All of them were princes. The prince of Bhirkot was captured one night when he had lost his way in the forest during a hunt and was led by a dog-headed being to the Mistress, whose lover he was for ten days. The prince of Tanahun was swallowed by an enormous fish while swimming in a river, and remained Nidhini's lover for one month. A wild elephant took away the prince of Dhvankot while he was sleeping in a forest, on his way to the Deughat place of pilgrimage. The last statue, the prince of Musikot, was taken away one night by Nidhini's daughter in her flying carriage while walking in his garden.

All human employees of the kingdom of Nidhini had also been captured. Thus Latamaya, a Newar maidservant, met Nidhini when she was crossing a bridge over the Bagmati, and Bangali, another servant, was summoned by the magic formulas of the Mistress who had gone to the cremation field of the terrible Kamaksha goddess, leaving doubt as to whether Bangali was dead or alive. In addition to these abductions of men by spirits, the novel also mentions cases of unfortunate people who penetrate spirit kingdoms inadvertently, and are then mercilessly eaten once they had been fattened. The characters are never kidnapped from the closed and safe spaces of their homes but always outside, on a journey, when crossing boundary zones such as rivers, paths and forests, and especially during the night, clearly delimiting the spirits' fields of intervention. As far as this belief is concerned, the novel does not highlight any new element, but makes the largely widespread beliefs relating to the supernatural realm more explicit.

Kidnappings take place with the help of wild assistants, especially animals, such as tigers, wild elephants, enormous fish, or those auxiliaries called the Vīr, half-human and half-animal beings. The call of the spirits is truly initiatory, as in shamanism. The weak ones succumb to it and do not return from the world to which they were called, while the hero discovers a new maturity and learns how to control treachery. Thus Agnidatta, who is presented as a teenager, acts as an adult upon penetrating the kingdom of Nidhini. The initiatory journey reverses roles: it is the teenager who takes the initiative and saves his parents from danger in the other worlds, while the latter recover their role and authority as soon as they are back in the human world. This first initiatory journey leads to others: back from Nidhini's domain, the hero seems attracted by these strange worlds in which he moves skilfully, thwarting obstacles and understanding tricks. The initial entry into the world of Ban Jhankri and his spouse Nidhini gives rise to a series of similar experiences, at the end of which the hero has subdued all the worlds and 'bound' them.

The 'worlds apart' possessed by spirits thus act as centres of attraction towards which select people are led without their knowledge by the spirits who control the borders of the human world. In these antechambers of the hereafter, they set in motion apparently fortuitous and 'natural' circumstances, controlling from a distance the unsuspecting humans. The novel presents two opposite types of summons: the election of a man called to reign over the spirits, and the capture of people aimed at their subjection. We will see that these opposing attitudes are associated with two distinct categories of spirit, which maintain contrasting relations with high-caste Hindus.

LUSTFUL FEMALES AND CANNIBAL MALES

The capture of men by female spirits seems to reflect, in reversed form, the common practice of capturing a spouse, which is still practised in the Himalayas. In the novel, few women are kidnapped by spirits, and when they are, it is with the purpose of turning them into maidservants. Male spirits clearly do not seem to have the same sexual appetite as their female counterparts, and this feature must be understood as yet another inversion of human characteristics.[17] Beyond the recurring and typical inversions, the clear difference in the behaviour of male and female spirits vis-à-vis human beings perhaps also underlines a logic of alliance specific to them, which we now examine. Female spirits are lustful and choose beautiful men as lovers. This union leads to the lover's ruin, as he is either transformed into a statue, or quite simply eaten at the end. Thus, one of the petrified princes delivered by Agnidatta is later captured by a spirit-shaman who dopes and buries him. He is then dug out from his tomb by Tibetan and Thakali women, who lead him to a lady.

She was sixteen years old, her face was luminous like the moon, her skin had the colour of a magnolia flower and her cheek that of a red rose, her teeth seemed to be pearls, her hair black like the hair of a bumblebee, and elegantly styled in a Chinese fashion, was hanging on the two sides of her face. Her breasts resembled lemons, and her waist was thin; she was wearing a yellow silk costume, a diamond ring and an emerald necklace....

This idyllic creature tells the prince that she is the daughter of the Mustang king, and that she wishes to become his wife. Although he was 'pierced by the arrow of the god Love', the prince is wary of her proposal and prudently obtains information about her. He learns from a Brahmin in her service that she is in fact the fifth wife of King Tukuca Prasad Danava, and is in charge of his kitchens. The Brahmin explains that the king ritually consumes 'Brahmin-Kshatri' meat before his meal, just as they, the Brahmins, purify themselves by absorbing a Tulasi leaf before eating. His fifth wife, who has to ensure that the king is given such meat for each meal, always manages to find Brahmin-Kshatri meat 'alive or buried'. In addition, she has a strong libido, and whenever possible fornicates with the Brahman-Kshatri for one month while taking care to fatten him at the same time, before killing and serving him to her husband. The old Brahmin has escaped this fate 'because he is old and thin'.

---

[17] The inversion of human features is typical of Himalayan spirits (M. Lecomte-Tilouine, 'Hommes/divinités de la forêt').

Thus, in the spirit world, men are reduced to their most physical aspect: an instrument of pleasure for the female spirits, and the favourite meal of the males. The spirits benefit from men, drawing from them all they can. After their brief amorous encounter, men are destined to nourish them or embellish their gardens by literally becoming man-objects. The spirits' attitude makes man perceive the painful image of his mere materiality. Selected when young and fat, they are not only the spirits' meal of choice, but also their ritual food. *Vir caritra* often dwells on this point: human bodies are cut up and cooked in Nidhini and Ban Jhankri's kitchens as well. In the cremation fields, Bhut-Pret and Masan feast on the hot flesh of the corpses, or follow the army for banquets on battlefields, so that any death, even natural, signals the transformation of human beings into food. In fact, cannibalism perhaps forms the single common denominator of all spirits, their distinctive feature. Furthermore, this act transforms man into an evil spirit, as if this formed the essence of their nature. It is striking to note that this characteristic had already been attributed to spirits in ancient India who went by the generic name of 'man-eaters'.[18] Male spirits are physically portrayed as carnivorous beasts, hairy, with long fangs.

The existence of cannibal spirits establishes man as a hunted hunter, and leads him to identify with them vis-à-vis his relation to his own prey, the animals, thereby underlining his own murderous and carnivorous instincts. Thus, in central Nepal today, one often hears villagers declare that they are Rakshas with respect to animals. The model provided by the spirits thus reflects a self-portrait of man in his relation to other categories of living beings. Brutality, unbridled female sexuality, butchery of humans, and anthropophagy reign among the spirits as an astonishing amalgam of the fear that the Other, in its various aspects, inflicts on man, and, more subtly, as an image of the appalling treatment of the Other by man. The spirits enable the human being to transpose his 'self' in the place of the Other: the hunter sees his 'self' eaten, men are captured by lustful women. The living, while being buried alive or fattened for the kill, are treated as if dead, and the dead, when called from the field of cremation to live with the spirits, treated as if alive, thus confusing

---

[18] W. Hopkins, *Epic Mythology*.

the borders of common registers. Lastly, the surprising modernity of supernatural worlds, which we will dwell on at length later, can also be seen to highlight the human beings' wildness.

ALLIANCES WITH THE SPIRITS

Being cannibal does not prevent the spirits from allying with human beings. Consequently, they not only cease to consider humans meat, but even take on their appearance and observe their food taboos. Thus, the Small Bhut[19] is allied with the hero and accompanies him in his wanderings in human form. When the time came for a combat in the forest, he resumed his spirit appearance so as to be recognized by a Rakshas, who then brings human and other animal meats, beers and alcohols in homage. Horrified at such food being offered him in the presence of the young Brahmin, the Bhut spirit insults the Rakshas demon, and summons him to take away this rubbish. He then literally puts himself in the place of the Other, that of the young Brahmin whose cause he has adopted. A two-way identification between men and spirits is thus possible (the Small Bhut transforms himself into a man while one of the two heroes becomes a Rakshas), underlining a common nature, or at least an easily crossed threshold between the two categories of beings. The proximity of men to spirits is also marked by matrimonial alliances between them, which, however, are always in the same direction, between a man of this world and a woman from beyond, underlining the spirits' lower status.[20]

The four princes who are rescued by Agnidatta begin to look upon him as their father. He later establishes each of his four spiritual sons at the head of a supernatural kingdom, a ritual that always follows the same procedure. Eliminating the demonic king, he marries the daughter of the latter to one of the princes, then blesses the couple and places them on the throne. No harm is done to the local population, which apparently is not regarded as evil

---

[19] The Bhut are spirits of violent or untimely death.

[20] Only isogamy and hypergamy are allowed in Hindu society. In both cases, the wife-giver is regarded as lower in status than the wife-taker. This fundamental rule perhaps also explains the absence of alliance and sexual intercourse between male spirits and human women.

even when they happen to consist of bloodthirsty ogres, if the king who controls them is righteous.[21] The first prince marries Nidhini and Ban Jhankri's daughter, the second Suna Jhankri's daughter, the third Kalu Prasad Danava's, and the last prince receives King Daitya Vajradatta's fortress and the king of Rukum's daughter, who was held captive there.

Thereafter, the hero Agnidatta himself becomes 'the spirits' son-in-law',[22] like a shaman, by successively marrying a Nag kanya (a female snake from the underground), a Rākṣasanī (demoness of the airs), and quite an earthly woman: the daughter of king Mukunda Sen of Palpa, a very powerful monarch from central Nepal. Through his alliances Agnidatta controls the three levels of the universe, but refuses to reign over them as according to him, temporal power is not appropriate for a Brahmin.

Between the spirits, alliances mainly take the form of ritual friendships. Several are mentioned: those that link Ban Jhankri and Suna Jhankri, Suna Jhankri and Ritthe Jhankri, Ritthe Jhankri and Tukuca Prasad Danava, Vajradatta Daitya and the Nag king. All the monarchs of the supernatural realm are thus bound by a ritual friendship, in the name of which they provide assistance to each other. On the other hand, no ritual friendship ties spirits and human beings together, perhaps because this relation both implies and induces some equality between the two parties.[23] On the other hand, for high-caste Nepalese, a matrimonial alliance

---

[21] This idea is explicit in the Gorkha chronicle (Naraharinath 2021 VS/1964: 60), where one can read this saying: *jasto rājā bhayā tastai prajā hunchan*, 'like king, like people'.

[22] According to A. de Sales' expression ('Actes et paroles dans les rituels chamaniques des Kham-Magar'). In fact, in the novel, Agnidatta is the only true son-in-law of the spirits, since his relations with his Rakshas mother-in-law and his Nag father-in-law are described in detail. The princes, on the other hand, do not have in-laws as they had been eliminated, and are consequently merely 'husbands of spirits'.

[23] Indeed, though this type of friendship can occur between individuals of different status, it creates a fictitious family tie between them, which induces the only form of equality I observed in central Nepal, manifested in the reciprocal and simultaneous handing over of the frontal *ṭikā* mark. It usually reaffirms an unequal relation between the donor and the receiver of the mark.

is seen as subordinating the bride and, by extension, her group, a fact that explains why matrimonial alliances are associated with the subordination of a kingdom. To be a son-in-law among the Magar tribal group, on the other hand, implies a radically different relationship since, for them, the son-in-law is an inferior. One seems to find traces of this tribal inversion of high-caste Hindu values in the spirits' practices as depicted in the novel. For the seductive female spirits, sexual union contains no aspect of subordination. They control any possible harmful consequence by eliminating their partner soon after. The matrimonial context within which sexual union is legitimate for high-status Hindus is proposed by female spirits only by way of a trick, as seen in this scene where Nidhini asks the hero to become her lover (p. 29):

AGNIDATTA: ...I am not married and cannot become your lover as long as my marriage has not taken place.
NIDHINI: If it is thus, marry me.
AGNIDATTA: I do not know your caste, *jāt*. How could I marry you?
NIDHINI: I am the daughter of the Ban Jhankri of the Sakhi Mount.
AGNIDATTA: In the *Dharmaśāstra*, the Brahmans only dealt with the marriage of the girls of the four castes: Brahman, Kshetri, Vaisya and Shudra. Ban Jhankri doesn't belong to these castes, nor does he respect the *Veda*, so how could I marry the daughter of such a person?
NIDHINI: No matter what the *śāstra* say, Chepang and Danuvar[24] eat out of Ban Jhankri's hand. And as for the laws concerning the marriage of one of Ban Jhankri's daughters, you do not know anything about it.

When it comes to matrimonial alliance, G. Joshi's novel is almost ethnographic, meticulously reflecting the rules of inter-caste relations. In this scene, the young hero reproaches Nidhini for being an outcast, for not belonging to the Hindu universe. She, on the other hand, clearly identifies with the tribal (Chepang and

---

[24] The Chepang are a group of hunter-gatherers who now lead a sedentary lifestyle, and the Danuvar is another small tribe living in southern Nepal. While it is interesting to note that Nidhini seems more particularly attached to these two groups, it is not possible to deduce that the Jhankris were specifically attached to them one century ago because the author may have referred to them to avoid criticism. It should also be noted that Nidhini is presented here not only as Ban Jhankri's wife, but also as the daughter of another Ban Jhankri, as if the female counterparts of these Jhankris were all Nidhinis.

Danuvar) groups in order to defend her status, and snubs the Brahmin who addresses her in a sententious way by pointing out that he knows nothing of tribal laws or their usages. Confronted with the young Brahmin who reproaches her for being outside the Hindu caste structure, Nidhini seeks refuge in her tribal origin, which confers upon her an intermediate but pure rank, and not an external position, within Nepalese caste society. It is interesting to compare this scene with the unions Agnidatta formed thereafter, for a fundamental difference between two groups of spirits is highlighted through matrimonial alliance. Thus, when the hero falls in love with an unknown girl who had sworn to marry only a god or a man, Agnidatta lets her know through the mediation of a third person that if she marries a Brahmin, her wish will be doubly fulfilled because 'Brahmans are gods'. Once the maid is convinced, it is the hero's turn to express reservations when he learns that she is a snake-girl, Nag kanya (p. 401).

AGNIDATTA: Me, I am Brahman and you, a daughter of Nag, our castes do not get along, what are we to do?

THE SNAKE-GIRL: Vedvyas wrote in the *Purāṇas* that the child born of a man and a daughter of god, of Nag or an Apsara, receives the same caste as his father. The child born of Sage Adhika and a Nag-girl was Brahman as well as the child of Sage Vasista and an Apsara. Therefore there would be no evil if you were to make such a marriage.

The snake-girl knows the Hindu rules well and the alliance does take place, but only after several adventures since Agnidatta learns that residence among Nags is customarily uxorilocal, a practice that repels him. The young hero, a good Brahmin, is very attached to his caste rules, and unwilling to live at his in-laws'. Thus, even among these spirits belonging to the Hindu universe, Otherness is marked by opposite practices relating to alliance (in this case, uxorilocality).

The novel draws a clear distinction between 'Hindu' spirits and the ones that can be described as 'tribal' spirits, that is, between those with whom a Brahmin can make alliances without his children losing status, and others with whom he cannot. However, Agnidatta does not hesitate to marry the prince of Musikot with Ban Jhankri and Nidhini's daughter. Again, in this case, the author does not invent anything, since there have been many alliances between Thakuri princes and tribal girls in the history of Nepal, which ensured the local legitimacy of the foreign Thakuri conquerors. Moreover, a child born of a Thakuri father and a tribal woman carries the status of his father, contrary to the Brahmins.

The difference in the way the two spirit groups—tribal and Hindu—are treated is also highlighted in the fact that the tribal groups see their kings eliminated and replaced by Hindu suzerains, whereas the king of the Nag not only continues on his throne, but even obtains an extension of his kingdom thanks to his daughter's alliance with the young Brahmin.

The alliance with the Rakshas demons is the most complicated and difficult to understand in the novel. At the very beginning, as we have seen, the hero's brother is turned into a Rakshas by the goddess of the Masan, and becomes their king. Throughout the novel he fights in the form of a demon at his human brother's side without knowing who the latter is, because the goddess of the Masan has asked him to. Thereafter, Agnidatta meets a female Rakshas in a cremation field who offers him her daughter in marriage. Agnidatta accepts at once, specifying, however, that since she is not of his caste, he will not marry her in a Brahmanic ceremony, but in a short ritual called 'Gandharva marriage'. Here again the text presents no discrepancy because it is then a second marriage for the Brahmin hero and, while it is essential that the first alliance contracted be within one's own caste, the following ones can be with women of lower rank. The son whom he begets from this union does not have his father's rank, in accordance with Hindu laws; however, it is not known whether he is regarded as a Rakshas or forms a different, bastard caste. At any rate, when the hero has to appoint one of his sons to succeed to the Rakshas throne after his brother recovers his human form, he declares (p. 507):

My eldest son is called Kumardatta. However, as he is Brahman, it would not be fitting for him to become king of the Rakshas. It is advisable to place my son Jvaladatta who was born of a Rakshasani.

It is only at the end of this long novel that one understands the reason for the repeated alliances between the Brahmins and the Rakshas demons, headed by Masan Devi. When the two brothers find themselves face to face and about to fight following a misunderstanding, the goddess Masān Devi once again emerges from the ground and addresses Agnidatta in these terms (p. 505–6):

Hey grandfather[25] Agnidatta! I am the Kalika goddess of the village of Baglung which your ancestors venerated. Because your younger brother was weak, at the time when Yamaraj[26] was about to carry him away, by the force of yoga I turned him into the king of the Rakshas and have so far kept him under my protection. From now on, his harmful days are over. I entrust him to you.

The Rakshas spirits are subordinate to the Tantric goddess venerated by the hero's ancestors. She misleads death by temporarily turning Vishnudatta into a demon, in order to protect him. Thus the repeated alliances with the Rakshas spirits is explained. Not only does the Goddess save the life of one brother by this trickery, she also sends him with the whole demoniac army to provide assistance to her Brahmin devotees in the struggle that places them in opposition to the 'tribal' spirits: the Jhankris, Kalu Danava (surrounded by Mustangis and Thakalis) and Vajradatta. The other brother marries a demoness who bears him a son, and the son later reigns over the demonic realm. In this scenario, the Rakshas appears as an agent of Hindu power, controlled by the Goddess for the benefit of her best devotees, the Brahmins of her locality. The relationship with the Rakshas takes the form of a circular exchange with the Brahmin-demon who comes to fill the vacant throne of the demons finally being replaced, after being restored to the human world, by a demon-Brahmin, the hero's son. The whole is presented as a series of exchanges of services centred around death and royalty in the struggle against tribal enemies, embodied by shamanic spirits and cannibals. In a certain sense, *Vir caritra* can be read as an allegory of the conquest of Nepal's tribal territories and their subsequent Hinduization, since all the shamanic spirits are finally destroyed or brought under the control of the young Brahmin, while he becomes the ally of the harmful Hindu spirits: demons (Rakshas), spirits of the dead (Bhut), and divine snakes (Nag).

---

[25] Even very young Brahmins are addressed as 'grandfather' as a sign of respect.

[26] The god of death.

THE SHAMANS' KINGDOMS

A central feature of Girishallavabha Joshi's novel is the abundant descriptions it provides of the kingdoms of the spirits. As weird as the descriptions may sometimes appear in our eyes, it is clear that they were not born entirely from the author's imagination. I will deal only with the kingdoms of the shaman spirits or Jhankris, while noting that these are hardly different from those of the other classes of spirits. The worlds of the spirits are in the form of fortresses, *killā*, an image found elsewhere in Asia, which at the same time indicates their inaccessibility, their power, and their insular character. Set apart from the normal world, they are true worlds within the world, and the majority of them are located underground.

In the kingdom of the Shaman of the Forest (Ban Jhankri), it is his spouse Nidhini who rules over daily affairs, while the ruling shaman spirit remains confined to a cave which he leaves only once a year, to distribute the ṭikā.[27] Many groups live in this kingdom: the Tharu, Chepang, Bangali, etc. Its garden is a paradise, abounding with flowers that release delicious perfumes, and lotus-covered brooks and ponds. Here and there groups of musicians play traditional (*pañcai baja*) and foreign instruments (organ, harmonium, guitar). It is also a very modern place, equipped with electric lanterns, tables with paper, ink and pencils, and paths covered with brick dust. The place is marvellous, replete with human and animal shaped fountains, and marble, copper, silver and golden statues.[28] Everything seems artificial: the mountains, bushes and animals are false, and even the light is electric.[29] In the first garden, which one reaches from a cave, a column opens onto a staircase leading downwards. On the lower floor is another garden containing a bungalow reserved for the hero and his parents. A little distance away, a gate dissimulated at the foot of a tree opens onto another deep staircase. Once down, 'one still does not see the

---

[27] Frontal mark that chiefs and kings give their subordinates during the Goddess festival.

[28] This paradise-like garden brings to mind the hanging garden of Bombay, with its broad alleys, its bushes cut in the shape of animals or human beings, its arches and fountains.

[29] Even today, large parts of Nepal have no electricity.

ground and looking towards the sky, one does not see stars either, but only electric bulbs shining in lamps and lanterns. In such a light [Agnidatta] was carried from this intermediate world, while flying away' (p. 22). After a long journey through the air the hero and his witch-guide land in a small garden. There, his guide, the witch Dankini, explains to Agnidatta (p. 23):

All the plants which you see in the neighbourhoods are made of paper. The lights lit here and there are made of bronze. The pond that you see is of glass. There is no water inside....

Only Vir, Chauda, Bhut, Pret, Pisac, Sahakada, and Dankini spirits live at this level, and human beings are not allowed to reside here. It is here that Nidhini, the Mistress, lives, making her home each day in a different house.

Of forty or forty-five years, wearing black Tibetan silk clothes, with brown and enamelled hair parted in two by vermilion powder, her moulded chest displayed two breasts similar to two grain measures of four litres. Dressed in a Chinese fashion, she was holding a gold-plated skull from which she drank alcohol (p. 24).

For the peasants of central Nepal, Nidhinis are the spirits of women who died during childbirth: bare breasted, they haunt forests which they cross at great speed, despite their backward-turned feet, in search of male prey. As with the royal figure of Nidhini, the villagers underline the size of their breasts: so heavy and pendulous are they that in order to escape, one must run down the slope.

In the novel, the court of Nidhini is worthy of a queen. Dances and concerts are performed before an assembly of rich ladies of all nationalities: Parsi, Nagarni, Marhatteni, Panchabini, Kasmiri, Madesani, Tharuni, Bangali, Udeseni, English, French, German, Italian, Russian, Tibetan, Chinese, Japanese, Malaysian, Burmese, and Singhalese. However, features that are odd for both the hero and the Nepalese reader are added to this familiar princely framework. Thus, the custom of bowing does not exist, but one has to greet another person from afar. When it comes to consulting Agnidatta's parents, it is his mother who is consulted and not his father, because, as the witch says: 'women are by nature sharp and enlightened, they speak as is appropriate'. Lastly, it is a woman who controls the kingdom while her husband stays confined to a cave.

The kingdom of Nidhini and Ban Jhankri is composed of three levels: first, a wonderful garden; the second level where spirits and men live; and the third, meant exclusively for the Mistress and spirits. However, this constitutes only part of the kingdom, which is furrowed by underground galleries, staircases, and secret gates. From the second level, where he resides with his parents, Agnidatta explores another part with a Newar maidservant. Through a doorway hidden in a blue mast covered with lianas, they enter a forest, in the middle of which they encounter an arch flanked by a gate. Upon striking its bell, a lion's head emerges from the door, which in its turn had to be struck before it opened onto a staircase. Below this, a plain crossed by three paths stretches out: one leads to the kitchens, another to the treasure house, and the third to the prison. The path leading to the treasure house goes through a long tunnel covered in velvet and lit by flashlights. It culminates in a gate decorated with multicoloured glass plates upon which, when black bean grains are scattered, a large poisonous snake appears. The maidservant informs the hero that if one manages to seize its tongue when it opens its mouth, the gate opens; otherwise, it cuts one's fingers. Behind the door, they discover a large house with a pile of riches, from where an underground gallery leads to the south, towards the kitchens. An iron gate, where an iron bear sleeps, guards its access. To open it, one has to recite a formula and tear off the bear's leg. The meat of human beings, horses, cows, dogs, pigs, elephants, tigers, crows, and vultures is prepared in the kitchens. An underground path leads from the kitchen to the west, and the prison. It makes its way through a plain covered by a lawn and lit by gas lamps, and then an iron forest, in the middle of which stands a huge black stone building, the prison.

Lastly, another path leads to yet another large forest, at the centre of which stretches a lake, with an island in the middle. On the island, the hero sees a platform surmounted by cannon-guns and gunners, with an arch and four iron masts at its corners. The place is lit up by large lamps containing electric bulbs. Iron men and animals stand on the bank of the island. This is the entrance to the den of Ban Jhankri, who reigns over this world. When the hero reaches the spot, he introduces himself by speaking into the ear of an iron dog, after which soldiers posted on the island strike the arm of an iron man seven times, causing one of the masts to drop, forming a bridge for the hero to cross. Once he crosses, he is greeted by a Vīr who throws rice on a pillar while reciting formulas, and then strikes the ground under his foot seven times. This action causes a gate to open in the pillar, which gives onto a very deep iron staircase that leads to a small iron room. From here, another gate leads to a stone tunnel lit by gas lamps, where the water lies knee-deep, and which finally opens onto a deep pond that has to be crossed in a skin-boat. On the other bank, a mountain covered with a thick forest of papaw trees heavy with fruit and scented flowers seems to be 'ignited by flashlights'. A long red stone staircase climbs up to a huge cave of polished marble. Seated beside a *dhuni* fire consuming enormous logs of juniper and sandal trees, Ban Jhankri looks eighty years old: his skin is black, his fangs reach down to his navel, and his messy hair down to his waist. He wears a tiger skin, a green stone necklace, a rosary of riṭṭhā seeds, and a necklace of snake bones. Sitting on a bearskin, he says his rosary. Remaining silent all the while, he speaks in signs to the hero, who is disguised as Ban Jhankri's ritual friend's messenger.

Some leitmotifs recur in the description of Ban Jhankri's kingdom, which combines demons and wonders. This parallel world is made partly of iron: iron gates, iron forests, iron animals, and iron men. This feature obviously recalls the iron body attributed to the shaman and the underground journey of the first Magar shaman, who emerges as a blacksmith. The kingdom is an illusory reproduction of the world: water, plants, animals, and even the light are all artificial.[30] The wild world thus conceals extreme

---

[30] This taste for the artifice was very much in vogue among Rana governors. Thus, this description of the Singh Darbar palace in the 1920s could be taken from the novel studied here:

Suddenly, I had the feeling that I was dreaming. While turning back, I saw General Krishna whose image was reflected in a mirror, but a convex mirror which stretched his silhouette in the funniest manner....The room of mirrors preceded a kind of gallery of normal mirrors where the Maharaja gives his official receptions, sitting on a throne flanked by the busts of Edward VIIth and Queen Alexandra. In the middle of this room with too much gold finery, there was a marble fountain surmounted by a basin of Venetian glass, with a complicated mechanism which makes it possible

sophistication in the form of a manufactured world, like an anti-nature into which one plunges from the wildest places: the caves, rivers, and forests. The geography of Ban Jhankri's kingdom evokes the infinite: the levels follow one another down to an underground cosmos that separates the private domain of the Mistress from those of the others. It is also a labyrinth of corridors, columns, staircases, secret passages, and initiatory gates guarded by animals, evoking a world where human spatial reference marks are mixed up, a world reserved for initiates. The maze of Nidhini and Ban Jhankri's world apart is made up of a network of other worlds apart, all connected to each other by thin and practically impassable passages, increasing the embedded effect and the intoxication that its description arouses. Only the hero's audacity and the tricks he plays in his successive disguises enable him to unlock its secrets, and it is perhaps his adaptability to Otherness that is underlined here.

SUPERNATURAL MODERNITY

When the reader penetrates Suna Jhankri's kingdom, he is led directly to his remarkable courtroom (p. 115):

Suna Jhankri, was holding an audience along with Ritthe Jhankri, Masan Jhankri, Khole Jhankri, Khate Jhanki, Rukh Jhankri, Bhir Jhankri, Serpha Lama, Murmi Lama, Khole Lama, Bhote Lama, Potale Lama, Guru Dhami, Magar Dhami, Hayu Dhami, Baramu Dhami, Pahari Dhami, Gurhaun, Tharu, Chepang, Gubhaju, Kusle, etc. and all kinds of exorcists (jhārphuke). All were drinking alcohol, smoking and joking.

This assembly of spirits and tribal and Tibetan mediums and intercessors gives a precise idea of the religious specialists Brahmins assigned at the time to the various population groups. All those named Jhankri are obviously spirits as their names do not refer to an ethnic group, but to elements of the landscape. Successively, the spirits were: the 'golden shaman', 'the Rittha seed shaman', the 'shaman of the cremation fields', the 'shaman of the rivers', the 'wandering shaman', the 'shaman of the trees', and the 'shaman of the chasms'. The association of Jhankris with the wild world is amply underlined, as it continues to be in central Nepal. In this

---

to suddenly start luminous fountains with interchangeable colours (M. Dekobra, 'Le Népal, royaume interdit').

area, as in the text, the term Jhankri sometimes refers to human intercessors or shamans, but it more frequently denotes a class of spirits related to shamanism. There then follows a series of Lamas, linked to Tibetan or Tibetoid names: the Murmi Lama (Murmi being an old name for the Tamangs), the Tibetan Lama, the Lama of the Potala, the Khol Lama.[31] Then come mediums or Dhamis, who are enumerated as: 'Magar, Hayu, mountain-dweller, Baramu and Guru', thus clearly associating them with the tribal groups of central Nepal, although spirit possession is quite important for high-caste Hindus of central and western Nepal as well. At the very end are mentioned the Gurung, Tharu, Chepang, Newar Gubhaju priests, and Kusle musicians and entertainers. These shaman-spirits, Buddhist priests, mediums and tribal people form a community in communion with alcohol, whose consumption is strictly prohibited for people of high castes. In the kingdom of Suna Jhankri, contrary to that of Ban Jhankri, there is no important female character, and the role of the shamans are developed more fully. Thus Suna Jhankri takes Ban Jhankri's pulse in order to treat him (although he uses ayurvedic drugs after his diagnosis). Later, Suna Jhankri asks all Dhami-Jhankris to locate his enemy Agnidatta with their art (*jokhānā herne*). He touches sacrificial rice grains and some money, which he distributes to each of them. The 'Dhami-Jhankris look at the rice', and they all declare that Agnidatta is staying near the Balahari river.

Surprisingly, the city of the Golden Shaman seems more familiar to us than the underground maze of Ban Jhankri's kingdom, since it happens to be a real modern city. On the other hand, there were several reasons why the Nepalese reader at the time would marvel at it (p. 92):

In the middle of the mountain stood a fortress, inside which a town of beautiful lime houses rose. Immense shops occupied both sides of the road. Buses, trams, and Victorias were running. On the sidewalks, pedestrians walked

---

[31] Kol or Khol are described by the Gurungs questioned by Dharmaraj Thapa (2041 VS/1984) as an anthropophagous group that had been living in their area before the latter established themselves there. In the western Himalayas, they are described as an extinct Munda population. The term may also come from the Nepali *kholā*, river.

while looking at the shops....Automatic fountains with water were laid out every fifty cubits. Car cisterns poured water onto the roadway. Street sweepers removed the refuse off the road and carried it away in a cart. Nepalese, Panjabi, Christians, French and people of all countries trade together....At the crossroads were very large towers on which there were clocks showing the time. There were theatres, cinemas, circuses and dance rooms. There were also civil and military courts of justice, banks, printing houses....Outside the city, on a plain, young English, Muslim and Hindu people played *bhakuṇḍo*, tennis, hockey, polo and other games. Under the fortress, steamboats and rowing boats sailed on the Modiganga.

Merchant ships travelling between Kagbeni, Tukuce, Dana, Modibeni, Ridi, Palpa and Dyaughat blasted their sirens. From the railway station, mail, goods and passenger wagons circulated from Meci in the East up to Mahakali in the West, blowing their whistles. Some Sahebs flew away to Mustang in a smoking balloon (p. 162).

The city, which clearly refers to British India, is in fact a very exclusive society of shamans since, with the exception of the merchants, 'only the Dhami-Jhankris can enter the town of Suna Jhankri' (p. 143).[32] The shamans lord it over as masters, controlling the government and education:

In the city, the Jhankris who had come to supervise the examinations in the schools, passed by in a buggy drawn by four horses. They were dressed in a skirt of Tibetan silk, necklaces of *riṭṭhā* seeds, a yellow satin cap, and were beating their *ḍhyangro* drums. As soon as the shamans' car approached, the merchants stood up and greeted them by bowing low.

[32] One again finds this curious mixture in Rana Nepal, as seen in this scene described in 1929 during the New Year festival in the very traditional town of Bhaktapur:

I expected to see emerging the imposing procession of the princes in sumptuous Nepalese dress, assembled on elephants caparisoned in gold brocart. But Nepal had reserved another surprise for me. The sons of the Maharajah appeared, on saddle horses, in elegant riding costumes provided by the best tailors of London....We exchanged handshakes. Was I in Bhatgaon or in the presence of perfect gentlemen riders frequenting Rotten Row? New amazement: three American sedans emerged, with lowered curtains...these cars, whose passengers were not to be seen by the crowd, transported the wives of the Maharajah's sons (Dekobra, 'Le Népal, royaume interdit').

One consequently begins to enjoy oneself by imagining what the school curriculum of the city's inhabitants must have been like.

However, one does wonder whether this mixture of modernity and shamanism is pure fabrication on G. Joshi's part and if it appeared incongruous to the Nepalese at the beginning of the twentieth century. At any rate, it is certain that the first part of the novel, which describes the shamans' realms and which was published separately at the beginning of the twentieth century, was a great success. The idea was thus acceptable, and its extensive development satisfying. Moreover, it is still frequently said in Nepal that 'the Americans only manufactured the machines that the Hindus had invented in their myths'. Do the gods not have extraordinary machines, flying carts and invincible weapons? In a even more direct manner, the association between Western modernity and the world of the spirits was laid out to me on several occasions in Nepal, where I was told by some old people that what they call *pātal*, the underground world where the spirits live, was in fact my country, the country of the white people. In Nepali, the term pātal indicates not only the underground, but also the West, as opposed to the East, which is paradise, *svarga*. This may reinforce the idea that Westerners are chthonian beings.

The representations of 'White people' match those of spirits on several other points as well: pale, they are compared to the dead, whose blood has left their faces, or to sick people, in particular those affected by amoebas. Hairy, they are compared to wild men or monkeys. Their ablutions are said to be 'reversed', and they eat the strictly prohibited flesh of cow, pork, horse... and people are never sure where the limits are drawn: at snails, cats, dogs, men? Their females are known to court men and have several husbands (if not to enjoy 'free sex', like Nidhini). Lastly, for those with only a muddled idea of the time difference, they live during the night. As shown in *Vir caritra*, this monstrosity is accompanied by extraordinary richness, marvellous machines and uncontested power over the world.[33]

---

[33] The limits to Westerners' knowledge and technology are also uncertain, as I realized when I invited a villager from central Nepal to France. Among the numerous instances that showed me that he thought that anything was possible there, I will quote just one. Once, as we were watching *Star Wars* with my children, my friend began asking questions about the strange creatures he

Structurally, the association of Westerners with spirits can perhaps be explained through a classifying logic based on the general principle at work in this novel: any form of otherness is put aside in the spirits' realm, where various strange and dangerous beings coexist: wild animals, tribal peoples (and their priests), as well as Westerners and other foreigners. This allows for a place to be assigned to everyone within the closed universe of caste. This process results in the formation of a very heterogenous category, within which, however, important distinctions are made between the Hindu and the non-Hindu. Thus, the novel distinguishes between two categories of spirits, which are placed in opposition to each other: the Hindu evil spirits are possible allies, whereas tribal spirits are neutralized through the replacement of their kings with Hindu kings. In this respect, too, the novel exposes a fundamental social feature: it is the king (or his substitute, the village headman) who is the ideal person to deal with the Other,[34] the foreigner, and this dimension reinforces his prestige. On the other hand, he entrusts the relationships that are to be struck with the evil spirits of the kingdom to specialists—ascetics and priests.

The adventures of Agnidatta are a peregrination through Otherness in all its forms, from which the hero rises all-powerful. His voyage to Ridi is fully shamanic. Saving men from perdition in the world of the spirits, the hero, disguised and crafty, passes from

---

saw on the screen. I answered quite simply until one of his questions made me doubtful as to how real the movie was to his mind. I then pointed out that this was all imaginary (*kalpanik*), to which he reacted rather angrily, saying that if it was imaginary, it was useless. Interestingly, he then chose to regularly watch *Microcosmos*, a documentary on animal life in a meadow, which offers a new and 'alterocentric' point of view that he enjoyed a lot, as it is shot on the scale of these tiny animals.

[34] As the preceding note underlined, the Rana leaders themselves were certainly perceived as belonging to an external world, as foreigners. This phenomenon does not date back to the Rana, however, since as early as the seventeenth century the sovereign of Kathmandu, Pratap Malla, had financed a monumental inscription in various foreign languages (including French and English) that he placed in front of his palace, as well as a bas-relief representation of a man holding a telescope. The king had received this telescope from the first Westerners who entered his kingdom, two fathers on their way to India from China.

the human realm to supernatural ones. He forms alliances within the hereafter, twice becoming the spirits' son-in-law, and controls the three levels of the universe, which he crosses, descending into its very depths to the Jhankris' kingdoms and flying away in the Rakshas' balloon. Like a shaman, his relation with the spirits is a struggle, but it takes a particular form here. This is not merely about fighting face-to-face, or disentangling oneself from attacking spirits as the Nepalese shamans describe it, but a gigantic organized combat, where large armies clash under the leadership of kings from competing worlds. In the same way, the weapons used are truly fantastic in this Nepal of 1900: rifles and revolvers, as well as bombs and torpedoes are used in this fight. These techniques strongly contrast with current ideas relating to the spirits, who are now presented as retrograde and scornful of modernity. This evolution undoubtedly reflects the extent to which the Nepalese, even in the remotest villages, have embraced modern technology; Otherness is now relegated to the wilderness. With this new association, villagers sometimes feel that they belong to this Otherness, and see themselves as wild, that is akin to forest spirits.

Like a shaman the hero is also neutralized for a time by the spirits. Struck dumb, he is locked up in an iron cage, and his person appears particularly attractive to the female spirits who court him. This is similar to descriptions of the shamans of central Nepal, who often talk about how they had been captured and struck dumb before managing to master their art, and how, thereafter, they became the objects of witches' obscene proposals.

Shamanic in nature, the Agnidatta epic presents the voyage as a peregrination in the Otherness of anti-worlds, and the alliance with supernatural beings as the guarantor of harmony throughout the universe.[35]

---

[35] Alliance with the supernatural is, for Roberte Hamayon (*La chasse à l'âme*, pp. 738–9), constitutive of shamanism:

> ...shamanism is a symbolic system based on a dualistic design of the world, implying that humanity maintains relations of alliance and exchange with the supernatural beings who are supposed more largely to control the natural beings on which its subsistence depends, and more generally the random factors of its existence.

Men's relationships with various types of spirits (and probably the human groups with which they are associated) are articulated through these alliances. However, the relations they express are not simple. Each group has its own values concerning food taboos and purity, as well as alliance rules, which are contrasted with those of the others. The account underlines the extent to which the spirits' logic organizes our phenomenal world without our knowledge; however, the hero stands out from ordinary men by thwarting these traps through a controlled adoption of precisely that Otherness, assuming various identities which enable him to appear as a tolerable intruder or intermediary in the field of the Other, for example in the guise of a messenger or an itinerant merchant. By adopting the logic of the spirits in order to mislead them, the hero manages to subjugate and impose Hindu command over them by means of repeated alliances.

Vir caritra thus comes across as a vast metaphor of the world as the Nepalese conceive it. It shows how chance plays no role in the phenomenal world as proof of the spirits' intervention. The Agnidatta epic is not a search through imaginary worlds; it does not aim to modify their nature but to bind them, to end the world in order to return to the starting point, in the way a simple point transforms the infinite line into a circle. This exercise of circumspection brings to mind the ritual process through which afflictions are treated by inserting people, through recitation, into a closed, ideal and mythical world that the shaman controls.[36] In this parallel world, the components of which have been mastered by the shaman, afflictions are reduced to manifestations of essential malignant causes: chance, the unknown, the inexplicable, do not exist. Thus, because of all these aspects and not merely because it takes place among the shamanic spirits, *Vir caritra* can be qualified as a shamanic account. However, the question remains open as to whether embedding defines this genre.

---

[36] This idea was developed by Maskarinec, *The Rulings of the Night*.

3: Dance for Shikari, God of the Hunt, during the Bhume Festival, Syaulibang, Pyuthan (Photo: M. Lecomte-Tilouine).

2

Hindu Power in a Tribal Territory
The Cult of Bhume among the Magars*

The military conquest of the Magarant, the Magar country, took place around the fifteenth century, when the Thakuri petty kings and their dependents (priests, artisans, and soldiers) settled in what today forms the central, hilly part of Nepal. The Magar resistance appears to have been weak due to their lack of unity, and the alliances the conquerors formed with some of them. The Magar people were quickly assimilated, adopting most of their Hindu neighbours' cultural traits, notably their language and religion. Nevertheless, they retained or developed particular rituals in their relationship with the earth, as is obvious from the rites they devote to Bhume. We should first emphasize that the name Bhume is itself Nepali, derived from the Sanskrit *bhū, bhūmi*. However, this goddess is neglected by upper-caste Hindus while she is central to the Magars. This paradox has two possible sources: the Magars might have identified one of their principal goddesses with a minor Hindu deity by virtue of a common relation with the earth, conferring unusual importance on the latter. Or they might have constructed a divine being on the basis of Hindu concepts, which could have stemmed from a newly found need to defend their rights over the earth in the face of Hindu

* Originally published as 'Le culte de la Déesse-Terre chez les Magar du Népal', *Diogène*, 174, 1996, pp. 24–39.

invaders. The second hypothesis seems more likely, since no trace can be found of a Magar earth goddess before Bhume. Even in regions where the Magars retained the use of their original language (such as in Palpa, Syangja, or among the Kham-speaking Magars) and where, consequently, some of the gods have Magar names, the earth goddess is given Nepali names such as Bhume, Bhuyar, or Bhayar. Furthermore, even if the Magars did once have an earth goddess of their own, the renaming of this deity would indicate a change in identity, given the importance of a divinity's name.

Other indications tend to support the idea that the goddess Bhume was created as a reaction to the conquest. For example, the Magars call themselves autochthonous and often describe themselves as 'elders by the earth', an expression obviously created later, based on the link between autochthony and power over the earth, the two central aspects of Magar identity. Their earlier settlement on the land, coupled with their martial character, earned the Magars the relatively noble position of lower Kshatriyas in the new society created during the sixteenth and seventeenth centuries. Their early settlement is a sign of prestige both among the Magars —who never tire of flaunting it—and in the caste society that acknowledges it. It is likely that the Magars found a Hindu deity, Bhume, upon which they grafted an ideology that equated rights to the earth with ancestral rights, placing people of high caste, the more recently settled, in a delicate position, analogous *mutatis mutandis* to that of the Aryans in tribal India. As the Magar example in Nepal shows, earth cults and the monopoly of the priesthood over earth deities probably reflect a reaction to an invasion rather than a set primitive tradition. Confronted with people who flaunted their superiority in terms of purity, the Magars countered this by claiming to be 'elders by the earth', and thus deserving of respect. The link between power and ancestrality on the other hand, which is clearly illustrated in the Magar word *mijār*, meaning both the elder of the founding patrilineal line and village headman, and which underlies the cult of Bhume, was not recognized by upper-caste people.

BHUME IN THE LOCAL PANTHEON OF GULMI

In a polytheistic culture as richly developed as that of central Nepal, where Hindu and Magar cultures (to cite the two being reviewed here) are inextricably bound together, the gods often lack distinct traits, and their functions are not clearly defined. Their nature can nevertheless be gleaned from their various associations, which are expressed verbally or manifested in rites. This is why I consider Bhume a special case in the local pantheon; in some ways she is identified with the evil forest spirits, while in others she shares certain characteristics with the great masters of the earth, the mountain ridge gods.

Of the three levels that make up the world, earth is the one shared between men, 'the kings of cultivated lands', and the 'petty deities', who are the 'forest kings'. This realm is ruled from high up by celestial gods residing on the mountain tops, the 'Kailash' gods, who govern the whole earth (prthvī) as well as great natural phenomena such as rain, hail and epidemics. Identified with ascetics, these gods are nonetheless described as owners of the earth, for example the god Malika, whose name means 'the owner'. Associated with extreme purity, their worship is reserved for society's elite, the high castes, and to a lesser extent the Magars. They are inaccessible to lower castes and women.

As mentioned earlier, human beings and their ruling deities share the earthly level with 'forest' spirits. The 'forest' world includes water, paths, and the underworld. The forest and the underground are part of the same 'low' level, and the gods associated with the earth are often described as evil spirits or forest deities. Bhume herself is conceived as such, but her position is unique; a wild goddess domesticated by man, she sides not with her own kind, but with the villagers who nurture and honour her. Her ties to the forest, where violent death prevails, are nevertheless emphasized by the fact that she is often described as a goddess related to death. This cannot be seen as a characteristic of an indigenous Magar earth goddess, dating from before Bhume, because the association of the dead with Bhume are found both among the caste people in central Nepal and in popular Hinduism in northern India.

Men and forest deities share a relationship that is competitive and malevolent. What differentiates them is the knowledge of agriculture, which men possess and which is unknown to the spirits. Forest divinities are much like hunter-gatherers, living as predators. As a matter of fact, groups of hunter-gatherers, such as the Rautes or the Kusundas, are today presented as forest divinities in central Nepal. During prayers to the forest divinities, men begin by offering them precisely what they lack, such as small shelters, the replica of movable sheds, as well as a miniature technical panoply (bow and arrows, a drum, kitchen paddles, yeast) and, in particular, a set of agricultural tools (hoe, swing-plough, beam, plane, etc.).

THE REPRESENTATION OF PLOUGHING

Among these agricultural tools, the plough is held in the highest esteem. It is the only tool to which prayers are offered before it is used, and the one that represents the highest achievement of their culture.[1] This is because the use of the plough not only distinguishes man from the spirits, it also defines a territory, and likewise a property. Thus, until the 1960s, non-cultivated private land was not considered the sole property of the owner. For example, in the village of Darling (Gulmi), anyone could gather fodder or firewood on private land. Similarly, itinerant farming did not correspond to ownership. It was only after ploughing the same spot for three years that someone was expected to pay taxes, and in this way assume ownership. In many regions of Nepal, such as the Terai or the Mahabharat, plough soles driven into the earth mark the boundaries of localities or properties. While ploughing distinguishes man as a peasant from the predatory errant spirits, that is, from the spirits inhabiting the earthly level, it also separates him from the other gods of superior rank who inhabit the mountain tops. Indeed, contact with the earth, of which ploughing is the most complete expression, is the lot of the ordinary man; Hindu gods never touch the earth, and ascetics (or the crowned king) keep their distance from it by wearing wooden sandals. Furthermore, it is written in the Śatapatha Brahmaṇa 1.9.1.29 that though the sacrificer may reach the heavens through sacrifice, if he does not return, he risks going

---

[1] Quite often a new plough undergoes a little ritual before its first use. Similarly, during the Tihar festival, the plough is the only farm implement that is venerated. It is decorated with a flower wreath and a ṭikā mark; in the Sallyan, Rolpa, and Jajarkot regions, householders remove the ploughshare and fill the blade slot with rice.

mad. To remain human, he must touch the earth. The Brahmins, who live on the earth in spite of their divine pretensions, nonetheless do not till it; they have neither the right to plough the land and nor can they enter it with the purpose of exploitation (for example, entering a mine).

Ploughing contains an important sexual symbolism. Valued for both its virile aspect and for the fact that this activity requires great skill—it is among those rare manual labours that men are proud to be photographed undertaking—it also represents, in Hindu terms, an impure task that might pollute a man of high caste. Sexuality and impurity in fact characterize both ploughing and the fruits it bears. People say that in order to avoid all contact with cultivated land (but might it not be sexuality that is referred to?), ascetics traditionally do not eat the fruits of ploughing, while Brahmins living in the world are content with avoiding any physical contact with the plough. Moreover, nubile women, in anticipation of the day of Rishi pancami—a ritual during which they purify themselves of their menses and recover their virginity—turn over small plots with hoes in order to eat pure rice from the unploughed earth on this occasion. The homology between earth and woman, between ploughing and the sexual relationship, is taken even further in certain regions of India such as Bengal, where men do not plough or have carnal relations with their wives during a ritual period of five days that correspond with the 'earth's menstruations'. This taboo is also present in Nepal, manifested during a day set aside 'to avoid the earth'. Significantly, the virgin and wild goddesses of central Nepal's mountain tops, such as Malika, must not be offered products from ploughed fields, and people must abstain from eating grains on the day they are worshipped. The sexual symbolism of the plough can again be found in a ritual practised by the shamans of Gulmi. This has to do with getting rid of the spirit of a stillborn child or a child who died young by sealing it within an earthenware pot, which symbolizes a womb, the opening of which is sealed by a swing-plough before it is buried at a crossroads.

Through the act of ploughing, man thus enters a special relationship with the earth. Women are excluded from all cults pertaining to the fertility of the fields, and the earth in general. They are not supposed to step over a plough or even an ox harness. Thus the plough belongs to the realm of the masculine as opposed to that of the feminine, to humanity and the cultivated world as opposed to the wild spirits and gods.

THE EARTH

The earth contains an intrinsic power that regenerates both men and demons. In the myth of the struggle between the first shaman and the nine witch sisters in the Gulmi region, the shaman is vanquished by sorceresses, who rip out his heart and roast it. The shaman nonetheless succeeds in eating his own heart and falls asleep, declaring his intention to 'entrust himself to the earth'. He lies down flat on his stomach on the ground for seven days, at the end of which he is reborn in all his glory. The power recognized in the earth can also be found among the Kham Magars, who call the ceremony they devote to Bhume a 'ritual of power'.[2] The earth's principle of vital energy is quite often used by demons, who come back to life or multiply when in contact with the earth, as in the case of Raktabija. Since the earth contains a formidable energy, ploughing is considered to be a gruelling activity, the only one that ends with the workers (and the oxen) being well-compensated for their efforts. However, the earth is not just a source of energy: its ambivalence is highlighted in the myth of Prithu. Usually depicted in Hindu mythology as a defenceless woman oppressed by too heavy a load, who begs the gods or the king to come to her assistance, the earth appears in this myth as a perfidious creature who swallows all the vegetation and causes the world to waste away.

The ambiguous nature of the earth seems to be initially related to purity. Unlike elements such as fire, which nothing can deprive of its pure character, the earth, while possessing the ability to absorb impurity and purify it, may also be polluted or contaminated. Hence high-caste women can be seen first washing themselves with earth, and then, once purified, avoiding contact with it by sitting on a banana leaf and not on the ground during the Rishi pancami rite.

We can identify two different attitudes towards these ambivalent aspects of the earth, which I call 'brahmanic' and 'royal' respectively.

---

[2] Sales, A. de, *Je suis né de vos jeux de tambours*, p. 93.

The former is respectful. One finds this attitude among the Brahmins of Gulmi, who explain that they do not plough in order to not 'wound their mother', the earth, and among the Brahmins of Maharastra, who apologize each morning before walking on the ground. The second attitude is much more complicated, as the myth of Prithu, mentioned above, shows. The king, generally depicted as the protector of the earth, here appears to dominate it. Earth swallowed the vegetation and caused the world to waste away until King Prithu forced it to return its bounty, levelled it out, and founded agriculture. In the Mahābhārata or the *Bhāgavata Purāṇa* Prithu is described as the father of the earth, but this descent is not so firmly established since *The Laws of Manu* portray him as her husband. Many facts indicate that the king shares a very intimate relationship with her, both protecting and dominating her, and that he is conceived of as her ploughman and husband. In classical Hindu mythology, the earth goddess Bhūmi, a young woman of great beauty, is in danger. She sinks into the depths of the ocean. The one who saves her is in fact the prototype of the ploughman, a wild boar. It has to be mentioned that the wild boar digs the earth with his tusks to hunt for food and that in the myths of central Nepal, it is often on land dug up by a wild boar that a hunter sows seeds and founds a village. It is significant that Hindu kings often identify themselves with the wild boar, saving, working, and loving the earth. The deep intimacy between Hindu kings and the earth is expressed through the Nepalese royal consecration, which is marked by anointing the king's body with earth from different parts of the kingdom, an unction compared to a union. Moreover, the king is frequently called *Bhūpati* (in the national anthem, for example), the master or husband of the earth.

The privileged relationship uniting the sovereign with the earth can likewise be read in the belief held among some Magars, according to which the king of Nepal would plough each year, followed by the queen who sowed the seeds. This ritual is supposed to take place at the beginning of spring to open the farming season. I was not able to verify the existence of a spring ploughing royal festival since the custom has not survived to the present day, but it has been ascertained that a royal rice planting ceremony used to take place within the palace during the nineteenth century, at the beginning of the rainy season.[3] Whether or not the king of Nepal actually ploughs or used to plough in the past is of little importance; what this belief does is underline the strict tie between the king and the earth's fertility in the eyes of the villagers. We should also point out that the king radically distinguishes himself from his peers through this act (or in the belief of the existence of this act), which is forbidden to Brahmins and Thakuris, the latter being the caste group the king belongs to. A famous example of royal ploughing occurs in the Rāmāyaṇa, which states that Sita was born from the earth when king Janaka made a furrow with his swing-plough, and the custom has been preserved in at least the ancient Indianized royal kingdom of Cambodia. Faced with the Brahmin's respectful attitude towards the earth, imagined as a descending filiation, the king, her protector, demonstrates his domination over her by taking on the role of either father or husband, and not a son. The Mahābhārata 13.8.21 clearly establishes the privileged matrimonial alliance between the earth and warriors: 'In the case where the husband is absent (dead), the wife marries his younger brother. In this way, since the earth cannot have a Brahmin, she takes a Kshatriya to wed.'

Let us now examine the agrarian rites that punctuate the agricultural cycle in central Nepal, before exploring the collective cults of the earth deities, who on this level are imagined as the protectors of a territory in connection with political power.

OFFERINGS TO BHUME AND THE EARTH DEITIES

The three main crops cultivated in the district of Gulmi are rice, maize, and finger millet. The oldest of the three crops is said to be finger millet,[4] but as this grain is eaten by poor people and is considered impure, its first fruits are rarely offered to Bhume. To my knowledge, only the inhabitants of the village of Darling offer four litres of it to the goddess after its harvest. The cultivation of maize probably dates back to the seventeenth century in Nepal, but its first fruits are offered in most villages and among all the groups. The

---

[3] Hamilton, *An Account of the Kingdom of Nepal*, p. 224.

[4] On the history of agriculture in Darling, see Lecomte-Tilouine and Michaud, 'From the Mine to the Fields', and in the Himalayan range, see Dollfus, et al., 'Les cultures à l'épreuve du temps'.

ceremony is simple. The divinity is represented by a stone in a field and is usually accompanied by Nag and Nageni, a couple of divine snakes, and Jhankri, the shaman of irrigated lands, as well as Sikhari, the divine hunter. A chicken is often sacrificed, and a libation of milk and the smoke of clarified butter mixed with Artemisia are then offered to the deities. Afterwards, an entire cornstalk is uprooted and the officiating priest, opening the husks, places it on Bhume's altar, 'ready to be eaten'. One ear is then grilled on the hearth, and a few kernels are mixed with butter and offered in three vessels intended, respectively, for Bhume, the divinities of the lineage, and the 'divinities from the outside'. More simply, the Brahmins of the village of Musikot are content with warning Bhume that they are going to harvest the field with the following phrase: 'Very well, now we are going to eat grain'. Apart from these widespread offerings of first fruits, after the harvest the villagers from Darling offer four litres of maize in the name of Bhume, but here again they are an exception. More commonly, in this region the four-litre offering involves only the rice crop. The grain is presented to a young virgin girl in each household on behalf of Bhume. The young girl disposes of it as she sees fit, eating it, selling it, or even turning it into alcohol if her caste allows it and she wishes to do so. This offering indicates that Bhume is conceived of as the daughter of the head of the household. This is unusual, since normally virgin daughters receive the food left over from an offering to the gods or a sacrificial wage; the young girl in this case is a substitute for the goddess herself, as the recipient of the offering. Worship to Bhume also accompanies the paddy harvest. It takes place on the threshing floor or in the field, and usually involves the sacrifice of a chicken.

Apart from these agrarian rites, two similar ceremonies in which Bhume, Jhankri, Nag and Sikhari are worshipped take place in the months of November-December (*mansir*) and April-May (*baisākh*). During these ceremonies, both compensation and restitution are offered to the earth deities. This is why the Brahmins of the village of Asleva leave a little chicken out in the fields so that it may go into the forest and become wild. In exchange for the fruits of the cultivated earth, the villagers give back to nature a small domesticated animal, so as to maintain equilibrium between the wild and the cultivated and appease the wild side of Bhume.

As we can see, it is mostly harvesting that prompts any worship of Bhume. This worship includes three other deities in the agricultural context. First, there is Sikhari, the forest deity presiding over wild animals and the hunt. The relationship between Sikhari and Bhume can be seen in the village of Neta, in the commune of Dibrung, where the Magars offer the heart, liver and pieces of meat from slaughtered game to Bhume (in her dual guise as Sime-Bhume) instead of Sikhari. The second deity accompanying Bhume is Jhankri. Jhankri is a generic term which, in Gulmi region, designates the forest divinities related to shamanism. Bhume herself sometimes qualifies as such. Jhankri or the Jhankri and Jhankreni couple, who accompany Bhume in the rites, preside over the muddy earth, such as irrigated fields, as well as the aquatic element in general. In the same way that Bhume appears to the Magars in dreams in the guise of a Brahmin's young and beautiful daughter, decked out in finery and with a dark complexion, Jhankri is imagined to be a rich man with black skin. He is a *lāgo*, a god who sends down calamities. A Magar once told me that after having ploughed his irrigated fields, he saw two beautiful women with dark complexions walking on it. The next day he fell ill and concluded that he had seen Jhankri's wives, who had sent him his illness. An irrigated field is considered dangerous. The Dogami Gharti Magar of Darling thus imagine that one of their ancestors died in his irrigated field when he tried to plough it, sinking into the mud with his oxen, where he remains to this day. Jhankri is the counterpart of Bhume, and complements her. Bhume herself is often called Sime-Bhume, although Sime, whose name means 'the one from muddy ground, from the source', never appears alone as an individual entity. Their inseparable nature is often used in verbal imagery. Hence a Kami artisan from Darling explained to me one day that the Kamis and the Magars were like Sime-Bhume, inseparable and complementary.

Finally, the last divine figure associated with Bhume is Nag, the divine snake living in the underworld. Like Bhume and Jhankri, Nags appear as bearers of wealth, and this feature seems characteristic of the earth and all who inhabit it, particularly in the region where mineral lodes are plentiful. Here, again, there are strong ties between Bhume and the Nags. Their figures are partially confused among the Kham Magars.[5] Likewise, in the village of Darling, someone one day told me that 'they were making a snake of ashes for Bhume', without making it clear whether the snake represented the divinity or was being offered to her.

Nag plays a special role in the agricultural cycle. He is the object of a well-known cult in the Hindu world, the Nag pancami, which falls on the fifth day of the dark half of *sāun*, June-July. On this occasion, all over Nepal and in the north of India, people paste drawings of Nags on the doors of houses and temples. In Darling, people say that this is the day that Nag and all other snakes emerge and rise out of the ground. For the villagers, it is also the beginning of winter, which indeed corresponds to the 'descending season' (*udāuli*), the season during which the sun begins its journey towards the North. The purpose of this ritual is made clearer through a comparison with its counterpart, Shri pancami, which takes place six months later, at the advent of spring and the rising season (*ubhāuli*). People say that Shri pancami marks the beginning of cultivation. Each person must then either plough his field or have it ploughed. The first strike of the plough is ritualized. First the 'snake is scaled', then 'split', and then 'cut into pieces'. The position of this snake in the field is determined by an astrological computation, and the ploughman must take special care to scale the snake by beginning with the tail. Once the snake has been cut into pieces, the field becomes 'homogeneous'. The presence of the snake in the earth is an obstacle to working the field, especially to ploughing. Once scattered, 'there are Nags everywhere, in a continuous fashion', people say, and working the fields may begin. The snake regulates the solar and agricultural calendar. Killed for the rising season and the agricultural season, it is reborn in the descending season to protect the crops as they ripen. The main role that the villagers attribute to the Nag is that of protector—he protects the crops from thieves and evil spirits. Interestingly, this role is also attributed to Bhume, and is taken much further in the case of the latter, since the deity assures the protection of the men who cultivate the fields as well. Thus a young Magar, frightened to see me walking around the village

[5] See Oppitz, *Frau für Fron, Die Dreierallianz bei den Magar West-Nepals.*

at night, advised me once that if I were to encounter an evil spirit, I should jump off the road and into a field, where Bhume would protect me. Her protection is more effective, he added, if the field belongs to you, which underscores the contract that independently links each domestic group with the form of Bhume presiding over its lands.

Akin to forest deities and those of the underground, Bhume appears as the daughter of the householder at the time that offerings of the first fruits are made. This idea, which is linked to the 'brahmanic' attitude towards the earth, coexists with the idea that the village headman, or *mukhiya*, is a substitute for the goddess. This is indicated, for example, during the symbolic purchase of a tomb site from Bhume, an act usually performed with the chief. In this instance, the Magar headman is no different from the Hindu king, who is often described as akin to the earth.

THE VILLAGE CULTS DEDICATED TO BHUME

Intimately linked to the founding of a village, the cult of Bhume remains associated with the first settlers. More often than not, Bhume's priesthood is conferred on a person of tribal lineage. In the village of Aglung, the inhabitants go so far as to hire an officiating priest from a neighbouring locality, a descendent of a group of Magars who, they say, once lived on their lands, but had been driven northwards at the time of their arrival. Four hundred households of Hindu caste gather together for this cult and offer an enormous sacrificial payment to the Magar officiating priest from the village of Kahare Darling, who receives half a litre of rice from each for his office. Should we view this as ritual compensation, guaranteed by Bhume, for lost lands?

At any rate, the collective cults dedicated to Bhume are intimately tied to power and political units. Bhume is an omnipresent deity, defined by the sociological group that worships her. Hence, in Darling one distinguishes the various 'Bhume(s) of each man's field', who are the recipients of the agrarian rites I mentioned, from the 'Bhume of the whole village'. One also finds this distinction among the Magars of Sikha who worship, on the one hand, a Mukhiya Bhume, the deity of the headman's territory, who is worshipped by the latter and who protects the people, the crops and prevents epidemics, and, on the other, a 'thum Bhume', which is placed at the head of the previous political Thum unit grouping together several mukhiya territories. Thus, in Sikha, above the individual and village cults, there exist larger territorial cults devoted to Bhume.[6] Conversely, in Gulmi district, the cult of Bhume is often based on very small territorial units such as the tol (quarters) or the ward, administrative divisions of the Panchayat. This can probably be explained by the fact that there are fewer Magars here. Hence, in a Panchayat such as Badagaon in Gulmi, where the population is largely made up of Hindu castes, only the Magar hamlet organizes the collective worship of Bhume. Until the reform of the Panchayats in 1962, in many Magar villages the officiating priest for the collective worship of Bhume was the headman, or mukhiya. This worship, intimately tied in with political organization, changes considerably with each political reform. Before examining its evolution, I will describe, as an example, the cult I was able to observe in 1990 in Syaulibang (Pyuthan district), where the former mukhiya continues to exercise his role of officiating priest as in the past.

Some time before the ritual, each household under the mukhiya's control sends him half a litre of maize, with which he makes beer. Then, three days before the ritual, the headman goes to the Bhume sanctuary outside the village, where he remains alone for three days and nights, sleeping on the spot. The villagers take turns to bring him his meals, which must include fish, supposedly the first catch of the year. The ritual takes place on the tenth day of the bright half of the month of mansir (November–December), at the beginning of winter and the fishing and hunting season. Hence, at one time it also opened the hunting season, since an animal killed in the forest was supposed to be brought to the mukhiya at the same time as the fish. During his confinement in the Bhume sanctuary, the mukhiya should not speak to anyone; and no one may touch the walls of his house in the village. When he returns home on the morning of the

---

[6] J. Kawakita, *The Hill Magars and Their Neighbours*, p. 345. To relativize this statement, it should be noted that the thum were of very different sizes, depending on the region. In Gulmi they were much larger than they were in the Tanahun and Gorkha regions, for instance, and corresponded to the ancient kingdoms. Perhaps this explains why they do not form a ritual basis in this region.

ritual, he sprinkles holy water along his path in order to remain pure. He then sits on a leaf on the veranda of his house, wearing a white turban on his head, and still not speaking. All the villagers gather in his courtyard, bringing rice as well as kid goats and sheep to be offered in sacrifice to Bhume. Damai musicians play their instruments, from which strips of cloth have been hung. A man from the mukhiya's lineage officiates as priest. He takes the twelve jars of beer made with the villagers' maize from the headman's house and places them in the courtyard. He then measures the rice brought by each person and pours it onto a large cloth placed on the ground, verifying that each family has indeed brought half a litre, and then transfers it all to a basket. The headman gives orders with a sign of his head and hands. He points out the priests and the Damais, signalling for them to leave. They go straight to the sanctuary, where the priest offers incense, milk and strips of cloth to Bhume. The headman then points to a man in the crowd who carries a bow and quiver. He comes to the centre of the courtyard and executes a very beautiful dance with his bow. Turning slowly, he removes an arrow from the quiver and pretends to shoot it in the four directions of the universe. With a wave of his hand the mukhiya dismisses him. This man is a Bhujel Magar, a wife-taker of the headman's lineage; he leaves the headman's courtyard to worship Sikhari near a spring. The priest then returns from the Bhume sanctuary and the headman orders him to leave again. Seizing the basket containing the rice, he goes back to the sanctuary. Finally, the twelve jars of beer are seized by different men at the mukhiya's command, and brought to the sanctuary (*thān*). The headman and the priest then wash themselves in the river, and afterwards all the villagers proceed to the Bhume *thān* with their sacrificial victims. Only the males have the right to approach the Bhume sanctuary, but they do not have the right to go inside. They prepare rice pudding in a large pot while the mukhiya, alone and still silent, takes a large sabre with a flared blade and decapitates the sacrificial victims one by one with great butchery, for the animals are not supposed to be attached and no one is allowed to help him. There follows a banquet in which the entrails of the victims are eaten with rice pudding and the corn beer offered by the community. Here again, the women do not take part in the feast, although it unites the men of all castes and notably the Damais, the very low caste of tailor-musicians.

This rite is enacted primarily by the village headman. Based on a script well known to all, since it takes place without words, it presents a pure chief of supreme authority: all the actors react to the slightest nod of his head. Here, one sees clearly how the role of village priest is attributed to the village headman among the Magars. During the time of the Bhume ritual, the headman enters an exclusive relationship with the earth goddess, with whom he first spends three days and nights in private, speaking to no one. Through this intimate contact with the goddess, he comes into a state of purity that cuts him off from the rest of the world, since when he emerges from his austerities he is still forbidden to speak to anyone and must particularly avoid contact with the soiled earth, purifying his way with water and sitting on leaves. In short, he is the only one who may enter Bhume's sanctuary and offer her sacrifices. This exclusive relationship with a deity is very unusual in central Nepal, and one can notice the quasi-matrimonial relationship that exists between the mukhiya of Syaulibang and Bhume, whom the headman's brother described to me as 'our wife' (since the headman himself could not speak to me).

In fact, information from the village of Darling indicates that the local 'Bhume of the whole village' was also, long ago, merely the headman's Bhume. The ritual took place in the very courtyard of his house, where he sacrificed a pig to Bhume with his own hands. All the village men, excluding the women, then ate the pig's flesh. The purification of the Syaulibang chief no doubt embodies a collective dimension, as does the Darling headman's cult of Bhume. Elsewhere, as in the Kham Magar village studied by A. de Sales, the whole village has to be purified before worshipping Bhume, and the villagers are confined to their houses.

For the Magars, the concept of the village community is thus partly structured around the cult of Bhume, in which everyone participates. In Sikha, where a certain number of people settled recently, the Bhume celebration defines the 'true villagers', differentiating them from those who do not participate and are not really part of the community. The cult of Bhume combines an ancestral connection to the earth with a recognition of an inherited power over the earth, the power of the mukhiya. A Sikha villager thus defined the *jagatko puja* ('cult of territory') in the following, negative terms: 'It is different from *Bume* [because] the mukhiya plays no role, in contrast to the Bume Puja....the mukhiya...happened to join it but not as a mukhiya, but as a mere individual'.[7]

The tight link between the cult of Bhume and political power is displayed in the modifications it has undergone as a result of political changes. Thus, in Sikha, the cult of Bhume was not performed in 1960, a date that corresponds to a major political change, one that led to the reform of the Panchayats.[8] J. Kawakita quotes a villager: 'We stopped performing Bume Puja in 1960, as the *mukhiya* accepted the suggestion of the younger generation to do so. Unluckily, epidemics, crop failure, hailstorms, etc. attacked our village since that time. Therefore the Puja was resumed in 1961.'[9]

Similarly, in Darling, the Panchayat reform in the early 1960s had an impact on the Bhume pūjā. Bhume's sanctuary was transferred from the headman's courtyard to the crest of the mountain. While the man elected as the head of the Panchayat still decided its precise date, he was no longer entitled to play the role of the divinity's officiating priest, because of which a Magar priest had to be chosen. More significantly, the cult of Bhume has to some extent been supplanted by that of a new divine figure, Grame, 'the villager', who seems to be for the Panchayat what Bhume used to be under the mukhiya's jurisdiction.

HIGH-CASTE GROUPS AND BHUME

The attitude of high-caste people towards the collective cults addressed to Bhume differs depending on the context. Kawakita showed how some of them refused to participate in Bhume's collective worship, which had been organized in the territory where

---

[7] Kawakita, *The Hill Magars and Their Neighbours*, p. 369.

[8] At the village level, the Panchayat reform led to a gathering of the ancient territories of the mukhiya headmen into larger areas called the Gaun Panchayat. Moreover, a person elected by universal suffrage (the Pradhan) replaced the traditional village headmen, whose authority used to be hereditary.

[9] Kawakita, *The Hill Magars and Their Neighbours*, p. 370.

they live in the region of Sikha. This extreme attitude may be linked to the fact that they were recent migrants. In the Gulmi region I did not encounter such rejection; on the contrary, I was struck by the fact that high-caste groups participated in the collective worship of Bhume organized by the Magars, agreeing to play the subordinate role of cook. We must note that this participation usually takes place in contexts where Magars are present in large numbers. However, I encountered an extreme case of a Bhume 'tribal cult' in a village only inhabited by upper-castes, but which was said to have been inhabited in the past by Magars. The attitude of the high castes towards Bhume is thus no doubt linked to the conditions of their settlement in tribal territories. In the zones of ancient cohabitation, a *modus vivendi* took root, bestowing a certain prestige on the indigenous people, or allowing them to believe that they still have a power monopoly over the earth.[10]

Regardless of the apparent disinterest in Bhume among the high castes, the religious practices in Gulmi district demonstrate that the deity is nevertheless present in some sanctuaries, and is collectively worshipped during the Dasain festival, the ten days dedicated to Durga, the warrior form of the goddess. Thus in Dasikot, Rupakot and Juniya, there is a Bhume shrine within the *koṭ* (temple arsenal) next to Khadka, the divine sword. Bhume is represented by a sacred rock driven into the earth. She must remain anchored in it, as the case of Rupakot demonstrates; here, Bhume's rock is situated on the ground floor, while the sanctuary containing the arsenal and the divine swords is on the first floor. Bhume worship, however, continues to have impure connotations in these cases. In Juniya, for instance, it is a low-caste Kami officiating priest who offers her chickens, or impure animals. In Rupakot, too, Bhume receives chickens. The Dasain festival, on the other hand, celebrates royal power through the mediation of the local chief. The very association of Bhume with the royal sword, a symbol of sovereignty, suggests that for the upper-castes, it is only the king, who is represented by the local headmen, who can establish the only truly divine relationship between man and the earth. Through the worship of Bhume, a direct relationship between the headman and the earth is formed

[10] M. Lecomte-Tilouine, 'About Bhume'.

among the Magars, while among the Indo-Nepalese of high caste, the relation to the earth is mediated by the king and the sword-gods, which embody royal military power.

Bhume is the spouse of the Magar headman, as she is of the Hindu king. She is the mother (or the virgin daughter) of high-caste groups and ordinary villagers. In this respect, one might interpret the royal ban on Brahmins and Thakuris from ploughing, and its severe punishment, as a way of distancing them from direct power over the earth.[11] Nevertheless, while the Hindu king's power over the earth is limitless—except in the case of the ocean—and relies on his military might, the Magars associate this power with the first occupation of a territory, thereby by definition restricting it.[12] This idea is obviously bothersome for high-caste immigrants, who arrived after the tribal groups, seized power, and never ceased to extend it. Thus in the *Gorkhā Vaṃśāvalī*, the lack of enthusiasm for the territorial expansion of Magars is invoked by two Brahmins when they discourage King Narabhupal Shah from appointing ministers from this group.

The supremacy of the Hindu king over the earth is nonetheless recognized by the Magars at the time of the Dasain festival. Until the Panchayat reform, the Magar mukhiya had been doubly legitimized: by a direct relationship with his ancestral land through the worship of Bhume, and as a representative of the Hindu king during the Dasain festival. This situation differs from that of the Limbus in eastern Nepal, who preserved two concurrent forms of legitimacy after the conquest of their territories: the one delegated by the Hindu king to the *subbā* chiefs, affirmed by the Dasain festival, and the one conferred upon the former *hang* chiefs by the power of the mountain.[13] The concentration of these two forms of power in the same person among the Magars probably dates back to their ancient contacts with the Indo-Nepalese, and the alliances their chiefs formed with them. Knowing nothing of the specifically Magar forms

---

[11] According to R.C.P. Singh (*Kingship in Northern India*, pp. 101–10), the Visvakarman Bhauvana myth offers a Brahmin representation of the land that stood in opposition to the pretensions of the king.

[12] Naraharinath 2021 VS/1964: 101.

[13] Philippe Sagant, 'Le double pouvoir chez les Yakhthumba'.

of rule before the conquest of their territories, the particularities they cultivate today during the cult of Bhume, in which the headman plays a large role, provide food for thought. Since the Magars claim to have originated from hunters and wandering clearers of land, the importance they grant to ploughing seems paradoxical, and contrasts with Limbu ideas of power based on the force of nature. One gets the impression that the Magars created their own royal Hindu model by rooting it into the earth, so as not to be driven away from it. On the other hand, if we refute the idea that the Magars created a later-day ritual in the case of Bhume, the conceptions of power over the earth and the source of the chief's power expressed therein manifest great similarities with Hindu ideology, which certainly helped in their Hinduization.

4: Weapons Kept in the Arsenal of Alam Devi, Lasargha, Syangja (Photo: M. Lecomte-Tilouine).

3

The Enigmatic Pig
On Magar Participation in the State Rituals of Nepal*

Once upon a time if a Hindu Nepalese happened to marry a Muslim or a Christian, the whole kingdom was considered polluted and the King himself had to undertake costly ritual proceedings in order to purify the country. Francis Buchanan Hamilton[1] witnessed such a ceremony in 1803 when the King reportedly spent a huge amount of money on this occasion. This anecdote has multiple symbolic

* Originally published as 'Entre orthodoxie hindoue et cultes tribaux', *Archives de Sciences Sociales des Religions*, vol. 99, 1997: 9–32. Translated and revised as 'The Enigmatic Pig: On Magar Participation in the State Rituals of Nepal', *Studies in Nepali History and Society*, vol. 5, no. 1, 2000: 3–41.

[1] Hamilton, *An Account of the Kingdom of Nepal*, pp. 20–1. This was true even when the culprit belonged to a low caste. In the manuscript of Francis Buchanan Hamilton's book, 'Some observations...' (folio 102–3), the ceremony is more detailed:

Any Musulman or Christian... who should cohabit with a Damai woman, would suffer death and the woman would be severely punished. When any woman has been discovered with a Musulman, the whole kingdom thrown into confusion....This can only be expiated by a ceremony called Praschit, in which the Raja or Rany washes in the river with great ceremony, and bestows large sums on the Bramins, who read the Muntres proper on the occasion. The expense of an expiation of this kind, which was performed during our stay in the country, was by my Bramin estimated at two thousand rupees: but the natives alleged, that it amounted to ten times this sum.

dimensions, revealing not only the extent to which Hinduism was the state religion of Nepal, but also the holistic nature of the society, within which individual deviations affect the whole, which is itself embodied in the unique person of the king. The king is the ritual embodiment of his subjects as well as the government he heads, for both are known by the same name, *sarkār*. When he wears his crown, the king uses the first person plural, because 'he speaks in its name'. In the same way that Louis XIV is well-known for his statement, 'L'État, c'est moi',[2] the king of Nepal is the monarchy incarnate, and was the incarnated state until recently.[3] On the basis of these equivalences, I shall here consider the royal dynasty's religious practices to be forming the nucleus of Nepal's State religion.

Since its establishment in the latter half of the eighteenth century, Nepal has been an explicitly Hindu kingdom. Prithvi Narayan Shah, its founder, describes it as such in his *Divine Teachings*: 'Our garden will be a real Hindu kingdom for the four classes [*varṇa*], high or low, and for the 36 castes [*jāt*]'.[4] This founding statement has persisted till date, and even survived the 1990 People's Movement which led to the new 1990 constitution in which, despite considerable debate, Nepal was still defined as 'a multiethnic, multilinguistic, democratic, free, indivisible, sovereign, Hindu Kingdom ruled by constitutional monarchy'. The king is himself defined as being 'of *ārya* culture, Hindu religion, from the Gorkha dynasty and from the descendance of Prithvi Narayan'. Hindu kings of a Hindu kingdom, the sovereigns of Nepal have frequently used religion as a tool with which to cultivate their 'garden'.

A HINDU KINGDOM

Hinduism was used as a catalyst to solidify the sudden unification of numerous kingdoms and ethnic groups into Greater Nepal at the end of the eighteenth century. This process had already begun

---

[2] 'The State, it is me'.

[3] He officially lost this position when he introduced the Panchayat system in 1962 (under which the vote was first introduced), and then more effectively after the 1990 People's Movement, which greatly reduced the king's role in the governance of the state. Chapter 7 describes the more recent fate of monarchy in Nepal.

[4] Naraharinath 2016 VS/1953: 20.

within these petty kingdoms since at least the fifteenth century. The most striking rite, both in its breadth and symbolic efficacy, is without doubt that of Dasain.[5] On this occasion, from at least the nineteenth century onwards, it was mandatory for all government representatives to worship the Goddess and pay homage to their hierarchical superiors. Until 1963, authority was delegated from the centre, that is, the sovereign, and had to return to him during Dasain in the form of offerings, *prasād* or *olāk*. The birth of the centralized state thus linked all the ancient sites of power to the new capital through the elaboration of the gigantic pyramidal ritual network of Dasain. The delegation of royal power to the officials was clearly indicated by their wearing an 'official's crown' as a royal symbol. In any case, this power was contractual and annual. If the king's power was automatically renewed by the Goddess at the time of Dasain, the officials' position had to be renewed annually by the king during an assembly called *pajani*. On this occasion, all the positions were either reconfirmed or were not, and those who were dismissed had to return their crowns at the feet of the king, in itself a highly symbolic gesture.[6] The contractual and annual nature of power was one of the Hindu king's weapons, with which he could easily rid himself of undesirable or incapable people.

The king utilized another Hindu conception to reinforce his sovereign power: the idea that he owned the land, which was an essential source of income until the twentieth century. This concept is clearly expressed in an edict attributed to Ram Shah (r. 1614–36): 'The land belongs to the king'.[7] Any resident in the kingdom was thereby placed in a state of dependence. Land was managed through a complex system of tenures. If *raikar* landowners had rights akin to property, State officials were extremely dependent on the king through *jāgir* tenure, which consisted of land allotted and rescinded along with one's function, as a salary. Royal families, influential

---

[5] On the Dasain rituals, see Krauskopff and Lecomte-Tilouine (eds), *Célébrer le pouvoir*.

[6] As described by K.P. Malla in an interview with David N. Gellner ('From literature to linguistics to culture').

[7] In a long proverb, he specifies what falls to the different members of the government, starting with 'the king's earth', *śrīrājāko bhūmī* (Naraharinath 2021 VS/1964 : 23).

people and Brahmins were equally dependent on the royal gift of *birtā* lands. Taxes on land—and other natural resources—were conceived as a kind of rent for exploiting the king's properties.[8]

Richard Burghart has shown how this prerogative positioned the king as the supreme dispenser.[9] The king offered lands to temples and priests in particular, thereby becoming the patron of all the great temples and rituals of the state. Through these gifts of land, the king alienated a share of his rights to the benefit of the gods, who thus became 'as kings'.[10] Perhaps this procedure should be considered part of a more general identity between the king and the divinity. Not only were parts of territories commonly offered to the gods, but there were even cases where the whole territory was given to them. According to different chronicles, Bali Raja did not agree to directly accept a kingdom from the king of Jajarkot, but asked that it be given first to his ritual friend, an astrologer, as a birtā grant.[11] The great king of Jumla thus ruled over a huge birtā land grant. In the same vein, Hamilton[12] retells the story of the kingdom of Gor Samaran (modern-day Simraongarh and the ancient capital of Mithila) whose king, Shivai Singh, abdicated in favour of his tutelary deity, Kangkali, when the Muslims attacked him. The goddess took control of the kingdom and pushed the enemy back. If the gods

---

[8] For more information, see M.C. Regmi, *Land Tenure and Taxation in Nepal*.

[9] The gift of land was a king's privilege (except for royal authorization). Brahmins received land on specific occasions, such as lunar or solar eclipses, to restore the cosmic order, or at the end of funeral rites to ensure peace for the dead. They also received such a gift to ensure the king's celebrity, prosperity or victory. Ascetics did not receive land, but revenues (Burghart, 'Gifts to the Gods', p. 260). (Some people had royal authorization to offer land themselves.)

[10] Burghart, 'Gifts to the Gods', p. 260. Cf. Bouillier, 'The Royal Gift to the Ascetics', for a case study of the limitations in the practice of the relinquishment of royal privilege in the name of the gods.

[11] The first inscription of the Malla kings also shows Krachalla offering the entire territory he had conquered from the king of Kartikeyapur to the temple of Balesvar Mahadev, in ad 1223. Cf. Vajracarya 2028 VS/1971. More recent studies on this inscription can be found in Mahes Raj Pant and Maheswar Joshi's chapters in M. Lecomte-Tilouine (ed.), *Bards and Mediums*, forthcoming.

[12] Hamilton, *An Account of the Kingdom of Nepal*, p. 48.

are assigned worldly power, the kings and queens are deified in a process of reciprocation. Apart from the usual assertion that the king is an embodiment of Vishnu, numerous stories abound of royal personages who turned into deities after their deaths—like Mukunda Sen, who turned into a black stone venerated at Deughat, or the queen of Ram Shah, who became the Goddess Manakamana. The two phenomena probably stem from the same idea and highlight the significance of royal gifts: kings and gods were analogous both as landowners and prosperity givers.

Brahmins were the main beneficiaries of royal land gifts; these lands were frequently the newly conquered ones on tribal territories.[13] The offering of these newly conquered territories to Brahmins or gods may have concealed a number of motives. It was perhaps a magnanimous gesture of gratitude to the spiritual actors who had made the victory possible; or a way of sanctifying or Hinduizing 'barbaric' territories and their dangerous chthonian gods; or a kind of renouncement that increased the king's merit and power, since ascetic practices were one way for the king to increase his powers of aggression.[14] In any case, the establishment of Brahmins in the newly conquered territories ensured the Hindu king's power as well as the propagation of Hinduism. More practically, Brahmins also served as a human shield, because the murder of a Brahmin was the most severely punished crime. This role of human shield made itself manifest when Brahmins were placed as real inviolable guards to protect, for example, the Malla kings or the Jesuit Fathers

[13] V. Bouillier, 'Du bon usage des brahmanes'. Thus, for example, the Ghimire family received as a birtā grant a Ghale king's territory, which had been conquered with their help by the king of Lamjung (Thapa 2041 VS/1984: 313–15).

[14] Thus Ram Shah retired to the forest with his friend the king of Parvat in order to please the god Gorakhnath and accumulate power (Naraharinath 2021VS/1964: 17–18). In the oral tradition of Lamjung, Drabya Shah is said to have been victorious, in contrast to his neighbour the Magar king of Gorkha, because of his austerities: 'The neighbour king of Gorkha was Mansingh Khadka. He drank spirits and beer....But Drabya Shah, even when king, was an ascetic. He was the first devotee of Gorakh Nath and this is why he was always victorious in battle' (Dharmaraj Thapa 2041 VS/1984: 312).

during the Gorkhali conquest of the Kathmandu Valley.[15] For the same reason, they made ideal spies.[16] Nevertheless, Brahmins were at an advantage only when serving the king's interests. Otherwise, they stood to lose, as shown by the case of the Brahmins attached to the Malla kings, whose birtā properties were confiscated by the Gorkhalis and distributed among the latter's soldiers after the conquest of the Kathmandu valley, or that of the thirty-two Tirhutiya Brahmins of Nuwakot who were dispossessed by Prithvi Narayan Shah.[17]

The establishment of Hindu kingdoms in the central region of contemporary Nepal is relatively recent, dating back to the fifteenth century. This territory was at that time mostly inhabited by tribal groups which did not follow any named religion, had no script of their own, and probably had not formed state societies.[18] The place of tribal groups in the newly formed Hindu states was complex. If the Hindu kings favoured 'cows and Brahmans' to their disadvantage, they also at times adopted a policy of integration, providing them with important state functions and worshipping their gods.

[15] According to Father Da Rovata, who had a good understanding of the Brahmins' role as state agents: '...it seems to me he [the king of Gorkha] thinks that we do for the English what the Brahmins do for him' (quoted in Stiller, 'A Letter of Fr. Guiseppe da Rovata [Dec. 29, 1769]', p. 10).

[16] The death sentence, abolished in the 1980s, was not applicable to Brahmins according to law. This fact perhaps encouraged their political activity. This was why Tanka Acharya, sentenced to death by a Rana trial, could not be executed (Fisher, Living Martyrs, p. 107). On the other hand, it seems that the state could on some occasions act secretly, contrary to the law. One of my Nepalese friends told me that his father, who was a judge, died of anguish after he had to secretly sentence a Brahmin, who had tried to place a bomb in the royal palace, to be hanged in prison.

[17] Cf. Hodgson Papers, Vol. 14, folio 94, India Office Library, for the first case, and Wright, History of Nepal, p. 15, for the second.

[18] Here, I will use this expression to designate the groups that share these characteristics in the Himalayan region, in order to juxtapose them against the caste groups and the Tibetan communities. Since 1990, the tribal groups have been calling themselves 'indigenous peoples' in English and Janajati in Nepali.

HINDU LAW, KINGS AND TRIBAL GROUPS

The encouraging of Brahmin settlements and the institution of Hinduism as the state religion led the government to take special measures to make tribal groups respect certain Hindu principles. Among them, two were particularly difficult for tribals to accept: the sacredness of the cow and the kinship rules of the high castes.

Tibeto-Burman groups commonly consumed beef, and they had to renounce the slaughter of cows or be severely punished.[19] Sexual union with this animal—a crime apparently known as there is legislation concerning it—was also severely punished, as was the castration of bulls, for which crime the culprit's hand was cut off.[20]

The Nepalese legal code (Mulukī Ain) of 1854 also condemned hypogamy, according to the definition provided by the Indo-Nepalese[21] rulers concerning the hierarchical order between wife-givers and wife-receivers. The former were considered inferior to the latter, and only a wife of inferior or equal rank was to be taken as a spouse, as the wife-receivers would otherwise be placed in a paradoxically inferior position. This definition, however, happens to be the opposite of the one held by numerous Tibeto-Burman groups, such as the Magars,[22] who view wife-givers as hierarchical superiors. In such societies, hypergamy is thus logically reversed. Raising the Brahmanical kinship system to the status of universal law has resulted in the Hindu government imprisoning and severely punishing tribal groups regarding this matter.[23]

[19] Abandoning cow or bull sacrifice was particularly difficult for some northern Magar clans, such as the Budhathoki of Maikot, who had to offer these animals to their lineage god.

[20] According to an edict dated 1856 VS (1799) (Naraharinath 2013 VS/1956, Vol. 2, Pt. 2).

[21] French anthropologists conventionally designate as 'Indo-népalais' those Nepalese groups of Indian origin who do not possess any group name apart from their various caste names.

[22] The Magars form the biggest tribal group of Nepal, numbering one and a half million in the 1991 census. A minority among them still speak a Tibeto-Burman language.

[23] In 1986, I met in Darling (Gulmi district) an old Sris Magar man who had spent several years in jail for having married a Chetri woman.

THE OUTLAW KING

The king is an outlaw himself because law is not applicable to him. His crimes are not judged by men, but by gods. Thus Pratap Malla, who according to chronicles[24] killed a very young girl during a sexual act, expiated his crime by simply performing some rituals. As a Hindu ruler, the king of Nepal must ensure respect for the law, but may also modify it in any respect according to his will. He has the ability to change even the socio-cosmic order of castes; for instance, when raising an untouchable group to a pure rank as a mark of gratitude for a favour.[25]

Paradoxically, because of his divine nature, the Hindu king is not an orthodox follower of Hinduism. Prithvi Narayan, for instance, took numerous religious liberties when he decided to change his *gotra*, or when he secretly adopted a new preceptor,[26] provoking

[24] See, for instance, Hasrat, *History of Nepal*, p. 76:

Pratāpmalla made a vow to cohibit [sic] with 100,000 woman [sic]; but when he had corrupted the chastity of 30,000, one night a virgin was brought to his bed who was too young and died by the force of his lust. Rajah much repented and to atone for the crime he performed a Kotyāhuti sacrifice to Paśupatināth...

[25] The king was master of the caste system. He could elevate an entire caste to a new status. Conversely, one of the punishments often ordered by the king was public degradation. He was also endowed with the power to purify the pollution affecting status. Thus it was that the delegation of twenty-seven people, who had to take a tribute every five years to the Chinese emperor, could regain their caste status at the end of their travels merely by receiving water from the personal water pot [*lota*] of the king (Cavenagh, *Rough Notes on the State of Nepal*, p. 69). While many of these powers have been superseded or rendered moot, at least formally, by the civil legal code and the constitution, the royal family remains 'above' or 'outside' the law—that is, immune from prosecution—even today.

[26] The episode of the change of gotra figures on p. 125 of the *Gorkhā Vaṃśāvalī* (Naraharinath 2021 VS/1964), and the clandestine change of guru on pp. 105–6. Gotras are mythical clans, theoretically grouping descendants of the disciples of different sages. In ancient India, only the Brahmins, who alone received such instruction, had a gotra. Since that time, all pure castes possess at least a gotra name, which helps to define their group identity. It is normally impossible to change one's gotra, which is inherited along with lineage and caste names. This change of gotra, unique to my knowledge, shows that nothing is impossible for the king. But his motivations are more

the anger of the royal priests. According to oral tradition, he even destroyed the temple of the Goddess in Belkot after the difficult conquest of the site.[27] His grandson went further when he organized the funeral of Taleju, the tutelary goddess of the kingdom, to punish her for the death of his wife. Moreover, the alliance he had concluded with his wife, a Brahmin widow, was already a double infraction—against the rule of hypergamy and the remarriage of Brahmin widows.

The Hindu king obviously displays arrogance, even vis-à-vis the gods. He may go as far as refusing to eat their prasād, those blessings reposing in the food left over from the offerings made to the gods, and which, like any leftover, may be considered 'polluted' food.[28] This point of view is presented in an extreme case in an episode of the *Gorkhā Vaṃśāvalī*, where the prasād is regurgitated by the god. The young Prince Prithvi Narayan Shah refused to eat the yoghurt vomited by Gorakh Nath, as ordered by the god, and thus lost part

---

mysterious. In the Gorkha chronicle, Prithvi Narayan informs his surprised brothers that in this way, he wishes to gather the eight ṭikā of their clan into one. According to M.S. Thapa Magar (Bista et al., 'Vartaman Rajako Purkha Magar Hun ya Ksatriya?'), Prithvi Narayan changed his gotra because his previous one was not famous, being a Magar one. Though pleasing, this idea is strange, given that the Magars have lately adopted gotra names from high castes, and thus there is nothing to distinguish a Magar gotra name from those of high castes. It is also often said that Prithvi Narayan changed his gotra to facilitate his attack of the Shah of Lamjung, thereby avoiding the crime of *gotrahatyā*, killing someone from within the same gotra. However, this contradicts the idea of a larger group sharing the same gotra, as then chances of gotrahatyā would increase.

We may wonder, on the other hand, whether the meaning of gotra in this context was the same as what we understand today. It seems that Prithvi Narayan's purpose was to unify the different branches of a group conceived as one family in order to establish a unique power. In the same way that Nepali texts and people often refer to the four jāt and the thirty-six varṇa when relying on the Indian conception of the caste system, which presents the reverse (that is, four varṇa and 36 or a multitude of jāt), perhaps the gotra indicated in this context a branch of a common line.

[27] Cf. Pfaff-Czarnecka, 'A Battle of Meanings', p. 64.

[28] Between human beings, leftovers can only be consumed by the wife or young children (except the *bhānjā*, nephew, who is of superior status). The attitude of the king reveals his pretension to equal status with the gods.

of the power which would have been conferred on him through this act.[29]

The duel between the Hindu king and the gods is in fact fairly equitable. Though the kings appear to be defeated more often by gods angered by their arrogance, they do sometimes succeed in subduing the divinity.[30] The conflict between them is also apparent in the structural rivalries between kings and priests. Omnipresent, this conflict is enacted on many occasions. The story of Matsyendranath represents one of them. To establish this god of prosperity in the Kathmandu Valley, the king and his priest sat before a pot in which the god, in the form of a bumblebee, had to be shut in. The bumblebee-god came twice, but the king, who had to shut him up, had fallen asleep. The priest finally hit the king's knee to wake him up when he saw the god approaching for the third and the last time. The god was thus captured thanks to the priest, but the king was so angered by the lack of respect shown by his priest that he conceived of a plan to punish him severely.

The complexity of the state religion probably stems from the antagonism between the priest and the king. However, the different powers of the kingdom were united against foreign religions, which were viewed as a greater danger. It is perhaps not mere coincidence that the centralized State, which emerged at the end of the eighteenth century, was constructed on the basis of a total closure of the country, justified in terms of the rejection of foreign religions—in particular Islam and Christianity—which were presented as such great dangers that internal rivalries had to be subordinated to the collective preservation of the Hindu policy. The unification of rival groups against a foreign religion is strikingly

---

[29] Naraharinath 2021 VS/ 1964: 95. A similar story is contained in the Annals of Mewar. Bappa, the founder of Chitor, became the pupil of Harita. When leaving the earth in a celestial vehicle, he sent his blessings by spitting in Bappa's mouth. 'Bappa showed his disgust and aversion by blinking, and the projected blessing fell on his foot, by which squeamishness he obtained only invulnerability by weapons instead of immortality' (Tod, *Annals and Antiquities of Rajasthan*, Vol. 1, p. 265).

[30] A legend in Arghakot, for instance, recounts how the king subdued the local Kalika goddess to found his kingdom (Ramirez, 'Luttes d'influence dans l'empire de la Déesse').

illustrated in the *Nepālko Itihās Rājbhogmālā* chronicle, where Newar and Khas protested as one against the Malla king who favoured the Muslims.

Strangely enough, despite the liberty he took with his family priest, Prithvi Narayan Shah narrates in his autobiography how he went to pray in a very humble way, remaining at the door of the temple of a goddess whom he describes as 'the daughter of a Rana [Magar]'.[31] It is she who had conferred upon him his exceptional power when, having taken the form of a young girl, she offered him a sword in each hand.[32] It is interesting to note that in his memoirs, Prithvi Narayan Shah recalls this divine gift without mentioning any encounter with Gorakhnath, whereas the different *Gorkhā Vaṁśāvalī*-s make no allusion to this goddess, but repeatedly relate the holy interventions of Gorakhnath, the eponymous saint of the kingdom.

TRIBAL GROUPS VERSUS STATE REASON

One of the peculiarities of the Nepalese social order, as codified by Jang Bahadur in the mid-nineteenth century, is the median position conferred upon tribal groups in the caste hierarchy.[33] This situation contrasts with that in India, where tribal groups are

[31] The various translators and editors of the *Divya Upadeś* note that this expression signifies that the Rana Magar are the priests of this shrine. However, it seems to me that it expresses a stronger link between the Magars and the goddess, because the expression is entirely unusual. Prithvi Narayan writes that when he saw the girl, he asked her, 'whose daughter are you?' and she replied, 'I am the daughter of the Rana priest' (Naraharinath (ed.) 2016 VS/1953: 11). I believe this indicates that Prithvi Narayan considered this goddess as a Rana Magar. Stories about a little girl belonging to a group escaping the house and revealing herself as a goddess on a nearby summit or cave are numerous. For one example, see Dharmaraj Thapa (2041 VS/1984: 125), about the Lamjung Malika goddess.

[32] On the royal symbolism of the sword, see Lecomte-Tilouine, 'Les dieux-sabres'.

[33] Tribal groups were all ranked as pure castes and were divided into two groups, those reducible and those not reducible to slavery. For the caste hierarchy in the *Muluki Ain*, see Höfer, *The Caste Hierarchy and the State in Nepal*. The Magars were considered a pure caste of alcohol drinkers not reducible to slavery. This position is lower than their rank in central Nepal, where they are considered degraded Kshatriyas and superior to other tribal groups.

integrated at the bottom of the hierarchy. This relatively privileged position within the Nepalese social order is the result of its political and religious history, which we shall analyse here with the help of the Magars as an example. The most ancient sources referring incontestably to this group are the chronicles.[34] In the *Nepālko Itihās Rājbhogmālā*[35] they are associated with the Khas, as in the expression 'Khas Magar', and are described as forming the army of the king of Palpa, Mukunda Sen. They entered the Kathmandu valley during the sixteenth century, and victory was theirs after their king's encounter with Matsyendranath's procession. Terrified, all the devotees ran away, leaving the foreign king alone with the god. Removing the silver necklace from his horse, he tossed it to the god. As a sign of acceptance, Matsyendranath inclined his head to receive it around his neck. He still wears this jewel and his head remains inclined, as if to mark forever the cowardice of his devotees and his acceptance of Khas Magar's power. The 'barbarous' king's devotion allowed his troops to enter the cities of the valley. However, their misdeeds were so numerous that they provoked Pashupati's anger; he sent an epidemic which exterminated them all, except for the king. In this episode, Khas and Magar are said to be without 'straight or right dharma', that is, immoral.[36]

King Mukunda Sen was assimilated to the Magars, who formed the majority of his subjects. He did have some Magar blood in him as his ancestor, Abhaya, had married the daughter of the Magar king of Makwanpur. As the *Sen Vaṁśāvalī* recounts, 'He married, following the tradition of Makvanpur, Kantimati, the beautiful daughter of Gajalakshman, the Magar king of Makavan. From her was born the great king of kings Bhattarajadeva.'[37] Moreover, one of Mukunda Sen's wives was the daughter of the Magar king of Parkogha: 'Mahadevi Suvarnamala, daughter of the Magar king of Parkogha was another queen of Mukundasen. She bore three sons: Manishya

---

[34] Aramudi, the eighth-century king of the Gandaki region mentioned in the Kashmiri Rajatarangini chronicle, may have been a Magar, as his name indicates. Several names mentioned in the Purāṇas may also have designated Magars.

[35] A chronicle relating the history of the Kathmandu Valley.

[36] *Nepālko Itihās Rājbhogmālā*, Part III, p. 6.

[37] Rajvamshi 2020 VS/1963: 2.

Sen, Imbarsen and Kuvar Sen.'[38] In a palm-leaf manuscript kept in the Kaiser Library, dated 1567 VS (1510), on which contemporary events have been added, Mukunda Sen is described as a Magar king of Palpa who invaded the Kathmandu Valley in 1581 VS (1524).[39] The Magars were powerful during the sixteenth century, as shown by the copperplate inscription of a treaty dated 1605 VS (1548), which states, 'If Magars come through Nuwakot or elsewhere, we shall remain united and offer resistance with due consideration to their strength'.[40] Mukunda Sen's arrival in Nepal (that is, the Kathmandu Valley) was marked by the removal of the big and powerful mask of Bhairav from the Matsyendranath chariot. It was set up in his own kingdom of Palpa, as the enemy's gods were more frequently taken away in a gesture of appropriation than destroyed.[41]

In the Gorkha chronicles, the Magars frequently appear in the enumeration of groups; ranked after the Brahmins and the Khas, they are the only tribal group to be mentioned. The chronicles invoke a Magar country, the Magarat, which was annihilated by the Shah ancestors. The vanquished Magar group seems to have been associated very early on with the new governments of their conquerors. In the kingdoms of Gorkha and Musikot, the Magars even seem to have taken part in their own initial defeat,[42] revealing both the weakness of their ethnic solidarity at that time and the presence of clan rivalries. Once the Thakuri kings had established themselves in the ancient Magar kingdoms, some Magar personalities were given important political and administrative functions. This, however, created conflicts, notably with the Brahmins. Thus, Narabhupal Shah, the father of Prithvi Narayan, had Magar ministers (*cautariya*).[43] But this situation was contested

[38] Ibid.: 4.

[39] Pant and Pant, 'King Mukunda Sen's Invasion of Kathmandu Valley', (7), p. 113.

[40] Quoted in ibid. (9), p. 132.

[41] For examples, see *Nepālko Itihās*, Part IV, p. 4, or Dharmaraj Thapa 2041 VS/1984: 303.

[42] On the role of the Magars in Drabya Shah's conquest of Gorkha, see Ranamagar 2054 VS/1997, and on the same phenomenon in Musikot, see Lecomte-Tilouine 2000a.

[43] The Magars were not the only tribal group to act as ministers for Thakuri kings. In the eastern part of present-day Nepal, the Sen kings had

by Brahmins, as shown by two discourses addressed to the king by Mahesvar Pant, aimed at dismissing these functionaries. In his speech, the Magars are said to be 'without caste' (*ajāt*), of 'low or vile caste' (*nic jāt*), 'prompt to anger', 'not strong and intelligent', 'in league with themselves', and even 'not able to work or to make the kingdom prosper'.[44] In a later episode, the Magars were expelled from the Gorkha kingdom after one of them, the *dvariya*, that is, the headman by function, opposed the young Prithvi Narayan. One day, Prithvi Narayan Shah wished to eat sugarcane after swimming in a river. He sent his people out to bring him some. They could not find any except in the dvariya's field, which they did not dare to cut. Prithvi Narayan then went to the spot and quarrelled with the dvariya, after which all the Magars, except for the Gyanmi clan, were expelled from Gorkha.[45]

Later, however, Prithvi Narayan Shah came to rely heavily on the Magars, who formed an important part of his troops, as can be seen from the numerous lists of the names of soldiers who took part in the various military operations, as recounted in the *Gorkhā Vaṃśāvalī*. He also demonstrated his trust in the Magars in a most respectful way by dismissing his absent-minded Chetri sword holder and entrusting a Magar with this task instead.

In his memoirs, Prithvi Narayan Shah recalls his Magar *dada*, the man who looked after him during his childhood, and declares himself 'the king of the Magar country'.

Surprisingly, the most famous holy man in the Gorkha kingdom was a Magar as well, even though it is extremely rare nowadays for a Magar to adopt the path of the renouncer. Lakhan Thapa was a spiritual guide for Ram Shah and had a very close relationship with the queen, who was considered an incarnation of the Goddess.

Kirant chiefs as ministers, 'to rule them more easily', according to Hamilton's interpretation: '...the Kirats formed the principal strength of these Rajput chiefs, their hereditary chief held the second office in the state (Chautariya) and the Rajputs, who were united with them, did not presume to act as masters, to invade their lands, or violate their customs' (Hamilton, *An Account of the Kingdom of Nepal*, pp. 7–8). Obviously, for Hamilton, 'not to act as masters' was one way to make the governing of a newly subjected population easier.

[44] Naraharinath 2021 VS/1964: 100, 103.
[45] Ibid.: 116.

His role and the consideration afforded him are other strong clues pointing to the importance of Magars in the Gorkha kingdom's religion, which in turn lies at the basis of the state religion of present-day Nepal.

MAGAR FEATURES OF THE STATE RELIGION

The Thakuris and the Magars are thus closely related historically, but it is still not clear how the Thakuris managed to establish their kingship in the Magar country. The answer will not be a straightforward one. We may isolate the main factors as: collaboration between some Magars and the Thakuris against the Magars in power and the Ghales;[46] matrimonial alliances; and finally, a most curious fact—the offering of power to the Thakuris by the Magars. In Gorkha, the role played by Gangaram Rana Magar in the defeat of the Khadka Magar king of Gorkha has been well analysed by B.K. Ranamagar,[47] and we may presume that internal conflicts among Magar clans generally led some of them to side with the enemy. Either for this reason or to reinforce their power, some prestigious Magar kings (or chiefs—the precise nature of their power is still unknown) concluded alliances with Thakuri princes, though always in the same way, that is, by offering them their daughters. It is well-known that the Sen of Makwanpur and Palpa concluded matrimonial alliances with Magar princesses. Here, it should be remembered that from the Magar perspective, wife-givers are hierarchical superiors, while from the Thakuri perspective it is wife-receivers who are the hierarchical superiors.

In addition to these marital alliances—and this is more unusual—many facts seem to generally indicate that the Magars were inclined to offer kingship to prestigious foreigners. Thus the Magars of Pyuthan are said to have taken away the youngest grandson of Pitambar and established him as their king in 1515 VS (1458).[48] In

---

[46] The Magars and the Gurungs seem to have fought with the Thakuris against the Ghales, established in the north of Lamjung and Gorkha. Numerous instances are reported in the *Gorkhā Vaṁśāvalī* and in Dharmaraj Thapa 2041 VS/ 1984.

[47] Ranamagar 2054 VS/1997.

[48] Giri 2052 VS/1995: 13. However, in a chronicle published in the same volume (Giri 2052 VS/1995: 156–7), it is written that Tara Can killed the Kham

the same way, the youngest son of Jaitamalla, the king of Rukum, was said to have been taken away by the Bhujyal of Nishibhuji, who made him their king in Dhoralthan.[49] Another such example may be found in Musikot. In this ancient royal capital, two officiating priests, a Magar and a Thakuri, assumed a kingly role during the Dasain rituals. The allotment of their respective responsibilities is striking, for it is the Magar 'king' who gives ṭikā to the Thakuri 'king', thus marking his own pre-eminence. The people of Musikot explain what now appears to be a discrepancy by referring to local history: the Saru Magar, kings of the place, would have given their throne to a Simha Thakuri and consecrated him with the ṭikā mark.

Finally, the Magars might have been in the habit of choosing their king by setting up a contest. The throne of Liglig was given for one year to the winner of an annual race.[50] As presented by Dharmaraj Thapa, the story goes as follows:

Drabyah Shah was sent to the East by his mother to prevent him from quarrelling with his elder brother. Now the Magars of Liglig had the habit of changing their king every year. The afflicted people from Liglig, wishing that next year's king would be from the Shah clan, went to the fort of Raginas bringing with them solidified milk as a present. They offered this present to Drabyah Shah but he told them that he was not willing to be their king and that they could take back their present. They went back with it to Liglig. The astrologers and pandits of Gorkha happened to know that Drabyah Shah had refused and told the people to go back to him, as he would accept this time. The people went to him again and he accepted. The day of the new king's election came. Starting from the banks of the Cepe, the one who was first to sit on the throne of the Liglig fort, after having jumped the river and climbed to the top of the hill, became king. It was the custom of Liglig. Drabya Shah

---

king of Bhitrikot and ruled afterwards, while continuing with the worship of the god of the Kham king.

[49] *Samālavaṁśāvalī*, Naraharinath 2010VS/1953, Vol. 1: 68-9. The name Bhujyal refers to all the inhabitants of the Bhuji khola, and not only to the Magars of this valley, located today in Baglung district.

[50] The local population of Liglig is described as Gurung in the Gorkha chronicle but as Magar in the local oral tradition, as reported by Thapa (2041 VS/ 1984: 311–12). The election of the king through contest is reported in the Annals of Mewar as well, where the local Bhils are said to have practised it (Tod, *Annals and Antiquities of Rajasthan*, Vol. 1, pp. 259, 262, quoting Abu-l Fazl).

came first in the contest and the people organised a vermilion-procession to consecrate him as their king.

These ritual details are clues suggesting that the Thakuris began by showing respect to local populations and their customs because, arriving in small numbers, they could not have taken power by force.[51] Whatever the reason for their close relations with the Thakuris—whether it be matrimonial alliances, internal dissension, or the custom of electing a foreign king—it is striking to note how the Magars have been in charge of the religious functions linked to the very source of Thakuri power, somehow relegating the Brahmins to a secondary role. This is true not only of the earth-god Bhume, in whose cult Brahmins are either absent or limited to participating in the accessory fire offering,[52] but also, in a less general way, in the case of the Goddess[53] and the sword-gods, whose cult confers power on Hindu chiefs and kings.

In the Arka locality of Pyuthan district, an important sanctuary holds two sword-gods. One day, or so local people say, a Brahmin thought it was not right for a Magar, who daily consumes such infamous products as pork[54] and beer, to be their priest. Having decided to replace him, he went to the river, purified himself, recited holy prayers, and walked up to the sanctuary wearing nothing but a white *dhoti*. As soon as he began his rites, however, the two sword-gods turned into snakes. Frightened, the Brahmin ran away and

[51] Few traditions report the massacre of local populations. The only legend I have encountered that talks about the extermination of Magars by Thakuris is from the remote region of Tichurong (Jest, 'Traditions et croyances religieuses des habitants'). Tales of Magar kings killed by Thakuri ones, on the other hand, are numerous. For examples from Pyuthan, see Giri 2052 VS/1995; for examples from Rukum see *Samāla vaṁśāvalī*, Naraharinath 2010VS/1953, Vol. 1, pp. 68-9; for Gorkha see *Gorkhā Vaṁśāvalī*, Naraharinath 2021VS/1964, p. 4.

[52] See Lecomte-Tilouine, *Les dieux du pouvoir*.

[53] The main priests of Kalika—the goddess protecting the kingdoms of Lamjung and Gorkha—are Bohara Magars.

[54] The ignominious nature of the pig is underlined in a procedure aimed at degrading a Brahmin: his sacred thread is first broken, after which food offered by a person from a low caste is put in his mouth, and he is finally paraded around the city with a piglet tied to his neck (*Hodgson Papers*, Vol. 12, Folio 80).

went to the Magar priest, asking him to pacify the angry gods. The Magar, who was drinking alcohol at the time, went directly to the shrine, his breath still smelling of alcohol. Seizing a white cloth, he covered the snakes, which soon recovered their initial form.

The same symbolic pattern is present at the site of Bijuli (Pyuthan district), where an old palace contains the Khadka Maharaj, 'the Great Sword King'. Each year during the Dasain ceremony five swords representing this divinity are taken out and displayed to the devotees on a 'throne'. Among the nine Brahmin, Chetri and Magar priests, none but the Darlami Magar, who is considered the main priest (*mūl pūjārī*), can hold the swords. Local people explain this by referring to the fact that the Darlami Magars were the first kings of Bijuli. A Thapa Chetri[55] is said to have fooled the last local Magar king by concluding a ritual friendship with him.[56] Taking advantage of their privileged relationship, he stole the Magar king's seal (*lāl mohar*) and his swords, the insignia of royalty. The story goes that when he then tried to re-establish the gods in a new sanctuary, there was a terrible storm. With a great crash, a light fell on the swords and carried them away to the sky. Everyone began searching for the swords, which were finally located in the branches of a tree. Unfortunately, nobody could reach them. At last a Darlami Magar was called, upon which the swords descended by themselves, and came to rest on his back. Even today, when the Darlami Magar priest

---

[55] A stone inscription in front of the temple of Palu in Bijuli attests to the ancient presence of Thapa Chetri in this locality. Dated 1893 VS (AD 1836), it indicates that an *umarā* named Jagavira (that is, Jangabir) Thapa built the temple. Tradition also attributes the construction of the palace to this man, who is locally referred to as the 'kaptan' (I am grateful to Mahes Pant and Ram Panday, who corrected my mistakes in the reading of this inscription).

[56] The creation of a ritual friendship may have been a common stratagem to seize power. It is well-known that the kings of Gorkha became the ritual friends of the kings of Bhaktapur before their conquest of the valley. And Dharmaraj Thapa (2041 VS/1984: 239) reports a story which is very similar to that of Bijuli, in which the Shah king of Lamjung, unable to win over a local Ghale king, decided to conclude a ritual friendship with him on a certain day on the banks of the Dordi river. However, he had had weapons hidden in the sand, and attacked the Ghale king and his men through trickery. This place is still called 'The pieces of flesh' (Krocapse, in Gurung), because of the mutilated corpses of the Ghales that were left to decompose on the spot.

holds the swords, they are said to move by themselves and dance around his neck. The priest of the swords claims that they are alive, to the extent that it is difficult for him to hold on to them. Their active aspect is equally underscored by a belief which states that they take on their warlike appearance only during Dasain, wandering in the form of snakes the rest of the year. The original Magar kingship, as well as the Thapa Chetri's infamy, is thus ritually displayed every year in Bijuli.

Whether as a result of the gods' will, or as a recognition of the group, the Thakuris have assigned to the Magars the priesthood of their most important divinities—the ones who confer power.

THE LASARGHA SHRINE

The most interesting site related to the history of the Thakuri-Magar relationship is certainly the Lasargha shrine. Magar and Thakuri elements are so closely interlinked there that some writers cite it as proof of the Magar origin of the Shah royal dynasty.[57] As a matter of fact, the place is linked to this family's origin, as shown in the chronicles that relate its history. Written in Sanskrit, Hindi, and Nepali, most of these chronicles were composed at the end of the eighteenth century and in the first half of the nineteenth.[58] However, it appears that the chroniclers tended to add new events to older chronicles rather than begin anew; the stories recorded may also have been based on similar oral traditions, as the bulk of the content of different chronicles is very consistent.

All the Gorkha chronicles locate the cradle of the Shah family of Gorkha in Rajasthan. They are supposed to be Rajput survivors of the city of Citaur, destroyed by the Muslims in 1303 and 1567. The chronicles claim that the Rajput survivors fled to the

[57] This matter, with examples taken from the Lasargha shrine, can be found in D.B.Bista, R. Shah, H. Budha Magar and M.S. Thapa Magar Lapha. However, this theory is neither new nor linked to ethnic revivalism: I heard people say long before 1990 that the King is a Magar because he uses Magar priests who offer pig sacrifices in his name. The trend is now to openly publish and discuss matters which were confidential before the 1990 'revolution'.

[58] Two chronicles, written by Chitra Bilas and Dharanidhara Sharma respectively, were composed under the reign of Ram Shah in the seventeenth century (Naraharinath 2013 VS/ 1956, Vol. 2, Pt. 3: 572–5).

northern mountainous countries to 'protect their dharma' and save their lives.

This is certainly a noble and honourable origin for a group that claims to be Thakuri. For this reason, it raised early doubts in the minds of scholars such as F.B. Hamilton and Sylvain Lévi. Even the Nepalese historian Baburam Acharya contested the Rajput origin of the Shah, considering them to have belonged to the Khas, as did Sylvain Lévi before him. Hamilton, however, suggested that the Shah were in fact Magar,[59] a theory popular today among members of this group. It should be noted, though, that Hamilton's informants came from the royal families vanquished by the Shah, who had taken refuge in India. Their place in this history meant they were perhaps not the most impartial people in this context. As for Sylvain Lévi, he is totally contradictory on this issue, using, whenever it suits his theory, one or the other view.[60]

In any case, my purpose here is not to judge the veracity of such ancient and uncertain facts, but to re-evaluate the much contested contents of the Gorkha chronicles, and examine the political reasons behind the adoption of Magar features in the state religion set up by the Shah. Although the itinerary of their peregrinations in India has not been given, one should nevertheless note that the Shah ancestors' specified entry point into Nepal is not western Nepal as commonly described in other high-caste genealogies, but central Nepal. One of the first Nepalese localities to be mentioned is Lasargha. In the texts, it is precisely situated in relation to other

---

[59] He writes: '...the royal family are in fact Magars, a Thibetian race' (*An Account of the Kingdom of Nepal*, p. 52).

[60] He sometimes considers the Shah to be Khas (Lévi, *Le Népal*, pp. 256–7), sometimes as being mixed with the Magars (ibid., p. 265), and on p. 262 Sylvain Lévi (ibid.) writes, 'It was the time when the Rajputs, oppressed by the Muslims, retreated into the mountains, engaged in the service of the barbarian princes, overthrew them, and founded Hindu states on the ruins of the indigenous feudal system.' In fact, Sylvain Lévi's information on the Hill population is not original. It is based on the chronicle published by Wright (*History of Nepal*)—as indicated by his use of the name Sargha for Lasargha—and on the works of Kirkpatrick (*An Account of the Kingdom of Nepaul*), Hamilton (*An Account of the Kingdom of Nepal*), Hodgson (*Essays on the Languages, Literature and Religion of Nepal and Tibet*), and Vansittart (*Notes on Nepal*).

localities, leaving no room for doubt as to whether it does refer to present-day Lasargha. Lasargha is located in the western part of Syangja district on a hill surrounded on three sides by the Kali Gandaki River. It is situated on a very ancient road linking Nepal to India, which goes through Palpa and Butwal. Prithvi Narayan Shah used this route on his journey to India. Thus, it should be noted that the route the Shah Thakuri followed in his mythical travels was not whimsical.

Their first stop in Nepal is, moreover, supported by a number of facts, for instance regarding some features of the sanctuary of Lasargha and local oral traditions, which sheds new light on the events narrated in the *Gorkhā Vaṁśāvalī* about this period well before the establishment of the Shah family in Lamjung and Gorkha. Unfortunately, few chronicles describe the early history of the dynasty. The period we are dealing with, that between the hypothetical departure of the Shah from Rajasthan and their attested settlement in central Nepal, is, when it does find mention, not very detailed. However, the chronicles do contain two versions of the arrival of the Thakuris in Lasargha. The most famous one concerns the story of the Rajputs from Citvar, fleeing with their tutelary deity. Recent history has retained this version as it obviously serves a purpose—that of providing the Shah dynasty with a noble Rajput and Hindu origin. The second account is more anecdotal, and makes the settlement out to have been partly accidental. It is recounted in an old chronicle attributed to Dharanidhara Sharma, which ends with the reign of Ram Shah (r. 1614–36) and was perhaps composed under his reign. According to this text, entitled *Gorakṣarāja Vaṁśāvalī*,[61] the founder of the dynasty is Varavum, sovereign of the Jambira fort. He was succeeded by Amvum, Audumbarai, Bhattarai, Jillarai, Ajita, Alavum, Vimikirai, Harirai, Kanaka, Brahmanika, and Manmatha. This last monarch abdicated in favour of his eldest son and left for the forest, accompanied by his youngest son. He settled in Bahradarlam Jṛṣṛṅga. This toponym probably corresponds to the Resunga hill, located in south Gulmi and a one-day walk from

[61] Published in Naraharinath 2013 VS/1956, Vol. 2, Pt. 3: 573–5. I would like to thank Maheshvar Joshi and Mahes Pant, who helped me with its translation.

Lasargha. It is also near the village of Darlam, which is where the Darlami Magars originated.

There, the old king passed away and his younger son, Jaikhan, after completing his funeral rites, proceeded to the village of Lasargha.[62] Jaikhan married in Lasargha and people consecrated him as their king (or chief). His son was named Suryakhan, and founded the city of Khilung, etc.

This chronicle presents numerous likely facts. Ridi and Resunga are famous holy places mentioned in different Puranas, and local oral tradition states that the great ascetic king Visvamitra practised austerities there. There is nothing surprising, then, in this narrative of an Indian king spending his last days there in the company of his son, nor in the alliance concluded by the orphan prince in the foreign country. The story does not say whom he married, but we can suspect that it was a Magar princess. Finally, in the absence of a son, the transfer of power to the son-in-law is common in the Himalayas. Despite its reasonable and probable nature, this version of the facts is not repeated in either later texts or oral tradition. It is perhaps too commonplace. It does not glorify Rajput heroism, does not present divine will in the choice of the new site for settlement, and cannot reinforce a national feeling. Briefly, this myth of origin is not 'good to think', in contrast with the other story of the Rajputs fleeing the Muslims.

The version that provides the most extensive account of this crucial period—from the escape from Rajasthan up to the settlement in Nepal—is found in the manuscript of a chronicle taken to London in the nineteenth century by the British Resident Brian Houghton Hodgson. This chronicle first describes Rajput life and their relations with Muslims, evoking thirteen generations of independent kings of Citvar, who held the title of Bhattarak; followed by four generations of Rajputs kings vassalized to the Muslims, with a Rana title; and then sixteen generations who had the privilege of using the title of Rava. It so happened that Phattyasim, the second son of the last king among the sixteen Ravas, had a

---

[62] According to J. Gurung (2036 VS/1979), Jaikhan chose this site because it constitutes a natural stronghold, surrounded as it is on three sides by the Kali Gandaki River.

beautiful daughter named Samdamla. The Muslim sultan wanted to marry her and Phattyasim was offered whatever he desired in exchange, but he preferred to go home to Gadh Citavar to hold a council with the Rajputs. They decided that this alliance would be like letting 'vermin enter their caste', and refused. Consequently, the emperor attacked Citvar. Numerous Rajputs were killed, 1300 queens committed *jauhar* and the beautiful young girl jumped into boiling oil. Among the survivors, Udayaban Ranaji took refuge in Udayapur, and Manmatha Rava Ranaji fled to Ujjayini. The latter had two sons: Brahmanik Ranajirava and Bhupal Ranajirava. The Hodgson chronicle then recounts:

As the two brothers did not get along, the eldest stayed there and the youngest left for the mountainous countries of the North. He arrived in Ridi. While leaving Ujjayini, his elected divinity (*iṣṭa devatā*) told him: 'Having taken me away, we will settle on the empty soil (*khali bhaimā*) on which you will set me.' From Ridi, he arrived in Lasargha in 1417 Sake [1495]. He was exhausted and set down the divinity, who established herself there. He also stayed there a few days, but it was not possible to live there, and for the sake of convenience, he went to cultivate fallow lands in the place named Bhirkot Khilung where he settled. He had two sons named Khacha and Micha. They made their *bratabandha* initiation and [their father] asked for two Raghuvamsi Rajput girls from the plains and married them [to his sons]. Then Khacha the eldest went away with his wife, and having killed the Magrat [that is, annihilated the Magar country], he reigned over four countries: Grahon, Satahun, Bhirkot and Dhor. Micha Khan the youngest, also went away with his wife, and reached Pallo Nuwakot where he reigned.

Micha Khan's descendants were Surjekhan, Vichitrakhan, Jayanta-khan, Michakhan, and Jagadevakhan, whose sons obtained sovereignty over Kaski and Lamjung.

This chronicle was translated into English by Munshi S.S. Singh and Pandit Gunanand, and edited by D. Wright.[63] This translation,

---

[63] *History of Nepal*, pp. 271–84. We will not discuss the historicity of the Rajput episode contained in the Nepali chronicles. It seems that the different sacks of Chitor have been confused. As this history is presented by Tod (1987 [first edn 1920], Vol. 1, pp. 301, 303), the third son of Samar Singh is said to have fled to Nepal during the thirteenth century. Then, in 1303, Alau-d-din destroyed the city after being refused a beautiful girl named Padmini. On this occasion, too, the son of the Rana escaped to the mountains. As for Jaimal and Patta, they fought against Akbar in 1567. During this battle, Udail Singh

apparently based on Hodgson's manuscript, is quite faithful to the original, but has a mistake in the name of the locality which is the focus of our concern. Lasargha is translated as 'Sargha' due to a misspelling in the manuscript.[64] It is precisely the name of that locality that constitutes the first link between the Gorkha chronicles and the data associated with the shrine of Alam Devi in central Nepal. Indeed, the hill in Syangja district, atop which the shrine is erected, is called Lasargha, and may correspond to the Lasargha mentioned in the chronicles. As in those texts, it is located near Ridi, the holy confluence, from where the Shah would have gone to Lasargha. There is a place called Vaigha adjacent to Lasargha. In the 'Early Gurkha Bamsavali from Nilrajah' the place is called Vaigha-Lasargha. The exact location of the place called Lasargha allows us to pinpoint the Shah's itinerary.[65] Apart from this toponymic

---

escaped and founded Udayapur. His succession provoked a quarrel between his sons.

[64] One reads, in the chronicle preserved in the *Hodgson Papers*, Vol. 51, Folio 2: *Riḍideṣi sāke* 1417 *sālasarghā aipugyā*, which was translated as 'In Sākā 1417 (AD 1495) he set out from Ridi and reached Sarghā...' (Wright, *History of Nepal*, p. 276). However, it seems that the 's' after the date 1417 should be read as 'm', which makes it: 'From Ridi, they arrived in Lasarga in 1417 sāke'. Indeed, the two letters 'm' and 's' may be confused. Furthermore, it is to be noted that nowhere else in this chronicle are the dates followed by the word *sāl*, that is, 'year', but by *mā*, or 'in'. Moreover, it seems that Hodgson took copies of manuscripts to London, and not the originals. The error may have been made by the copyist.

[65] Baburam Acharya (*A Brief Biography of the Great King Prithvi Narayan Shah*, Vol. 1, p. 7), relating the ancient history of Prithvi Narayan's lineage, notes that Jaina Khan settled in Lasargha on the hill of Vaigha, a small locality on the bank of the Kali Gandaki facing Ridi. He does not mention his source.

The chronicle Hodgson titled 'Early Gurkha Bamsavali from Nilrajah' (*Hodgson Papers*, Vol. 51, Folios 111–20) is a list of kings' names, successively associated with the following places: Gadhagira, Gadhachitavara ('the fort of Citaur'), and then Vaigha Lasargha. After reaching this place, the lineage split into two. The eldest went to Grahon and took the title of Khan, and the youngest went to Pallo Nuwakot, then Lamjung, and finally to Gorkha. This chronicle also briefly relates the myth of the origin of the family, in Nepali:

Because of the younger sister of Jaimal Sim Rana and Phaktye Sim Rana, there was a great battle with the emperor of Dilli. The emperor did all that was possible to marry her, but the Rana people decided that they would

demonstration, data collected in the Alam Devi shrine of Lasargha allow for a better understanding of the early encounter between Magars and Thakuris.

---

rather die than give a Hindu girl to a Muslim. They resisted for 12 years, but when he saw that there was no solution to the war, Phaktye Sim told Jaimal Sim and the queen: 'Take flight both of you into another country where you will be safe [...]'.

Another genealogy in the same Hodgson volume (Folios 200-1) also provides a list of personal names associated with toponyms: first, Bahra Darla Sringa (where the man in charge of the royal children became the minister), then Lasargha (associated with a Khan king and a Bhattacharya priest), then Isma, Khilung, Kaski, Lantarjang and Gorkha, founded by Drabya Shah.

Lasargha is also mentioned in the *Gorkha Vaṁśāvalī* published by Naraharinath (2021 VS/1964: 121):

What is the lineage of Sri 5 Maharaja Prithvi Narayan Shahadev [...]? In the city of Udayapur, was the king Ayutam Ranaji 1. His son was Sri Barabum Ranaji 2. Sri Kanakabum Ranaji 3. Sri Malokabum Ranaji 4. Sri Bhattarkabum Ranaji 5. Sri Ambar Raye 6. Sri Birbikram Raye 7. His descendents quarrelling, left Gadh Chitavar and went to the mountainous countries of the North, Sri Jillah Raye 8. Ajilla Raye 9. Sri Atal Raye 10. Sri Duta Raye 11. Sri Vimiki Raye 12. Sri Hari Raye 13. Sri Brahma Raye 14. Sri Vekhan Raye 15. Sri Manorath Raye 16. Sri Jama Raye 17. Sri Jagat Raye 18. Sri Bhoj Raye 19. Arrived in Lasargha Sri Bhupati Raye 20. Sri Brahmanik Raye 21. Sri Manmatha Raye 22. Arrived in the place named Khilung in the province of Bhirkot and reigned there: Sri Bhupal Raye 23. [...].

This chronicle also forms the *Hodgson Papers'* Vol. 45, where only minor differences in the names of the earlier kings may be found.

In the vaṁśāvalī entitled *Āṭha ṭikā Sāhavaṁśāvalī* (Naraharinath 2022 VS/1965: 67), one reads: 'The princes of Lasargha were two brothers, Jaita Khan and Mincha Khan. The eldest Jaita Khan became the king of Bhirkot, the youngest Mincha Khan king of Nuwakot [...]'. In another *vaṁśāvalī* published in the same book (Naraharinath 2022 VS/1965: 98), one reads that the sons of Ramasim, Ramanaranasim, Nathasim and Suraprasata came to Lasargha from 'Chitar': '[...] These ancestors came to Lasargha and settled there: Sri Jaipalamasim, Sri Phatasim, Sri Visnusim [...]', but it is not said if they reigned there, as they are supposed to have done in the next mentioned stop, Garum kot (modern-day Grahon). A mention of Lasargha is also found in the chronicle in Vol. 17, Folios 168-72 of the *Hodgson Papers*, and in the *Gorakādhiśacampu* (Naraharinath 2013 VS/ 1956, Vol. 2, Pt. 3: 603). In the same volume, it is said that Drabya Shah sent gifts (saugat) to neighbouring kings on the occasion of Dasain. 'To the king of Lasargha, he offered a Narsiṁ [a long and curved copper trumpet]' (Naraharinath 2013 VS/ 1956, Vol. 2, Pt. 3: 418).

On top of the hill of Lasargha, people worship Alam Devi. I first heard of this goddess in Asleva village, which is located on the other side of the Kali Gandaki. An old man from the village had pointed out the top of the denuded hill facing us, saying that the king of Nepal used to fly there in a helicopter to worship Alam Devi, his lineage divinity. Puzzled by these costly trips to such a remote place and one, moreover, not at all linked a priori to Shah history, I went there in January 1994.

Bordered by stately banyans and mango trees, the path leading to the shrine is spectacular and incontestably old. The site of the shrine is also remarkable, offering a boundless panorama on all sides and surrounded by the dark waters of the Kali Gandaki to the north, east and the south. But the shrine of Alam Devi is quite modest, as if to preserve the site's natural grandeur and fascination. The current building is composed of a concrete double square enclosure flanked by a door on each side. Bells are suspended from the walls and porticoes, as well as inside the shrine. In the centre of the double enclosure is a Bhairampati tree (*Budleia asiatica*), which grows on a slightly elevated platform. At its foot disparate idols are displayed: statuettes of Sarasvati and Durga made of Indian plaster and plastic, a circular stone coated with cowdung and clay, a half-buried bell held in great sanctity; and, more importantly, an orifice in the soil through which one is supposed to hear the Kali Gandaki flowing some 1000 metres below. Worship is performed daily by a young, virgin Magar boy, who has already received the tonsure initiation but still ignores the habit of 'singing', that is, flirting. After purifying himself in a spring (as the Magars consider spring water to be the purest),[66] and before he eats, he offers incense, flowers, strings, and half a litre of rice to the goddess. He then sanctifies the sacrificial victims brought by the devotees as *bhākal* (an offering made in return for a wish). All animals except rams are offered outside the temple, tied to a very big sacrificial post. Sacrifices are performed all year round, with the exception of Sora Sraddha, the ancestors' fortnight. Two *pauva* inns meant for pilgrims face the temple. To its south, an arsenal or *kot* contains weapons: two ensign pikes (*bhālā*), a score of *tarbār* swords, about thirty *khoḍā* swords, numerous kukhuris, two

---

[66] In contrast to rivers.

kric daggers, one *khaḍka* sword, and two rifles. A very heavy khoḍā sword is used for the sacrifices.[67] It is called the 'main khoḍā' and is said to have been the personal weapon of Ran Bahadur Shah, Prithvi Narayan's grandson, during whose reign the conquest of western Nepal, Kumaon, and Garhwal took place. In fact, people say that all these weapons were offered to the temple by this king upon his victorious return from the war in the West.

The sanctuary is particularly important for Thakuris of all clans—Khan, Malla, Sen, Shah, and Sinha—and only women of the Thakuri caste are allowed inside, while men of any pure caste can enter. It is said that women from other groups would disappear if they go inside, something that has already happened. The goddess is particularly important for the Shah, for she is their lineage divinity (*kul devatā*). This fact is attested to in various historical documents.[68] A Sanskrit inscription dated 1708 sake (1786), from Ran Bahadur Shah, is engraved on the *nagarā* drum played every morning before the temple by a Damai. It accords tax-free land (*guṭhī*) to the temple servants: 100 *muri* to the priest (pūjārī), 30 muri to the nagarā drum player, and 20 muri to the *karnal* horn player. Gyan Bahadur Maski Rana possesses three donation deeds (*lālmohar*) written by Ran Bahadur Shah. Two of them, written in Nepali, are dated 1843 VS and 1708 sake respectively (that is, 1786 in both cases). The other, written in Sanskrit, is dated 1857 VS (1800).[69] They concern *sri* kuldevatā, 'the venerable lineage divinity', and grant the same donation in all three cases.[70]

[67] The khoḍā is a heavy sword, with a large, curved blade widening at the end. The tarbār is a thin, curved sword and the khaḍka, a straight one.

[68] Gurung 2036 VS/ 1979. Besides the historical evidence set out here, readers should also take note of the interview with Rishikesh Shah published in the Magar magazine *Lāphā* (4 [12/13], 1995, pp. 7–8), in which this member of a collateral branch of the royal family recognized Alam devi as his lineage deity (*kulāyan*).

[69] A *lāgat* kept in the Guthi Samsthan (dirgha 415, dated 1996 VS [AD 1939]) and titled '*Lāgat* of the Lasargha *kuldevatā's guṭhī*, West n. 4', mentions a copper inscription dated 1708 (probably the drum inscription) and two *lālmohar* dated 1843 and 1857 (which are probably the two kept in the priest's house today). These texts have also been published in J. Gurung 2036 VS/1979.

[70] The two texts dated ad 1786 designate the divinity as kuldevatā. This date is anterior to the first attested mention of the expression in AD 1805,

The Thakuris do not worship Alam Devi collectively, and have no fixed date for the worship. According to Jagman Gurung, Alam Devi is not only the lineage deity of Thakuri groups, but also that of the Magars.[71] In the cult, it is said that pre-eminence is accorded to the oldest branch of the *āthaṭikā* Thakuris, the Bhirkote Khan. And according to villagers, the king must come at least once in every five years. He arrives in a helicopter accompanied by the queen and a priest. The priest performs a ritual inside the shrine, while the royal couple pay homage to the goddess and offer money to the local Magar pūjārī to pay for a sacrifice on their behalf. King Birendra's last visit is said to have displeased the population because he entered the temple without removing his shoes, and the crowd showed its displeasure when the helicopter took off.[72]

The link between the shrine of Alam Devi and the Lasargha mentioned in the chronicles is thus firmly established. This, however, is still more obvious in the myth of the origin of the shrine's priests, the Maski Ranas. This Magar lineage comprises nine houses in the locality and numerous households in neighbouring villages. All the males of the lineage may act as priests, but the eldest of the lineage is called the 'principal' (*muli*), and manages the temple. In 1994, I visited the muli, Gyan Bahadur Maski Rana. No sooner had I sat on his veranda than he began to tell me his family's story:

From the place called Chitorgar, our ancestors or the royal family ran away... those of the Shah family thus fled Chitorgar and came bringing their goddess. Five brothers of the Shah family came, carrying Alam Devi. These five brothers finally reached Ridi. When they arrived there, they had to cross the Kali

---

according to K.B. Bista (1972: 130). This author believes that the cult of the lineage deities, as performed today, is recent, and linked to the first use of the expression. For K.B. Bista, the concept of iṣṭa devata, tutelary or elected divinity, is anterior.

[71] In fact, it is more complicated. The Maski Rana consider Alam Devi to be associated with them, but not as their lineage goddess. Niranjan is worshipped as their lineage deity through the sacrifice of a white cock and a ram, following a specific mode of calculation, increasing and then decreasing the number of years separating the occurrence of the cult: five years, seven, nine, then seven, and again five. The cult is not performed inside the Alam Devi shrine but nearby.

[72] Here, we have here yet another example of the liberties the king may take with the gods.

Gandaki. As they were trying to cross, what happened? The boat stopped, it did not move anymore. The Bote boatmen were doing their best to row, but it did not move. So they asked what was going on and the Bote told them that the divinity called Vaghe had stopped the boat and that it was the custom to offer him a pig in sacrifice. 'The boat will not move until we make a *pūjā* to Vaghe'.[73] Then the brothers wondered, who will be the *pūjārī*? The third-born brother was simple and slightly foolish, so the others told him, 'go ahead, you will perform the *pūjā*'. Because they made him their *pūjārī*, this brother accomplished the sacrifice. He was a fool and did the *pūjā*. [He then asked]: 'And now, who has to eat the *prasād* [remains of the sacrifice]?' And he was ready to give it to his brothers. But they told him: 'Only the *pūjārī* shall eat *prasād*, it is not necessary for the others'. So this foolish *pūjārī*, this third-born brother ate the *prasād*. Having eaten it, he lost his caste (*jāt*).

Afterwards they crossed the river. There, on the opposite bank of Ridi, is a big stone, with an image of Hanuman on it. It is at this place that we offered our sacred thread (*janai*). Since that day, we have lost our caste. Having left his *janai* there, he and his brothers took to the road again. They arrived here and settled for the night at the spot where there is now the Alam Devi shrine. They rested the palanquin of the goddess on the Bhairampati tree which is now in the centre of the temple. The next morning, when they decided to go further, the goddess was not there. They searched everywhere, but could not find her. She had disappeared in the hole which is still there [in the temple]. As it was late, they had to go, but someone needed to worship the goddess. So they said to their third-born brother: 'Why don't you stay here, you, you will enter the service of the goddess'. The other brothers went to the east, towards Gorkha, but the third-born stayed here. The others became kings in Gorkha, and from Gorkha, they went further east and made Kathmandu their capital. Later, from there, Ran Bahadur Shah came back here and settled his soldiers near the temple. He gave us a *guṭhī*. What happened to us then? We settled here and concluded an alliance with the Magars. This is why, though we are Rana, we are Magar. But here stands the lineage deity of the king.

This myth has strong similarities with the Gorkha chronicle, to such an extent that it is possible to consider it a recent construction based on written texts. However, this hypothesis is unlikely, because

[73] The Magars of the neighbouring village of Pyungha worship Wa Ghay, who is considered a malevolent spirit (*bayu*) fond of pork, whose cult should be performed outside the house and whose prasād should not be eaten by women. In the nearby village of Asleva inhabited by Brahmins, Oghe is defined as a bhut (malevolent spirit) of the forest; his attacks render one mad, blind, or covered with virulent pimples. He is offered a bow and arrow, as well as a chicken, which is set free in his name (personal communication, Olivia Aubriot).

the Hodgson chronicle has never been published in Nepali. Even in English, this is a book that does not have a wide distribution, especially outside the Kathmandu Valley. The muli has not heard of it and neither does he speak English; he has heard this story from his father. Furthermore, the name Lasargha does not appear in the English translation, as noted before, and this myth of origin is widespread among other Maski Ranas as well. The story, as told by a villager in the nearby village of Pyungha, was very similar, except for the origin of the royal family, which was said to be 'Sudra Paschim' (the far west) or the region of Surkhet, which they fled after the Muslims attacked. Then one of them is said to have killed a pig because he was terribly angry about having been defeated by Muslims. After that, he left his sacred thread on the same stone on the bank of the Kali Gandaki.[74] This huge stone, referred to as *janai dhungā* or *janai lung* (in Magar), that is, 'the sacred thread stone', faces Ridi, on the opposite bank of the Kali Gandaki.

The existence of similar yet distinct versions of the same myth, known among unrelated people, proves that it is not a recent fabrication. An individual may have elaborated the myth, but at a date far enough back in time to allow for its dissemination. As it is unlikely that the myth was derived from a written text, it is perhaps the *Gorkhā Vaṃśāvalī* which stems from the oral traditions and was written down relatively recently,[75] rather than being

---

[74] The gesture should be understood as a provocation directed towards the Muslims.

[75] Another quite recent history (since it mentions Gandhi and Nehru) of the Shah dynasty was published by D. Pant in 1992 VS/1935. Vikram Rana (later called Bhupal Rana in the text) from Mewar walked towards the North, fleeing the Muslims. The night before his departure he saw his iṣṭadeva in a dream, who told him: 'Take me with you. In the place where you will be tired and where you will put me down on the earth, I will not move, if you stay there you won't find many things'. The prince reaches the Kali River and puts his deity on the ground to drink and refresh his body. He then remembers the dream. Out of fear, he pours water on his head and recites the mantra, which helps him cross the river. But when he reaches Lachārkhā, he is so tired and thirsty that, despite the fact that the place is a desert and dry, he leans on a flat stone and falls asleep. When he wakes up, the deity is stuck to the earth and remains immovable despite his efforts to lift it. The prince, along with his ministers, decides to attack the neighbouring king of Dhurkot to conquer a better territory, but the latter offers him the hand of his daughter,

literary fantasies concocted with the aim of glorifying the royal family's past, as Sylvain Lévi believed. 'Glorification' has been more a matter of emphasizing certain details (like Rajput origins) and glossing over others (the close association between Thakuris and Magars, for instance), while not erasing them entirely. It is obvious that *Vaṁśāvalī*s have been used for ideological purposes, but this instrumentation should be nuanced with regard to their real content. Thus a striking counter-example of the usual glorification of the dynasty is the famous part of the *Gorkhā Vaṁśāvalī*[76] where the great king Prithvi Narayan is said to have suffered diarrhoea, while camping in Butawal on his way back from India. He went to defecate late at night and made such a noise that the Palpali soldiers who were hunting around there heard him and started fighting with him. Interestingly, this episode is qualified by B. Acharya[77] as 'Most irrelevant', 'ridiculous', 'painful', 'surprising', 'not possible'. It obviously appears difficult to accept as historical stories that are either too prosaic or too glorious.

The oral version of the myth is very rich, and provides an explanation for several cultural enigmas: the puzzle of the royal family worshipping a Magar goddess as their lineage divinity,[78]

---

along with the villages of Bhirkot and Khilung. The variant name Lachārkhā mentioned in this text is close to the one mentioned in the procedures of the royal coronation, which stipulates that Mahakali, the svakula devi of the Shah dynasty residing in Laskara-pradesha, should receive two dināra during the introductory rites of the royal coronation (Witzel, 'The Coronation Rituals of Nepal', p. 437).

[76] Naraharinath 2021VS/1964: 138.

[77] *A Brief Biography of the Great King Prithvi Narayan Shah*, vol. 1, p. 112. One may quote as another counter-example to this alleged glorification the incident reported by the *Gorkhā Vaṁśāvalī* (Naraharinath 2021 VS/1964: 28–30) when king Ram Shah sent a delegation to India to make inquiries about the Shah identity (specifically their title *prasasti* and their tutelary god, kul devatā). Whereas the chronicle relates how they received this information from the emperor of Delhi, Sylvain Lévi (*Le Népal*, p. 257), who until this point had summarized the *Gorkhā Vaṁśāvalī* edited by Wright, reports that the delegation returned without the information because their bastard rank was revealed to the emperor (an anecdote he found in Hodgson 1874 II: 38).

[78] A lineage deity according to the local Magar tradition and the donation deeds of Ran Bahadur Shah; an elected, or tutelary deity according to the Gorkha chronicle preserved in the *Hodgson Papers*.

especially one located in a region they had conquered recently, according to official history; and the fact that the priests of this goddess are Magars and that some Magars, including the priests, bear a royal title as a clan name.

With regard to the first enigma, the goddess episode is only briefly developed in the Gorkha chronicles. It is because they were exhausted that the Rajputs rested in a place described as inhospitable, and unsuitable for forming settlements. But divine caprice being what it is, the Goddess appreciated the place, and decided to stay there. In popular etymology the goddess's name is linked to her disappearance: *ālam* is locally associated with *alap hunu*, 'to disappear', or with *harāunu*, 'to lose' [the divinity]. However, the word *ālam* also signifies 'banner' in Nepali and in the nearby locality of Argha, nine banner sisters called the *Nau bahini ālam* are worshipped during Dasain. They have achieved great fame as they are invoked in a large area around their shrine. However, no connection is drawn between the Argha ālam and Lasargha ālam. Thus, despite being close etymologically to the word 'banner', which is the attested signification of the word ālam[79], the name of the goddess is not understood as such. It is still taken in a sense that reveals her nature (disappearance), however questionable such a usage might be from a linguistic point of view. Thus, my repeated remarks about the common meaning of the word ālam did not meet with a response: it did not evoke anything specific vis-à-vis the goddess. This strange motif of the Goddess disappearing into a hole seems to be vital.[80] Through this loss, the four princes of the oral myth—or the solitary prince of the chronicle—are dispossessed of part of their identity. This feature recurs in the Gorkha chronicles,

---

[79] Though not an entry in any Nepali dictionary, the word *ālam*, of Arabic origin, is commonly used in the Nepali spoken in central and western Nepal to designate a banner. It has the same meaning in Arabic and the Indian languages that have borrowed it, such as Hindi or Nepali. I wish to thank Marc Gaborieau for the etymology of this word, and the confirmation of its use in western Nepal.

[80] The motif of the goddess residing in hole in the soil is a common one. For instance, Guyesvari appears out of a hole (*kuṇḍa*), and the goddess Kali in Argha was shut up in a well under the palace (Ramirez, 'Luttes d'influence dans l'empire de la Déesse').

and Ram Shah, being obviously ignorant of such details, is even said to have sent a delegation to the Rajputs in India to inquire about the modalities of the worship they should perform to their lineage god.[81] The myth thus explains the Thakuris' ignorance of their own ritual procedures as they are described as, first, having left without their priests, and second, as having lost their god on the way.[82]

Despite having disappeared, the goddess is nevertheless present at the site. Thus, the villagers talk about how they sometimes see flames moving in the sky from the Alam Devi shrine up to that of Palpa Bhairav, as a manifestation of the visits that take place between the two divinities. The goddess is indeed there, but has implanted herself in the territory. In a sense, the country itself has been placed under her patronage, since she has become an integral part of it. Another oral version of the implantation of the Goddess in Lasargha states that when the princes searched for her, she spoke from the hole, asking them to offer her the following: rice from Ghangkur, three *bel* fruits from Bel Danda, and bananas from Gobar Gha, in return for which they would be made kings in Gorkha. These are the precise ingredients which are brought to her in the *phulpati* palanquin each year during Dasain, as though her devotees desire to fulfil her wishes forever.[83]

The other two enigmas may also find explanations in the oral tradition under discussion. The Rana Magar could be ancient Thakuri outcastes (vis-à-vis the state religion) because of their having come into contact with the pig—a circumstance that reconciles their royal title with their Magar status. While this myth claiming the Thakuri origin of Magars cannot be extended to the entire group because of the distinct difference between the physical features of the Mongoloid Magars and the Indo-European Thakuris, nothing can

---

[81] *Gorkhā Vaṁśāvalī* (Naraharinath 2021 VS/1964: 28–31).

[82] Usually, Thakuri kings are said to move with representatives of each caste as their followers—priests, soldiers and various artisan castes—as stated in the myth of origin of the Musikot Simha, for instance. Their ignorance of their own ritual procedures can also be seen as evidence of the non-Rajput origin of the group, and has been understood as such until now. See, for example, Lévi, *Le Népal*, Vol. 1, p. 257.

[83] Local oral tradition collected for me by Krishna Rana of Pyungha.

disclaim it at the clan level.[84] On the other hand, it is not clear how those degraded men could have been chosen as priests to the tutelary goddess of the dynasty.[85] In the oral myth, the disappearance of the goddess immediately follows the brother's trickery, and seems to have resulted from it. The Thakuri brothers are presented as unscrupulous men, abandoning both their god and their deceived idiot brother. More fundamentally, or so it seems to me, the oral version of the myth brings together the implanting of the goddess in the soil of the Magarant with the Thakuris' contact with the pig, the only episode involving the divinity before her disappearance.

As a matter of fact, the pig sacrifice is not absent. It is performed outside the temple on the eighth night of Dasain and called the *khaṇḍa* pūjā, 'the worship of the sword', as well as in the afternoon of the ninth day at the end of the sacrificial session. In both cases pigs are offered to Chandi outside the temple. Dor Bahadur Bista[86] succinctly describes a ceremony which seems to have been phased out now: 'Nowadays, he writes, a boar is used instead of a pig. It is given to a lame person in the name of the king.'[87] In the same article, Rishikesh Shah declares that the Rajputs do not even eat boar while pig 'works' (*caleko*) among the Thakuris; it is not clear, though,

---

[84] The mixture of physical types in both the Magar and the Thakuri groups show that there were many alliances between them.

[85] In the neighbouring district of Gulmi, degradation is followed or is marked by exclusion from participation in the lineage cult.

[86] *Lapha*, 4 (12–13), 1995: 5. Bista writes that a pig sacrifice is performed, but outside the temple. As is often the case, ritual precautions are taken in Thakuri rites to separate the pig sacrifice from the main god. In Lasargha it is offered to Chandi, and the blood of the sacrificed pig is not brought into the temple. In the Musikot and Lamjung royal rituals, a pig is offered to Bhairam outside the main temple dedicated first to the Sword-god, and then to Kalika. Bhairam and Chandi are terrible divinities associated with weapons. Chandi is of special importance for the Magars, who worship her at the full moon of Baisakh (called *Chaṇḍī purnī*) with an offering of a pig.

[87] This custom no longer exists. People say that it refers to a man whose leg was 'wrong'. He came to the shrine during Dasain, ate the prasād of the pig—sometimes called *sũgur* (pig) and sometimes bandel (boar)—offered to Chandi on the eighth night, and was cured. The man was supposed to take one leg of the animal to the king, but the priest told the king that his leg was painful. After being cured, he went to the king, who told him: 'I see that your leg is fine, now'.

whether by this he means that the pig is only offered in sacrifice, or whether it is eaten by them.[88] For his part, M.S. Thapa states: 'Rajputs do not sacrifice pigs and do not eat them, but the Shah offer a black pig to Kalanki, their lineage divinity—a cult for which they use Magars'. He goes on to declare, 'One has to be stupid to think, then, that the King's ancestors are Rajputs!' The impure nature of the pig, according to high-caste tradition, is invoked to demonstrate the necessarily tribal origin of a high-status group that comes into ritual contact with this animal. Yet, in James Tod's description of the Indian Rajputs, the boar hunt and the consumption of this animal represent ritual activities marking the beginning of spring. This hunt, led by the prince, mobilized the entire court, and the boar was killed in honour of the goddess Gauri. Thus, when Rana Partap Singh was crowned king of Udayapur, 'scarcely was the ceremony over, when the young prince remarked, it was the festival of the Aheria, nor ancient customs be forgotten: "Therefore to horse, and slay a boar to Gauri, and take omen for the ensuing year"'.[89]

The boar, which is equated with the pig in central Nepal where, until the recent introduction of a new species, domestic pigs where black and hairy, was clearly not absent in Rajput religious life.[90] Moreover, it seems that its sacrifice and consumption became a real bone of contention in the relationship between Rajputs and Muslims. Tod[91] mentions the case of the Shaikawat Rajputs, who gave up hunting and eating boar following the injunctions of a Muslim saint who had granted one of their member's wish for a

[88] According to butchers in the Kathmandu valley, the Rana of Nepal, when in power, were so fond of boar flesh that they caused the development of a new market. It is a general Hindu principle that the wild counterparts of domestic animals are purer than the domestic ones.

[89] Tod, *Annals and Antiquities of Rajasthan*, Vol. 1, p. 385. Other mentions of boar hunting appear in Vol. 2, p. 660, and Vol. 3, p. 1746. Tod also reports the story of Arsi, Rana of Chitor, who, entering a field in pursuit of a boar, met a woman who impaled the boar with a stalk. 'Though accustomed to feats of strength and heroism...the act surprised them. They descended to the stream at hand, and prepared the repast, as is usual, on the spot' (Vol. 1, p. 313).

[90] Numerous boar hunts are represented on the Rajput temples of Khajurao, especially on the Lakshmanan temple, built by the Chandela dynasty in the tenth century.

[91] Tod, *Annals and Antiquities of Rajasthan*, Vol. 3, p. 1381.

son. The myth of origin recounted by the Maski Rana Magar of Pyugha states that their Rajput ancestor had reportedly killed a pig in a gesture of anger at his defeat at the hands of the Muslims and thereby lost his caste. This tale voices the widespread belief according to which Muslims did not enter the Himalayan territories because these areas abounded with pigs.[92] This idea is found, for example, in the writings of Sikharnath Sharma Subedi,[93] who considers the Ale Magars to have been Thakuris who started to raise pigs in order to drive back the Muslims.

This idea has already been developed by Yogi Naraharinath and K.B. Gurung,[94] who are of the view that the Magars were originally Rajputs who began to raise pigs in an attempt to drive back the Muslims while in a state of 'dire-strait dharma', a state which allows any infraction of caste rules. In the myths' portrayal of history, the Rajputs seem to be caught between two fires: fleeing their enemies who held the pig in aversion, they reached territories where tribal groups conferred great importance on this animal, both as favourite food and privileged offering for the gods. In their own tradition, they practised a ritual consumption of boar, a tradition which those among them who had shown some compliance with Islam had renounced. Given this situation, it seems quite natural that the Rajputs, in opposition to Islam, would have elaborated a marginal ritual practice and raised it to the status of guarantor of their group identity, even if by doing so they became identified with tribals themselves—the same tribal people who ultimately became very useful allies.[95]

[92] Even Brahmins, such as the Ghimire of Bhirpustun in Lamjung district, are said to have used this protective strategy. According to the oral lore of that region, three Ghimire brothers are said to have fled India for Lamjung in the Uttarakhanda, 'to save their culture and their religion from the Muslims.... They established the Shah kings in the old fort of Lamjung and received, after the conquest of Ghermu, this territory as a birtā. Again, in order to prevent the Muslims from entering Lamjung, they offered a pig in sacrifice to the Turlungkot Bhairav. It may be why no Muslim so far lives in Lamjung' (Thapa 2041 VS/1984: 346).

[93] Quoted in H. Buda Magar 2049 VS/1992: 50.

[94] 2020VS/1963: 31.

[95] In the Rajputs' own history, the Bhil tribal group entertained close and friendly relations with them. See Tod (*Annals and Antiquities of Rajasthan*) on the subject, for instance, Vol. 1, p. 316.

CONCLUSION

Nepali state religion is a product of the history of group relations, and in the absence of written documents, the organization of the cults would have highlighted it. If the cases discussed here appear to have been documented by only a few written sources, we can rely on better-documented cases to verify our hypothesis. For instance, the evolution of the priesthood in the temple of Man Kamana follows the trajectory of the Gorkha dynasty's relations with the groups they subjected to their rule. The first priest of the goddess was the Magar saint Lakhan Thapa, and after him his descendants, who consider the goddess their lineage divinity (*kul devatā*).[96] It seems that soon after the temple was established, Brahmins were also appointed as priests to the goddess. Until the conquest of the Kathmandu Valley by Prithvi Narayan Shah, there were, as a matter of course, both Magar and Brahmin priests, who can be viewed as the original autochthonous priests and the priests attached to the Hindu kingship of Gorkha, respectively. More surprising was the initiative taken by Prithvi Narayan after the conquest of the Newar kingdoms: he sent a Tantric Newar priest to the Man Kamana temple to offer a human sacrifice in his name.[97] He thus ritually marked the assimilation of this newly integrated group by

[96] Perceived as the queen of Ram Shah, Man Kamana's special relation with the Magar ascetic Lakhan Thapa proves again the role played by Magars in the religion of the royal Thakuris. Like Mélusine, the fairy wife of the lord of Lusignan, the divine queen of Gorkha is compelled to abandon her human form when her husband, the king, discovers her real nature. Her faithful friend Lakhan Thapa then asks her what would happen to him, and the goddess answers: 'You are my devoted servant and what happened is not your fault. I will be reborn as Man Kamana, the goddess who makes wishes come true. I will manifest myself in the shape of a stone which will be found in your own field and you will continue to serve me as the priest of my sanctuary' (K.L. Shrestha, unpublished material). In this story, too, one may wonder if the divine queen herself is not of Magar origin, as she wishes to be reborn in a Magar's field. In a way that recalls the birth of Sita, the goddess is reborn in the form of a humanized stone which spurts blood when the plough hurts her. Her temple was built on the spot where she was found, that is, in Lakhan Thapa's field.

[97] This information is from Pun Magar (2050 VS/1993: 22–33). Regardless of whether this is true, this assertion, apparently based on oral tradition, is suggestive.

reserving it a place in state religion according to its competence and specificities—through the human sacrifice—which, if we may say so, characterizes the Newars in people's imagination in much the same way that pig sacrifice characterizes the Magars, or textual recitations the Brahmins.[98]

State religion in Nepal is merged with the royal lineage's religious practices, as only this lineage has the power to patronize and give particular practices the status of *state* rituals. This is quite clear as far as the conquests of Prithvi Narayan Shah are concerned because the sites are few in number, and religious history was clearly portrayed through the organization of the cults and oral traditions. Such facts became increasingly obscured in the Kathmandu Valley because the Shah policy of integrating Newar rituals was not sufficiently documented. We must nonetheless underline the Gorkhali government's intense patronage of the gods of the Kathmandu valley. To cite just one example, the Taleju temple in Kathmandu is financed by sixty-two state guṭhī, according to a register kept in the Guthi Samsthan. The Gorkhali state has thus taken upon itself the financing of this cult, which was previously closely linked to the power of the Malla kings.

The Thakuris brought in a certain diplomacy in their dealings with populations they subjected, including them in their government and adopting their religious specificities. They did so particularly with their allies; however, there were also powerful groups, such as the Ghales of Gorkha and Lamjung, who were vanquished and driven back or exterminated without being ritually integrated into the Thakuri governments or religion.[99]

On the basis of what occurred in the Kathmandu Valley after its conquest, we are tempted to read into the Magars' participation in state rituals and the strange pig sacrifice that it includes signs of the

---

[98] These symbolic associations are very strong in the discourses of the people of central Nepal.

[99] There have been no studies conducted on the Ghales. Nowadays often assimilated with the Gurungs, in the past they headed kingdoms in Gorkha, Lamjung and Manang. As described by Dharmaraj Thapa's informants (see 2041VS/1984: 285, for instance), some were Bhote and had Lama priests. This may partially explain why they found no place in the Hindu Thakuri kingdoms.

ritual integration of this strategically and numerically important group—who were, moreover, useful during the opposition against the Muslims—rather than the 'stigma' associated with the Magar origin of the royal dynasty. Indeed, nobody would call the king a Newar despite his patronizing the Tajelu cult, which is strictly performed by Newar priests and includes rites considered unusual for the Hindus of the Hills. The ability of the Thakuris to incorporate religious elements of the conquered population within their own religion forms one of its main sources of power. The pride of each groups is thereby potentially preserved. The Magars take pride in the fact that the king is one of them, and the Newar devotees of Taleju, buoyed by the feeling that nothing has changed, can continue to revive the golden age of the Malla kingdoms during rituals.

While there was clearly significant intermarriage between early Thakuri immigrants and the Magar elite, ritual practice suggests a distinct origin of the Thakuris (regardless of whether their claims of Rajput origin are accurate). When one combines the evidence of the Gorkhali chronicles and Magar oral tradition, as well as knowledge of the socio-cultural systems of high-caste, royal Hindus of India and Tibeto-Burman Himalayan groups, and then considers this evidence in the light of the socio-political situation during the early Magar-Thakuri encounters, the apparent enigma surrounding the central place accorded to Magars in the state religion does not appear quite so puzzling. It appears that the Thakuris, numerically weak and in flight, were initially willing to integrate local societies and had, in their Rajput past, entertained close relations with the Bhil tribe. Their circumstances appear to have mingled well with Tibeto-Burman practices of incorporating foreigners and placing them at a high level in their society. However, the opposing views of Hindus and Magars vis-à-vis the relative status of wife-givers and wife-receivers suggest that both groups may also have initially believed themselves to have been contracting alliances from positions of superiority.[100]

The sacrifice of a pig, performed by a Magar priest at the Thakuri lineage god's shrine, shows that at the very least, the Thakuris

---

[100] On this *quid pro quo*, see Lecomte-Tilouine, *Les dieux du pouvoir*, pp. 328–30.

had placed Magar rituals at the heart of their religious practice. Although boar hunting is prevalent in the royal Hindu tradition of India, the domestic pig was clearly differentiated as a polluted and polluting animal. It seems plausible that the Thakuris favoured the incorporation of pig sacrifice as a symbolic defiance of, or an act of protection from, the Muslims who had recently vanquished them. The liberties granted to the Hindu royalty in religious practice support this possibility, as does the more general dispensation of Hindus to break taboos in situations of 'dire-strait dharma'.

Once the Thakuris had consolidated their power, one might have expected the state religion to have been 'purified' of such unorthodox elements. The evidence from Lasargha shows, however, that this was not the case. The ongoing practice of pig sacrifices and the participation of Magar priests in key positions in royal religious practices indicates a pragmatic strategy—that of incorporating subject populations into the state religion, particularly those who, like the Magars, were numerous, and therefore crucial in their role of allies within the new Hindu state. Similar assimilationist and conciliatory strategies in relation to the Newars' religion also support such an interpretation. At the same time, this integration may also be interpreted as a royal will to divide the spiritual power or to subject it, and hence the recurrent aggression of Brahmins vis-à-vis Magar participation in state rituals.

5: Dances after Transplanting Rice in the Magar Village of Kolang, Palpa
(Photo: M. Lecomte-Tilouine).

4

Desanskritization of the Magars
Ethno-History of a Group with No History[*]

Make the glory of our ancestors' spilled blood shine.
Make the language and the culture which have sunk shine.

S.Y.K. Thapa: *Gyāvaṭ prati*[1]

For Michel Foucault, the conduct of the self (la conduite de soi) represents the individual's form of resistance to modern forms of power. Modern forms of power are by nature bio-powers, managing populations via education, medical standards and minimal incomes. The passage from royal sovereignty to bio-power, which occurred over the course of two or three centuries in the West from the seventeenth century onwards has now spread all over the world. However, it spread under such varied conditions and in so many different historical, social and political contexts, that the least that can be said is that it did not necessarily introduce the 'conduct of the self' as the only or the main form of resistance. Governed by an absolute monarchy and strictly guarded against foreigners until 1950, Nepal has undergone drastic political and social transformations

[*] Originally published as 'La désanskritisation des Magar, ethno-histoire d'un groupe sans histoire', in 'Tribus et basses castes', in M. Carrin and C. Jaffrelot (eds), *Purushartha*, vol. 23, Paris: EHESS, 2002: 297–327.
[1] Extract of a poem addressed to *Gyāvaṭ* (a term that means 'Light' in Magar), an annual newspaper published by the association of the Magar students of Bhairahava. This poem appeared on p. 1 of the first issue, published in 1993.

since then. The restoration of the royal dynasty in 1951 marked the advent of a constitutional monarchy. A short democratic period was followed by the non-party system of the Panchayats, imposed by the sovereign in 1961. After thirty years of existence, the regime was abolished in turn, following the popular uprising during the spring of 1990 and the framing of the new constitution in November 1990. The multi-party system and the form of democracy linked to it thus only date back to 1991 in Nepal.

Like in many developing countries, family planning, vaccination campaigns, compulsory education, and protection of the environment have been quite the trend in Nepal recently, and the number of non-governmental organizations (NGOs) promoting this new type of control literally exploded in the 1990s.[2] Bio-power can thus coexist with royal sovereignty since, parallel to this, the king of Nepal preserved a crucial position as head of the army (until 2006). Nor is it incompatible with the Hindu hierarchy since high-caste groups, particularly the Brahmins, enjoy an extraordinary political over-representation in the present democratic system. The situation of the tribal groups in this very heterogeneous context, which is at the same time marked by components typical of the Third World, of the Hindu monarchy and caste organization, is particularly complex. They have raised their voices only twice in the history of Nepal and this, during democratic periods, which were also periods of political instability and general societal disorder throughout the country. Indeed, Nepal began experiencing the beginnings of ethnic revivalism parallel with their first experiment with democracy in the 1950s. This movement was then vigorously revived following the popular uprising of 1990 and the setting up of the multi-party system.

However, since 1996, the revival of ethnic identities has been eclipsed, so to speak, by the forceful actions of the Maoists, who

---

[2] According to an article in *Ajako samacharpatra* reproduced in the *Weekly Chronicle*, 13 September 1999, there were at that time in Nepal over 10,000 non-governmental organizations, which received 7 billion Nepalese rupees annually from abroad, or 12 per cent of the country's total budget. The number of these structures literally exploded in the 1990s since, according to a reference quoted in S. Tawa-Lama, 'Political Participation of Women in Nepal', there were only 222 NGOs registered in 1990.

gradually attracted people's attention, including that of journalists and social scientists.

The Magars, whom we are concerned with in our analysis of the relation between castes and tribes, form the largest indigenous community in Nepal. They were also the ones who played a central role in the two great movements of ethnic revivalism and Maoist revolution. It would be tempting, in the light of the news that has recently reached us, to conclude that once again, ethnic revivalism has only been short-lived, and has already been caught up in or replaced by partisan politics. That would, however, undoubtedly constitute a rather sweeping statement.

All these innovations might just lead us to neglect the more traditional forms of power, which are still very important and perhaps even on the rise, if one considers the increasing role of Brahmins in politics. The 'traditional forms of power' have mainly to do with the authority that is conferred on the eldest males (and *a fortiori* on the eldest males of the eldest clans), and on those placed at the top of the caste hierarchy. This 'natural' authority in fact results from the two embedded strands of logic governing Nepalese society: the lineage structure and the caste system. Nepalese society can be defined by the prevalence of the lineage structure, which controls and regulates caste organization in a certain way, somewhat like the classes (varṇa) in India, which have only an abstract existence vis-à-vis the castes (jāt) provided with councils. In Nepal, the local segment of a lineage used to guarantee caste rules within the village. It is this authority that deals semi-officially with infringements of the caste rules of commensality and alliance since the promulgation of the 1963 code, which prohibits any judgement with regard to caste. This situation is what the first social anthropologists who carried out fieldwork in the hills of Nepal observed. They then concluded that there was a real difference between the natures of Indian and Nepalese caste organizations, whereas the observable differences were perhaps a consequence of the recent regulations with regard to caste in Nepal. In any case, it appears that authorities created with the purpose of managing and controlling the behaviour of individuals belonging to the same jāt or jāti have flourished in Nepal since 1991, similar to what had taken place in India at an earlier date. The terms jāt or jāti, employed almost randomly in Nepal, mean 'birth'[3], and indicate, like in India, a group status corresponding to caste or tribe. Ethnic movements were born or expressed through organizations grafted on the traditional groupings, and intended to manage, promote and control them. From the tribal perspective, social groupings are not only represented (and reinforced or even constructed) by a great number of these associative structures called *guṭhī*, *samiti* or *saṁgh*,[4] but also by a confederation of more than one score of them: 'the great association of the nationalities', or the Janajāti Mahasangh. Within this framework, opposition to the State is obviously translated as a conflict between castes and tribes, a conflict that is itself reduced to racial opposition between the Aryas and Mongols. This opposition is translated more precisely as a virulent attack of what is called brahmanocracy (*bāhunvād*). In fact, castes and tribes behaved rather differently in the construction of their respective organizations. While tribes operated within this framework by gathering around the jāti, perhaps for the first time ignoring their internal status hierarchy related to locality and behaviour (such as ritual and food habits), the high-caste groups grafted associative structures either on the basis of vaster groupings, or, more frequently, on more restricted units than the caste. Thus, to my knowledge, there is not a single association bearing their jāt

---

[3] According to E. Benveniste (*Le vocabulaire des institutions indo-européennes*: 258), in most ancient languages membership to the same 'birth' is the basis of a social group.

[4] The Magars are not the precursors of this field, although they formed an association early on, between 1955 and 1957 according to sources: for Suresh Ale Magar (2050 VS/1993), the first Magar meeting was held in 1955 in Mahottari, and the Association for the Reform of Magar society was created the same year by Giri Prasad Budhathoki to unify the Magars and put a stop to their bad habits (*kuriti*, *kusaṁskār*). According to D.B. Rana Magar (2052 VS/1995), the first meeting of the Magars took place in 1957 in the village of Kulang (Tanahun), and in the same year the 'Great Magar Conference' was held in Bharse (Gulmi), where the Association for the Reform of the Magar society, or Magar Samaj Sudhar Samgh, was born (Licchavi Magar 2050 VS/1993). Gathered around Giri Prasad Budhathoki, and then around his son Shri Prasad Budhathoki (Minister for Tourism), the Magars of Bharse were the first to publish a book in Nepali on their village and their clans. After a long hiatus in Magar activities, the 'Langhali family' was created in 1971 in Kathmandu. Finally, in 1992, the Nepal Langhali Sangh became the Nepal Magar Sangh, and the activities of the association developed considerably.

or jāti name (Bahun or Chetri, for example). On the other hand, some of their associations gather them into one block, like the Arya Society (Arya Samaj), or the Society of the holy-thread holders (Tagadhari Samaj),[5] while the majority sponsor various clans, such the Nyaupane, Pokharel, Bagale, etc.

The study of the relationship between castes and tribes in Nepal is particularly interesting for three main reasons. First, the encounters between these two social groupings are of more recent provenance here than in India, and thus enable a better historical study of their relations. Second, Nepal is the only country to have produced a code legislating the interrelations between and status of all its population groups, which offers a global vision of the society and provides a solid basis for its analysis. Lastly, the popular uprising of 1990 marked the starting point for a sudden revival of ethnicity, the formation of ethnic associations, the organization of meetings, and the production of abundant literature, about which we are relatively well-informed. In this context, the Magars form one of the most interesting groups because of their very deep and old acculturation to the Hill Hindus' culture. This acculturation is so old, going back as it does to at least the fifteenth century, that their rejection of Hinduism and return to an authentic and original culture (two components of a process I propose to term desanskritization, although in the end it takes the form of a para-sanskritization) is necessarily close to a pure and simple invention. Invention, of course, has no place in the ideology of a return to authenticity, forcing the group to engage in some complex historical reworking, whose mechanisms we shall examine in the content of the ethnic claims and discourses. We note that for the first time in Nepal, cultural organizations born after the ethnic boom, assumed control of the jāt or jāti. There had previously been a control exerted either by the State, or by the local sections of the clan or lineage (the two characteristics of caste society in Nepal). Some jāti associations went as far as devising fines that were to be charged to those who deviated from their rules, especially those in India, but also among the Tharus of Nepal and, more recently, among the

---

[5] According to G.B. Khapangi Magar (2053 VS/1996), who stresses the importance of the clan (*thar gotra*) for people of high caste.

Magars.[6] While the associations usually did not go that far, they did not hesitate in their meetings or their printed texts to preach a code of good conduct for their members, endorsing some behavioural norms and proscribing others, separating (*chuṭṭāune*) what is 'good' from 'bad', 'authentic' from 'alien' and, somewhat ironically, what is 'pure' (*śuddha*)[7] from what is not. In Nepal, the individual's insertion within collective structures is thus reinforced by the most recent developments in society, confirming (if still necessary) Louis Dumont's thesis, according to which the fundamental difference between Western and Indian societies resides in the opposition between individualism and holism. Characteristically, the 'conduct of the self' does not feature on the agenda of the Nepalese political scene: opinions and voting intentions were firmly upheld in the 1990s and generally posted on the walls of houses, showing the single political colour of the household. In general the votes were largely controlled by the 'great men' of the villages, who received payment in exchange for the number of votes they ensured through their influence—a practice they did not even try to hide.[8]

The 'conduct of the self' is not part of life in Nepal not so much because democracy is new as because of the ideology it implies: an individual attitude is not associated with modernity but with a form of selfishness, from which it is necessary to free oneself before pursuing any political career. Even the 'conduct of us' in ethnic associations is often subjected to strong criticism: they are qualified as egoists and communalists. Their nature thus limits them to their

[6] See Krauskopff, 'An "Indigenous Minority" in a Border Area', about the Tharus. A Magar lady of Tulsipur, Dang, told me in 2006 that 'the Sangh', that is, the Nepal Magar Association, had declared that any Magar with the *ṭikā* frontal mark during the Dasain festival would have to pay a fine of Rs 5,000 to the association.

[7] The term śuddha indicates a particular register of purity, non-deterioration, authenticity, while purity in the sense of not being mixed, is expressed by another term, *choko*.

[8] The Maoist revolution put an end to these practices, first by terrorizing the members of other political parties, and then by preventing the elections from taking place. As a result, the only political party that was highly visible between 2000 and 2006 was the CPN (M), whose flag flew on the roofs of several houses in rural Nepal.

sphere of political activity. However, in this concept of 'sectarian' or 'communalist' (*sāmpradāyik*), ethnic associations have also found one of their weapons - turning against the government (which is said to be controlled *in fine* by the Brahmins),[9] the same arguments with which the latter attempt to curtail their movements. Thus, S. Guruchan Thapa Magar talks about how the Magars found it difficult to create an association in the Tanahun district because they were reproached for being communalist, sāmpradāyik. He reacts:

As for *sāmpradāyik*, they understand it in this way: [it indicates] those who try to dominate the others while trying to promote their self and their *jāti* only. In this country where only the sons of Upadhyaya Brahmans are allowed to enter the Sanskrit university of Dang or the Sanskrit school of Pashupati, who is communalist? Is it the Brahmans or the other *jāti*?[10]

As a member of the Magar student association of the Tansen campus, Om Bahadur Gharti,[11] retorted:

One reproaches this kind of association for being communalist and for wanting to raise itself, while fighting against the others. But the Magar student association aims at defending a language, a *dharma* and a culture which are denigrated by those who govern, at learning the history of the Magars and at helping the weakest among the Magars. One cannot but describe as sectarian (*sāmpradāyik*), the *jāti* of Nepal who, saying that they are at the top, exploit [lit. 'drain'] the other *jāti*, those who, pretending to be gods born from Brahma's mouth, exploit the guileless and honest (*sojhā-sidhā*) *jāti* in the name of sacrificial wages. One cannot say that the bees in league against the hornet that is trying to steal their honey are sectarian (*sāmpradāyik*). What is sectarian is the hornet, which drinks the sweat born from the bees' pain.

From this answer, it appears that the author can legitimately fall back on the *jāti* community only when the group is exposed to danger; and (as the first part of the argument shows) while specific ethnic features, such as language, religion, culture, are put forward, it is finally the fact of the group's economic exploitation that seems to justify its defensive attitude. This resentment against economic

[9] Shivalal Guruchan Thapa Magar summarizes this idea (2047 VS/1990, p. 20): '...in this country the king controls the people, but the Bahuns control the king'.

[10] 2047 VS/1990, p. 18.

[11] 2052 VS/1995, p. 2.

exploitation present in all ethnic literature perhaps sustained the troops of the People's War, launched by the Maoists in 1996. The People's War thus benefited from ethnic revival and may be viewed as its latest incarnation.

GUERRILLAS AMONG THE GURKHAS

There exists certain bonds and commonalities between ethnic claims and the Maoist movement, including the composition of population in areas where it rapidly expanded, which includes a high percentage of Magars, as seen in the fact that the armed forces of this guerrilla include numerous Magars, and in the arrest of certain influential members of Magar ethnic associations on the charge of being Maoist activists.[12] Following the increased violence in the context of the People's War, representatives of Magar associations even felt the need to publicly request to cease assimilating their ethnic group with Maoist actions. Finally, certain features are identical in both ethnic and Maoist written products, in particular the notion that violence is the only means available to weak people, and to those deprived of history. In order to stick to its initial '40 proposals',[13] the Maoist movement seems to have assimilated every popular claim, those of the poor, of women, of the 'untouchables', as well as of ethnic minorities. The appropriation of the latter's main demand perhaps pulled the rug out from under their feet.

The twentieth of the forty proposals presented as an ultimatum to the government in February 1996, before the launch of the People's War, is significant: 'All kinds of exploitation and prejudice based on caste should be ended. In areas having a majority of one ethnic group, that group should have autonomy over that area.' Although it asks for caste hierarchy to be abolished, the movement not only recognizes the specificity of the ethnic groups, but also intends to reinforce it by promising them territorial autonomy. In an interview

[12] One can quote the case of the poet Jit Bahadur Sinjali Magar, active defender of the Magar language and culture, who joined the Maoists and suddenly disappeared while wanted by the authorities (S. Lungeli Magar, 2054 VS/1997), or the successive arrests of Suresh Ale Magar, secretary to the Great Janajāti Association, for participating in Maoist activity.

[13] These forty points are listed in P.N. Maharjan, 'The Maoist Insurgency and Crisis of Governability in Nepal'.

published in February 2000, the Chairman of the Communist Party of Nepal (Maoist) [CPN (M)], Comrade Prachanda, was more prolix on the question of 'nationalities', which he claims 'to have solved' by preaching autonomy. He reveals the presence of many Magars in his armed groups, and repeats the most common stereotypes concerning them:

And in western Nepal there are the Mongolian ethnic groups—you saw how all our comrades there look Chinese. These nationalities are so sincere and such brave fighters—historically they have had this kind of culture. And upper caste chauvinism and feudal ties do not prevail in these nationalities....and in the family background in these nationalities, there is a kind of democracy, a primitive democracy. Even male domination in these places is weaker.

According to Prachanda, many ethnic associations were born from the People's War and are mere satellite organizations, like the Magar National Liberation Front, the Terai National Front, and the Newar Khala. He adds:

The reactionary ruling class feels that if these forces grow and develop it will be very dangerous for their whole system. Therefore they try to manipulate the people. They try to make some concessions to the oppressed nationalities and say they will do all kinds of things for them.[14]

Therefore, in many respects it would be tempting to see in the Maoist rebellion the last form of ethnic revivalism. However, though the CPN (M) has many Magar members (especially in the army) and may find it prudent to please potential recruits, it cannot be regarded as an ethnic movement. It should be underlined that the movement is led by high-caste men, Brahmins, more precisely; more importantly, its goal is to seize power and change the structure of society. On the other hand, Nepalese ethnic associations such as the Nepal Magar association preach no political transformation, no economic reform (except in putting an end to the payment of sacrificial wages to the

---

[14] Remarks taken from 'Red Flag ...', as well as the passage below:

Peoples of the oppressed nationalities—the Mongolian peoples, the Terai peoples and the far western peoples—have been very sympathetic to the People's War. They feel it is the only alternative for them. And this is also a big victory for the People's War and a big defeat for the reactionary ruling class. So many new organizations among the oppressed nationalities developed after the initiation, like the Magar National Liberation Front.

Brahmins) and, finally, little social change, except for a better social position for their group.

Certain Magar associations, such as the Magarant Liberation Front, claim autonomy for their territory, the Magarant, which comprises the twelve districts of Tanahun, Syangja, Parvat, Myagdi, Baglung, Gulmi, Palpa, Arghakhanci, Pyuthan, Rolpa, Rukum, and Salyan. The request was officially made to the government in 1993 during the Year of the Indigenous People, organized by the UN.[15] The creation of an autonomous territory was, however, not a popular item on the agenda of the main Magar association, with the majority of Magar publications placing greater stress on cultural, linguistic and religious aspects. The declarations of Prachanda presenting a certain number of ethnic movements born from the People's War was undoubtedly a form of propaganda, aimed at including dissatisfactions of all kinds. It is in any case certain that the Magarant Liberation Front existed officially before the People's War. However, most recent developments have shown that the Magars finally did create an autonomous territory within the CPN (M): its forty-seven member government was apparently elected by the population, and although there is a lack of field observations, written Maoist sources indicate that all inhabitants of the Magarant autonomous territory received their new ID from the Magarant State, the school curriculum was changed, and that even a new code of law was introduced as early as 2004.

To understand this unprecedented creation, the views of the CPN (M) are of course essential. However, the CPN (M) seems to have exploited the pre-existing ethnic revival, which should therefore be examined first. More generally, it is necessary to start with a short analysis of the history of the relationship between castes and tribes in Nepal.

CASTES AND TRIBES IN THE HISTORY OF NEPAL

In the works of Magar authors, a common assertion states that the caste organization in Nepal was introduced by Prithvi Narayan Shah at the end of the eighteenth century, or perhaps even later, by Jang

---

[15] M.R. Josse, '"Magarant" State Demanded By Liberation Front', *The Independent*, 17 February 1993.

Bahadur Rana in the mid-nineteenth century, when he instituted the code of the country (*Mulukī Ain*). In the same way, a number of writers speaking on behalf of the minorities claim that caste was imposed on populations in a sudden and authoritative manner. This sudden imposition of Hindu order is called 'hinduification' (*hindukaraṇ*) by Magar activists, a term defined along the lines of the 'unification' (*ekīkaraṇ*)[16] of Nepal undertaken by Prithvi Narayan Shah, albeit one opposed to it, as it offers a different historical point of view. Other authors, however, believe that the code was not strictly applied in areas far from the Centre.[17] With regard to the last point, I would like to quote, in the absence of an exhaustive study on the question, a telling example: when I arrived in a remote village in northern Gulmi[18] in 1986, with little knowledge of the history of Nepal and its civil code, I was astonished and even sceptical when I heard the old Mukhiya headman tell me how painful his position had been. Born in 1899, this old Magar, who was compelled by authorities to accept the position of Mukhiya after his father's death, recalled that he was often obliged, for example, to make sure that someone whose cow or ox had died while still attached, mourned his animal by being attached himself in the cattle shed, his mouth full of grass for a period of eleven days. Cases of misalliance were more severely punished, by castration or even execution, and the chief, who represented the State, was likely to be severely punished himself if he was caught covering for those at fault, or if he failed to disclose the offences. At the age of fifteen, he inherited the chief's duties and, being extremely reluctant, sought a way out; however, soldiers sent by the central government convinced him otherwise. The code that he had to apply against his will, and much to the disbelief of the young people of the village, was that of Jang Bahadur, the Mulukī Ain of 1854, which, while being slightly revised at various periods, remained in force till 1963.

[16] Euphemism used to describe the conquest of about sixty kingdoms by this king and his immediate successors.

[17] For an example of this point of view about the northern fringes, see Höfer's fundamental study on the Code of Jang Bahadur, *The Caste Hierarchy and the State in Nepal*, Introduction.

[18] Darling is three days' walk away from Tansen, which was only connected by road to the capital in the second half of the twentieth century.

There is no doubt that Magar kingdoms or chiefdoms of central Nepal had been conquered during the early Chaubisia period, around the fifteenth century, when the Hindu royalty was established in the hills. Few documents provide information on this period, but the organization of the rituals attached to these Hindu petty kingdoms, in particular the Dasai, stemmed from the caste system, which was based on a hierarchy of complementary roles assigned to the various groups of population at the time of the celebration of the warlike power of the sovereign.[19] There exists some tangible evidence of the existence of caste organizations within the various kingdoms that were unified during the second half of the eighteenth century by Prithvi Narayan Shah and his successors. Thus, we know from a late edict that in Jumla, 'During the time of the Kalyal kings, people who were guilty of prohibited sexual relations with relatives or other persons, *or with persons belonging to a higher caste*, or cow slaughter, or homicide, were punished with fines or death'.[20] But the most documented kingdoms are certainly those of the Kathmandu valley, where sixty-four groups were listed (or placed) in hierarchical order under the reign of Jaya Sthiti Malla during the fourteenth century, and, to a lesser extent, that of the Gorkha, one of whose monarchs, Ram Shah, published an outline of a code in the form of twenty-seven edicts in the seventeenth century. The edicts of Jaya Sthiti resemble the Mulukī Ain much more than do those of Ram Shah; however, they do not hold the same interest for our study.[21] Ram

[19] One should not conclude from this that we are facing a perfect illustration of the Hocartian model. Indeed, for Hocart, it is above all the notion of impurity that leads to ritual speciality and the priesthood hierarchy, from which, by extension, derives the caste system. For the Indo-Nepalese, impurity is dealt with mainly within kinship: among all the status groups, the in-laws (or uterine nephews) deal with the impurity of death. There is no specialist for cremation or tonsure. In the same way, the majority of groups call upon their uterine nephew to deal with the impurity of birth (see Chapter 6). The ritual service organizes the entire society in only one context: the celebration of warlike and royal power during Dasain (see Chapter 7).

[20] My emphasis. Interestingly, this text, dated 1885 VS (1828), is a petition from the people of Jumla and Humla, who ask: 'Now that Adalats [tribunals] have been established, we pray that these traditional arrangements be reconfirmed'; *Regmi Research Series*, 17 (11/12), 1985.

[21] For Jaya Sthiti's code, see S. Lévi, *Le Népal*, Vol. I, pp. 230–7, and D.R.

Shah's edicts cover various subjects, such as the establishment of weights and measures, interests, priorities at the fountain or the mill, the sharing of water, protection of trees and pastures; it also deals with a mark of status that seems essential: the wearing of gold on various parts of the body. One learns in edict 17 that only the royal family can wear gold on their feet, while the other castes, Brahmins, Khas and Magars, do not have the right to wear any, not even on their hands, without royal authorization. The Hocartian model developed by D. Quigley, in which the king is detached from the rest of caste society, is clearly present in this edict, where the unmentioned top part of the body seems the only authorized place to wear gold for groups not close to the sovereign. Edict 15 however, distinguishes Brahmins from the others: they form a category that one should not kill, along with the gotra brothers and the renouncers.[22] The following edict (16) mentions another category, whose neck must be slit in the event of guilt: the castes (jāt) of the Khas, Magars, and Newars. In this case, as in edict 17, the Magars appear among the groups called jāt, a term designating with no distinction castes and tribes which, as in the Mulukī Ain Code, are located in the middle of the caste hierarchy.

However, the Gorkha society is also very strongly marked by a clan structure, which finds mention in the edicts. Ram Shah mentions the 'Six' clans, whose role it was to warn the king of possible plots staged by his entourage. Elliptic and thus mysterious, edict 24 refers to two other groups of clans: the 'Twelve' and the 'Eighteen'. These thirty-six clans[23] of the Gorkha, Brahmins, and

---

Regmi, *Medieval Nepal, Part I*, pp. 641–61. In an unusual way, these edicts present, at least in the chronicle published by Wright (1993, pp. 185-7), a hierarchy of the castes in reverse order, starting with the lowest groups and ending with the highest ones. S. Lévi presented them in an order more familiar to us. The first two of the sixty-four castes listed by Lévi or the last two in Wright are *varna*: Brahmins and Kshatriya, as if there was at this level no internal hierarchy but only a clanic organization. In comparison, the rest of the society is divided in an incredibly meticulous way into sixty-two castes, which are in turn sub-divided.

[22] They were thus shaved and exiled, but as this edict specifies, 'shaving is equivalent to death'.

[23] 6+12+18=36 (Lévi, *Le Népal*, I, p. 286).

Kshatriyas, undoubtedly bring to mind the *janapada*, the clanic society of northern India, as described by Romila Thapar.[24] The Magars seem to have acted as right-hand men for these clans of high birth, in particular the royal families.[25] Even today, the Brahmins and Kshatriyas commonly speak of 'their Magar', *āphno magar*, a term synonymous with service man or ploughman, as well as with 'man of confidence'. In fact, like all tribal groups, the Magars formed a reserve of slaves for high-caste groups until the 1830s.[26]

Several texts dating from the rather interesting Shah period, which starts with Prithvi Narayan Shah and ends with Jang Bahadur (from the mid-eighteenth to the mid-nineteenth century), show that the strict rules relating to commensality and alliance were not invented by the Jang Bahadur code, but existed prior to it. I will quote as an example one rather eloquent case relating to the Magars: in 1805, a slave was condemned to be castrated, to have his eyes enucleated, and his nose and ears cut off because he had fornicated with an unmarried Magar girl.[27] In the same way, the Jang Bahadur code ratifies the recent privilege granted to the Magars during the Shah period. Several texts dating back to 1822–36 show how, in every area beginning with Myagdi, the Magars obtained royal grace exempting them from being reduced to slavery.[28] One does not know what justified this measure, but it is certain that it contributed to accrediting the State's account, since it was a custom to levy a tax—called salāmī—in return for a privilege.[29]

In fact, this measure was part of a series of exemptions and fines addressed to several population groups. Obviously eager to fill its

---

[24] Thapar, *From Lineage to State*.

[25] See Chapter 3.

[26] Despite the numerous royal exemptions of the first half of the nineteenth century, in 1920, 46,064 slaves were listed in the country, comprising five and a half million inhabitants (*Regmi Research Series* 5 (4), 1973, p. 65).

[27] *Regmi Research Series*, 20 (8), 1988, p. 147.

[28] As illustrated by four texts dated 1879 VS/1822, 1889 VS/1832, 1893 VS/1836 and published in the *Regmi Research Series*.

[29] As M.C. Regmi states: 'The measure was obviously aimed at raising revenue, for officials deputed to collect the fee were instructed to transmit to the central treasury a sum of Rs. 10,000 from the Marsyangdi-Pyuthan region alone'; *Regmi Research Series*, 17 (11/12), 1985.

treasury, the State had two means at its disposal: to give privileges to or punish a group. While the Magars were suddenly exempted by the State and removed from the list of potential slaves, the Jaisi Brahmins were heavily fined for assuming the prerogatives of full-status Brahmins (especially in the western part of the country). Fines were also imposed when allowing rejected practices. Thus, the Khas and Magar groups had to pay for practising matrilateral cross-cousin marriages not at the time of such alliances, though, but in general, because it was considered the group's normal practice.[30] Finally, the unification of the country and the succeeding decrees of the Shah period illustrate the importance of territoriality in caste society beyond the caste-based structure common to the various Himalayan Hindu kingdoms. Conquest seemed to have brought society back to square one: thus, interests on loans were suddenly cancelled so creditors thereafter could only recover their capital on behalf of their debtors, and all privileges related to customary law and even crimes were erased. Royal donations were initially renewed, but later, when the Gorkhali State needed money, it started requisitioning the least legitimately acquired land in the annexed kingdoms, that is, all the royal birtā donations that were not acquired through bravery.

While the structure of the Jang Bahadur code was very clearly inspired by the Indian varṇa model, it differed from it in many aspects: first, the first two varṇa were merged into one category, the 'holy thread holders', in which the Brahmins were not gathered at the top, but interspersed with Kshatriyas. Thus, in hierarchical order, the list reads: full-status Brahmins, Rajput, Jaisi Brahmins, Chetri, Newar Brahmins, and lastly Indian Brahmins. The tribal groups, called by a generic name—'alcohol drinkers'—are divided into two groups occupying the middle rungs of the hierarchy: those not

---

[30] Apparently the royal caste of Thakuri also practises this form of alliance, but I never came across any mention of the taxes they would have had to pay. A text dated 1832 (*Regmi Research Series*, 17 [11/12], 1985, p. 190) mentions three taxes addressed to the Magars of Myagdi that the editor did not know how to translate: Farnyaulo, Waksyo, and Gwasyo. I am unaware of the meaning of the first term, but the second means 'pork meat' and the third 'chicken meat' in the Magar language spoken in the Palpa and Gorkha areas. It is interesting to see that these food practices were taxed, and especially to note the use of the vernacular by the central government.

reducible to slavery (like the Magars), and those who are. Except for this regrouping, there appears to be no difference in the way castes and tribes are treated. Two categories whose generic name begins with *pānī nacalne*, '[those from whom] water cannot be accepted', are then distinguished. In the code, there therefore exists something of a variation on what is ultimately a ternary model, distinguishing the twice-born, the alcohol drinkers and the pānī nacalne. This structure has currently re-emerged in the form of the three groups that have been formed since 1990: the Bahun-Chetris or high castes, which are dissociated from the rest of society (notably because they are held responsible for all the country's evils); the janajātis or 'nationalities' linked together in their Great Association as were the Matwali in the Code; and finally the Dalit, the modern name for the pānī nacalne.

The question of hierarchy in Nepalese society is extremely interesting, particularly from the point of view of the janajāti groups. Viewed as the basis of caste by the majority of specialists, hierarchy—though not so much the castes in themselves, and even less so its most modern and authorized form, the janajāti or 'nationality'—has been vehemently attacked by contemporary Nepalese intellectuals.[31] The meaning of the term janajāti is so vague that many Nepalese are unclear about who it is that actually takes pride in being a part of it. It originally indicated groups conceived of as 'primitive', such as the hunter-gatherers, but since the 1990s it is used to refer to tribal groups or indigenous peoples, and can also mean the (oppressed) minority. The term, first translated into English as 'nationality' and then as 'indigenous people', does not exclude the recent settlers in Nepal such as the Sherpas, nor the groups organized into castes like the Newars. These two groups are generally counted among the janajātis because of their mongoloid physical type and their Tibeto-Burman language. Even the high-status groups of western Nepal, the Khas, can be included among the janajātis because their establishment dates back at least to the twelfth century, and their

---

[31] The oldest occurrence of the term janajāti that I could find dates from 1986, in J.B. Hitan Magar (2043 VS/1986). This author claims to have been the first to use it in as early as 2036 VS (1979); see J.B. Hitan Magar (2056 VS/1999).

distinct Nepali dialect. Conversely, some groups among the janajāti such as the Sherpas are considered less legitimate because of their relatively recent presence on the territory they occupy. As for the Magars, they exemplify every condition required to be part of the janajāti ideology: uncontested autochthons, they were oppressed to such a great extent that they were almost absorbed within high-caste society.

The janajāti like to be presented as a society composed of distinct groups affiliated with the great Kirant or even Mongol family, where no internal hierarchy prevails. Perhaps with this model in mind, or the two phenomena may be part of the same line, a non-hierarchical caste structure is apparently being considered by high castes as the future solution, made apparent by the many newspaper articles that condemn, for instance, the ostracism of low castes, or, more generally, all markers of caste status.[32]

The janajātis and others hold high-caste groups, particularly the Brahmins, responsible for the caste hierarchy they are said to have imposed on society. Ethnic literature makes this point amply clear, and as an illustration I will quote here a stanza from the poem 'I am of high-caste' by Omu Thapa Magar:[33]

Bow at my feet
Plough my fields
Carry my belongings
For I am of high caste.

Though it goes without saying that high-caste groups have benefited from this situation, their responsibility for the forms of hierarchy

---

[32] To take one example, an article titled 'Fight untouchability', published in *The Kathmandu Post* on 22 June 2000, considers untouchability the most heinous crime against humanity and states: '(...) the country will continue to remain backward as long as discrimination based on the caste factor continues'. It is not just untouchability, but the caste structure as a whole that is seen as an evil which must be stamped out (*The Kathmandu Post*, 29 November 1999). A *truly universal* declaration of human rights appears in the first reference: 'We, the members of modern society, have also forgotten the true and original religious and spiritual teaching that not only accepts but also declares that all creatures of this world, *and even beyond*, are equal and the same' [my emphasis].

[33] *Magar jagaran*, 1, 1, 2052 VS/1995, p. 13.

observed within tribal groups in Nepal is perhaps less certain. Ethnic activists who do not wish to tackle questions likely to divide their ethnic group, which has suddenly unified in the face of adversity, in fact deny the existence of internal hierarchy within their group. Several texts, however, show that the State had ensured that tribal groups did not develop an internal hierarchy. Thus the exemptions and other regulations concern all Magars, even those of a lower rank, like the Athara panthi and Agri.[34] Still more striking is the fact that the State did not want to see any internal hierarchy within what it considered a single body, a jāt, in regulations concerning the Tamangs, Bhotes and Gurungs. In 1810, King Girban wrote to the Tamangs and Bhotes stating how he had learned that in their groups, some people used a Lama for the rites of purification during births and deaths, while others did not have recourse to this. He adds: 'Fines must be imposed on those who observe two habits (*thiti*) in the same caste (jāt)'.[35] Similarly, according to a section of the 1927 Code, all Gurungs are equal, and ostracism within them would be severely punished.[36] The Nepalese State thus seems to have taken care to see

---

[34] In return for their new privilege, the Magars were supposed to pay a salāmī.

Not all Magar households actually paid the fee, however. A fresh royal order was therefore issued on Chaitra Badi 6, 1887 [1830 AD] reconfirming the rates. Two officers were sent to collect the fees, Arjun Gharti and Maniraj Gharti. Even then, a large number of Magar households defaulted. On Bhadra Badi 1, 1889, therefore, Maniraj Gharti and Srikrishna were sent to that region to collect the fee from all Magar households, including agri, mahar and atharpanthi (*Regmi Research Series*, 17 (11/12), 1985, pp. 189–90).

I do not know who the Mahar are, but the Agri are miners, with a low status similar to that of slaves, and the Atharpanthi, or eighteen clans, were in the 1980s considered lower than the twelve clans. In Gulmi, the two groups did not intermarry.

[35] *Regmi Research Series*, 4 (3), 1972, p. 44.

[36] 'Throughout the dominions of Gorkha, there is only one Gurung name and caste (jāt) all members of which can take cooked rice from each other, even if alliances are made with girls or widows. In case, therefore, any Gurung claims to be of a higher caste status than others, or ostracizes another Gurung in respect to cooked rice, he shall be punished with fines according to the law relating to marriage expenses' (*Regmi Research Series*, 20 (8), 1988, p. 148).

that its jāt did not subdivide as the inevitable result of the differences in their practices, the jāt being a status group based on both birth and practices (dietary, marital and religious). Contrary to current opinion, the Hindu State perhaps contributed to the harmony and highly praised equality that prevails within the Nepalese ethnic groups. On the other hand, the tribal groups, or, rather, those who think and speak on their behalf, were obviously petitioning the State to obtain legislations concerning their group. This is testified by certain documents in the case of the Magars. One can quote, for example, this text dated 1837 (Phalgun 1893VS), addressed to the Magars of the eastern half of Nepal, from Marsyangdi up to Meci:

From former times, people belonging to your caste have been offering your sons and daughters on bondage and receiving payments in money. Some of them have also been taking rice boiled without using purifying (ghee) from the hands of people belonging to inferior castes. *Accordingly, people belonging to the Magar caste held consultations among themselves and prayed: 'Regulations have been promulgated for all other castes, but not for us. There must be regulations for our caste as well.'* This request was conveyed to us by Bahadur Rana and Purnabhadra Desuwa. We hereby accept the request. We now order that irrespective of what may have been done in the past, no Magar shall be offered or accepted on bondage in the future. No Magar shall take food from the hands of people belonging to inferior castes. In case any (caste) stricture is violated unknowingly, the offender shall be taken back into his caste after performing Niti or Samriti rites. Any Magar who wilfully takes food (from the hands of people belonging to inferior castes) and keeps his offence secret, or offers or accepts anyone on bondage, shall be severely punished. [37]

REPRESENTATIONS OF THE MAGAR GROUP

The Magars constitute the largest janajāti group in Nepal, numbering approximately one and a half million individuals according to the 1991 census. This first representation of the group is contested by Magar activists, who are suspicious of any initiative of the government, which is perceived as a high-caste machine and the instrument high castes use to ensure their domination. Suspecting that their population was intentionally underestimated, they place the number at two and a half million. This point is not all that anecdotal in a communalist country with transitory governments, where the

---

[37] *Regmi Research Series*, 17 (11/12), 1985.

census seems almost as important as elections, in that it highlights the real political weight of each group. It should be noted that the first 'communalist' census, that is, by caste and tribe, dates precisely from 1991, the year of the promulgation of a new constitution and the advent of parliamentary democracy.[38] Ironically, the hierarchy of the Jang Bahadur code was preserved in the enumeration of groups, listed in this order for the hill area: Brahmins, Chetri, janajātis, and finally the low castes.

Thereafter, the Magar association wanted to present a controlled image of their group, as testified by the instructions concerning the 2001 census.[39] However, the results did not attest to any striking impact that ethnic action might have had, except on the question of religious affiliation. The total population of the group was probably not underestimated in 1991 (at least when compared to 2001); the number of Magar language locutors did not grow, but 25 per cent of Magars declared themselves as Buddhists in 2001, with Buddhism as a religion being promoted by their ethnic association. However, an even greater percentage (75 per cent) declared Hinduism as their religion in 2001. In comparison, the emphasis on ethnic identity is much stronger among other janajātis: thus 86 per cent of Limbus, who had been depicted as Hindus in the past, declared their religion as Kirant in 2001.[40]

Described as 'alcohol drinkers' during the Shah and Rana periods, the Magars were classified as one of the 'military tribes' by the first Britishers writing about the Nepalese population at the beginning of the nineteenth century. The Magars were and still are privileged recruits in the Nepalese, Indian and British armies. Their martial ideology and the alliances they concluded with Thakuri

[38] Since the publication of this census, one of the favourite exercises of Nepalese scholars has been to evaluate caste and ethnic representation in all possible fields.

[39] *The Kathmandu Post*, 4 December 2000:

Members of Magar community from more than 50 districts assembled in the capital to participate in a National training camp to generate awareness to the purpose of providing correct information during the national census 2001 ... the three day training was jointly organized by Nepal Magar Association, Magar Society and the National Census Committee....

[40] Dahal, 'Social Composition of the Population'.

families who seized power in Nepal during the medieval period led them to identify with this group, whose degraded descendants they used to claim to be, until recently. There have been many myths of origin related to this degradation, at least since the opening of the country's border in 1951. They display a uniform structure: for religious and/or inevitable reasons, some Thakuris were obliged to move away from the rules of their caste, thereby creating the Magar group. Before 1990, the Magars hardly wrote about themselves,[41] and for a long time their group was presented either in accounts collected by army men, or in those written by Western researchers and high-caste Nepalese. Since then, there has been an abrupt reversal. The Magars have begun conferring great importance on the production of their selves. In this literature, they usually lean more towards the past and sometimes towards the future, rather than focusing on a description of present circumstances.[42]

The principal claim of the Nepalese janajātis, to which the Magars belong, is not about economic equality, but political representation, access to education, and perhaps, especially, to recognition.[43] The

---

[41] A Magar from Gorkha answered Hodgson's long questionnaire on customs and habits. In this first half of the nineteenth century, the questionnaire already presents an extremely Hinduized group. After 1980, a few ethnic journals, such as Koṅgpī—whose editorial committee was mainly Rai, but where all Nepalese groups, Brahmins included—carried articles on them. The first Magar journal, Laṅghālī, was created in 1981. The 1990s was when a true explosion of ethnic literature took place, among whom (with special reference to the Magars) are the following: Lāphā, Gorākh, and Sonī, created in 1992, Gyāvaṭ in 1993, Kanuṅg Lām and Sār in 1994, Im and Magar Jagaraṇ in 1995, Soro in 1996, Mirmire and Rāhā in 1997, Konja marum in 1999 (this list can be supplemented with the one published in Lāphā, 1 [6], 2050, p. 16). The oldest journals were cultural in nature, those created in 1992–5 polemical and politicized, while the most recent ones also demonstrate an educational character through the publication of articles in the fields of health, physics, electricity, etc. The publication of books on the Magars by Magar authors follows the same trajectory.

[42] The most obvious counter-example is that of K. Baral Magar, Palpa, Tanahu ra Syangjaka Magarharuko samskrti.

[43] The ten requests placed before the government by the Nepal Magar Sangh after its creation in 1993 were: the nomination of Lakhan Thapa as First Martyr; a series of linguistic requests (broadcasts in Magar over the radio and television, creation of Magar schools, nomination of Magar as a

Magars consider themselves to have been absorbed, dispossessed by Hinduization, and lost the use of their language; and in many cases even their patronyms do not help to distinguish them from Kshatriyas. All these features are currently viewed as alienating by those Magars who express themselves publicly.

THE DISAPPEARANCE OF THE JĀTI, THE LOSS OF SELF

There are many aspects to the Magar search for identity. In several texts one can read real anguish relating to the nature of the Magar being. Ethnic organizations, particularly the historical research they undertake, are entrusted with the task of filling this existential vacuum. Tek Bahadur Rana Magar[44] expresses it clearly and concisely: 'the purpose of the Magar association is to answer the question of the Magars: "who am I?"'

This feeling of having lost their identity is apparently related to the disappearance of the jāti, itself seen as one unified group. The jāti, on the one hand, is distinguished from other groups through a particular language, religion and habits, thus allowing an individual to be defined as a member of this group. The Magars reproach those in power for having promoted their sole culture—jāti—to the extent of rendering others invisible by absorbing them within their fold, and sometimes even proceeding in a Machiavellian way to achieve this aim. This crime is equated with genocide, since jāti diversity is described as 'the country's most invaluable wealth'.[45] Personal attachment to the jāti and its values endows the individual with vital characteristics, as expressed by T. Pulami Magar,[46] who claims to be apprehensive of the possibility of his jāti's disappearance, as

---

national language); the publication of the (real?) number of Magars in the 2048 VS/1991 census; and finally, the removal from school syllabi of the play *Śilanyās*, as well as a passage from the geography text meant for the ninth and tenth grades, which states that carrying loads is one of the Magars' principal activities (cf 'Hamro 10 vata...', 2050 VS/ 1993).

[44] 'Jātiya utthanko lagi "Nepal Magar samgha" ko sthapana'.

[45] Om Bahadur Gharti Magar, 'Nepal Magar vidhyarthi samgha ra Magar jātiko samksipta cinari', p. 1: '...by losing its culture, language and religion, a jāti disappears. At the same time, it is the country's most invaluable wealth which disappears'.

[46] 'Im'ko dhoka kholi herda', p. 3.

it, along with its language and culture, is 'dearer to him than his life'. The acculturation of the Magars is often described as a plot, carefully thought out and implemented by the Brahmins. Om Bahadur Gharti[47] offers a good example of this point of view when he quotes Machiavelli in Nepali: 'if one wants to dominate a jāti, it is necessary to eliminate its language, its religion, its culture and its history...'. This author perceives the strategy employed by Brahmins vis-à-vis his group, and continues by saying:

to erase the Magar culture, they transformed Magar place names: Baglung for Balihang, Gandaki for Gânadi....In the same way they regarded the Magars in high positions as Chetris, because they knew that there would be revolts in the group if one lowered individuals of high position.

For many Magars, the most complete mark of alienation resides in their own religious practices, in particular the rites of the lifecycle (saṁskār), which are strong markers of group identity. 'Today the Magars are controlled by Hinduism so much so that their rites of birth and death are performed in the Bahuns' manner'.[48] The categorical rejection of everything they inherited from Hinduism obviously leaves a great vacuum, which is filled by various theories on the Magars' religious practices before their meeting with the Hindus[49] (which is dated very differently depending on the author, from 3000 BC to the unification of Nepal at the end of the eighteenth century), and more generally by theories concerning the origins of the group, which appear to bring Magars closer to a solution by rephrasing the famous questions 'who am I?', to 'where are we from?'.

In this search, the Magars seem to have adopted a new ideology based on racial theories, which were elaborated before the advent of the now widely accepted genetic theories. In addition, they attach great importance to names and what they reveal, not only the names

[47] 'Nepal Magar vidhyarthi samgha ra Magar jātiko samksipta cinari', p. 4.

[48] Hira Thapa Magar, 'Magar jatima hindukaranko asar'.

[49] According to different authors, Magars were originally followers of animism (or 'natural religion', prakṛtik dharma), of shamanism (jhāṅkrivād= Jhankrism), of Buddhism, or of Bon.

of groups, but also place names as well as certain words in their vocabulary which are considered true 'ethnic markers'.[50]

THE ETHNONYM AS GUARDIAN OF GROUP IDENTITY

In the same way that names of gods reveal information about their being,[51] the identity of a group, that is, its ultimate origin and even its nature, must be sought in its ethnonym and what it suggests. Thus, Magars are attached to the 'Mongols', from whom they derive their name. Starting from this linguistic index, all kinds of historical scenarios have been elaborated. Thus, for H.B. Buda Magar,

In the 5th century after J.-C., on the plains of Russia and China was a group, the 'Tarkomangol'. Among this group (*jāti*) was the sub-group (*thari*) of the Huns. Today Huns can be found from Hungary and Romania as far as Beijing. The Magar army of Mongolia, or the army of Magar Mangol, conquered Tibet and central Nepal.[52]

This scenario also allows for a historical connection between the Magars and the Magyars, repeating, one century later, A. de Csomos' famous quest, albeit in the opposite direction. The proof of this common origin is reinforced by homophonies: 'Two Magyar women having emigrated from Venezuela to Kathmandu met an Ale Magar and some terms of their two languages correspond'.[53] This additional proof reinforces the necessarily rich homophony between the two ethnonyms Magar and Magyar.

The ethnonym Magar is also situated in relation to the Magadha region in northern India, which is said to have been originally populated by Magars.[54] Born in a kingdom located between

---

[50] Speculations relate especially to the word *di*, which means water, river in Magar (and in several other Tibeto-Burman languages). The occurrences of this phoneme, in particular in toponyms, are interpreted as proof of Magar origin.

[51] M. Lecomte-Tilouine, 'The Avatars of Varaha in the Himalayas'.

[52] *Kirat vams ra Magarharu*, p. 46. Mongol is also often taken as meaning Mongoloid, as Gopal Gurung explains (quoted in ibid., p. 41): 'Kiranti are in fact the Mangol *jāti*. Among the three *varṇa*: Japhetic, Semitic and Hemitic is the Mangol *jāti*, this is why one replaced the term of Kiranti by that of Mangol. It does not mean that they come from Mongolia.'

[53] Ibid., p. 46.

[54] Ibid., p. 48.

Magarant and Magadha, Prince Siddhartha, who later became the Buddha, is also regarded as a Magar. Magar is also sometimes connected with *markat*, a term that designates the monkeys in Rama's army, which is said to have comprised Magars.[55] Finally, the name Magar contains the two Nepali words *ma gar*, 'I make', which indicates the Magars' benevolent and prompt disposition to work, and recalls how they agreed to undertake tasks repugnant to high castes, that is, to go to war or sacrifice a pig in their stead. This animal, which stigmatizes the Magar group in the Hindu social hierarchy, found an honourable place in the Himalayan range, as a defensive weapon protecting the Hindus from the Muslims:

...Bahuns fled the Muslims from India...and penetrated the Mangol kingdoms, but the Muslims did not stop pursuing them and it is only after they entered the country of the Magars of Gorkha, that the Muslims moved away when seeing the Magars' pigs. Thus the lives of the Bahuns were saved.[56]

HISTORY AS IDEOLOGY AND AS ULTIMATE SCIENCE

The Magars' attitude towards history is two-fold. On the one hand, they have no confidence in official history, which is viewed as an instrument of brahmanocracy. On the other, they manifest a salutory expectation with respect to the historical research undertaken by their group's intellectuals. This new, correct form of history would soon tell them, once 'enough research will have been carried out', who they are, what their religion is, where they come from, and why they are exploited today. Only then will they have the means to rise collectively. All this is clearly laid out in the editorial of the first issue of *Magar Jagaran*:

We the Magars, are the descendants of heroic ancestors, we the Magars, are the first inhabitants (*adibasi*) of this country, we the Magars, formerly ruled over this country. Why are we today absorbed and controlled in this country? Why do we have to survive as ploughmen or porters? Why are the Magars not part of the government? To find any answers to these questions, we must study Nepal's ancient history. But the historians of this country are full of caste prejudices. That means that no one has given a place in history to the Magar ancestors' heroism and love for the nation.

[55] D.P. Sris Magar, '"Magar" jat nam kasari utpati bhayo ta?', p. 5.
[56] H. Thapa Magar, 'Magar jatima hindukaranko asar', p. 7.

The ultimate discovery of their true identity is announced as imminent and inescapable:[57] 'Magars are searching for their *dharma*, their culture, their texts, their writing and their history. The day is close when the Magars will meet their essential origin in its true shape.'

This discovery, as stated earlier, will deliver the group from the uncertainty into which it has plunged: who is it? Where does it come from? What is its religion?

One of the most widely popular theories about the Magars' origin talks about the existence of a golden age where Magars were Buddhists and reigned over their territory. O.B. Gharti Magar, following the theses of the most famous book on the history of Magars,[58] calls this golden age the 'Licchavi time': 'The Licchavi time was very happy, there was no trick, no high or low status, no anger....All were Buddhist. All were equal.'

From this point an entire cultural arsenal was reconstituted with the active participation of M.S. Thapa,[59] a militant Magar historian, and delivered to the Magars via meetings and publications. It includes the original alphabet or Akkha lipi, the Magar calendar, the handbook of lifecycle rituals in Magar, as well as worthy icons of the group, in particular a Buddha with Magar features and the martyr Lakhan Thapa.[60]

In return, Magars were asked to clearly display their identity by adding the name of their ethnic group at the end of their patronym (as my bibliography testifies); by writing, speaking or learning their language; and by boycotting Hindu rituals, in particular the national festival of Dasain. The janajātis provided this festival with a new interpretation: it would celebrate the victory of the Aryans over the Mongols, the latter's spilled blood symbolically exhibited by the former through the red rice marks worn on their foreheads.[61] Violent practices, such as the animal sacrifices, are said to have been

---

[57] Ibid.

[58] M.S. Thapa, 'Pratham Sahid Lakhan Thapa Magar', quoted in O.B. Gharti Magar, 'Nepal Magar vidhyarthi samgha ra Magar jātiko samksipta cinari', p. 3.

[59] See M.S. Thapa, 'Pratham Sahid Lakhan Thapa Magar'.

[60] On Lakhan Thapa, see Chapter 5, this volume.

[61] *Lapha*, 7, p. 6.

imposed on Buddhist Magars by Hindu kings, who even checked to see that a bloody sacrifice had indeed been offered in each house during this festival.[62] The negative connotation now attached to Dasain is proportionate to its importance in the Hindu State. On the other hand, the Tihar festival, which celebrates prosperity and the brother-sister relationship, has been declared originally Magar, and its celebration strongly encouraged.[63]

THE ETHOS OF THE ETHNIC GROUP

While religious practices are subjected to detailed attention, more generally Magar ethnic activists morally evaluate the customs and habits of their group, underlining their negative (the most numerous, and which are to be eradicated) and positive aspects (to be developed). The negative characteristics listed most frequently are: very little importance attached to education; ludic or 'lazy' practices (like dancing, singing, etc.); 'useless' expenditure (on alcohol, cigarettes, feasts, jewels, etc.); divorce; polygamy; and superstitions. All this signifies ethnic puritanism. The last of the thirteen negative points listed by Lila Kumari Gharti Magar[64] is, on the other hand, particularly remarkable, as it mentions the absence of historians as one of the weaknesses of the group: 'the fact that the bravery of the Magars does not have a place in history, and that the Magars do no historical research themselves are also weak points in Magar society'. This point is also highlighted by Hira Kumari Thapa Magar[65] in the list she compiles of the features that caused the Magars to fall 'behind':

The Magars are left aside from education and on the other hand they prefer to enrol in the army because one earns more there than a university professor. And those who study only aim at passing the 'certificate'. Under these conditions, how can one protect its language and culture, how can one write its history? So far all the historians have been Aryas.

---

[62] According to M.S. Thapa Magar ('Ke Dasai Tihar Magarharuko Cadparva Ho'), the handprints made in pig's blood outside Magars houses were what allowed the king to check that everyone had indeed made a sacrifice on the occasion of Dasain.

[63] M. S. Thapa, 'Dasai Tihar Magarharuko cadaparva ho ki hoina?', p. 10.

[64] 'Magar samajma bhaeka kamajoriharu ra kehi ramra paksaharu', p. 34.

[65] 'Magar jatima hindukaranko asar', p. 39.

This author also mentions the importance placed on the political party over the jāti as one of the aspects that contributed to weakening the Magars.[66]

Among the positive aspects to be encouraged are women's autonomy, equality, mutual aid, and a willingness to work. The texts aimed at drawing up a list of ethics for the group are in fact often contradictory, at least in their form. Thus, G.J. Rana Magar[67] estimates that the Magars '...could not develop because they destroyed their old habits' while at the same time condemning shamanic practices: 'Magars first perform exorcisms (jharphuk) then only after, if the person is not cured, they take him to the hospital'. He also condemns the ostentation of the worship addressed to the lineage gods, and finally concludes, in a rather radical way: 'Young people say that these are "blind beliefs" and want to get rid of them to develop Magar society'. In this respect, he is only one example among many others, such as E. Ale Magar, who states[68]: 'we should separate good and ill deeds', 'it is necessary to uproot...bad life cycle rituals and to throw them away', and suggests that 'If today the Magars are exploited, it is because of the bad habits (kuriti) and superstitions: this is why the jāti should be educated'.

DESANSKRITIZATION

The phenomenon of desanskritization in Nepal is endowed with a literal meaning in addition to its metaphorical one. Sanskrit texts, the Sanskrit language, the places they are taught at and those who both teach and learn them, are targets for ethnic activists. Spectacular and forceful actions like the burning of Sanskrit books and bombing of Sanskrit schools exemplify their violent discourse. The Magars' resentment, like that of other ethnic groups, originates in the content of several Sanskrit texts, and in the very use of this language.

One of the most frequent janajāti claims has to do with abolishing the compulsory teaching of Sanskrit at schools, a subject that the janajātis are uncomfortable with because, as they iterate,

---

[66] Anonymous, 'Magarharuka kamajoriharu ke ke hun?'.
[67] 2050 VS/1993, pp. 21-4.
[68] 'Kuriti hatau, samajlai bacau', p. 7.

their language does not differentiate between dental and retroflex consonants. Hindu sacred books are constantly compared with the missionaries' Bible as a tool to seize power.[69] Moreover, it is the content that they were compelled to internalize that is denounced today. Many Magar authors simply quote extracts of Vedic and Puranic texts to emphasize their unacceptability in the current context, extracts that need no annotation to prove their point. For instance, 'the Brahmans possess all the goods of the earth', or 'the best among men are the Brahmans', or 'if a Vaishya or Shudra secretly listens to a Master who teaches Veda to his disciple, he goes to hell'. As a counterpoint to the rigour of these texts, the Brahmins' casuistry is an object of indignation and derision for Magar activists, who advocate the abolition of any sacrificial salary or gifts to Brahmins, and the employment of in-laws as domestic priests. This denunciation of the Brahmins' practices and ideology reinforces the Magar self-portrait: 'straight and frank[70] as opposed to the Brahmins, who are considered 'malignant and crafty'; illiterate when faced with learned pundits; dispossessed vis-à-vis the Brahmins, who are said to do nothing but store wealth; the Magars are autochthonous while the Brahmins are viewed as Hindu

---

[69] Om Bahadur Gharti Magar ('Nepal Magar vidhyarthi samgha ra Magar jātiko samksipta cinari', pp. 1–5): 'In the same way that the Christian Fathers entered India, carrying the bible in the name of religion and seized all the country, in the same way, Aryas entered the Magar kingdom carrying Vedas, *Purāṇas* and the Laws of Manu'.

[70] These two features are often said to come from the sedentary character of the Magars, in opposition to the high castes, who migrate and are consequently more skilful and cunning (M.S. Thapa Magar 2050 VS/1993, pp. 5–6). This idea is developed in this historical fresco:

Because of the climate, men were differentiated by their being black, white, yellow, small and large. While walking during a hunt, they left their territory. There was sexual intercourse between people of different colour and other physical characteristics. This gave rise to different *jāti* and from these *jāti* were born *upajāti*. From hunters, people became itinerant farmers. They formed villages of the same *varṇa* and of the same *jāt*. Some *jāti* leave their territory and migrate: they are better farmers and are more cunning. The *jāti* or *samāj* which do not migrate are *sojhā* (honest), *sidhā* (frank), *milānasar* (friendly)..., like the Magars, Gurungs, Rais... (S. Ale Magar 2050 VS/1993).

colonialists; Magars are courageous and handle weapons, whereas the Brahmins never, by definition, risk their lives, and only handle the feather.

This last feature is of cardinal importance for Magars, who view courage and bravery as particularly positive values. They wonder why these values are not recognized, particularly by the government. Why, asks a Magar author, does one publish stamps representing writers, poets, and artists but not valorous soldiers? The Magars always have a garland of 'brave Gurkhas' portrait surrounding their calendar, written in Akkha lipi.

The importance of the gift of oneself, the blood offered liberally by Magars for the sake of the nation and its defence, also appears in ethnic poetry in either exalted stanzas:

...we offer our warm blood
to save our mother Nepal.[71]

Or, on the contrary, in bitter and disillusioned ones:

the ancestors, faithful to the salt,[72]
were the goats of the sacrifice,
the lucky ones were cut into pieces....
Search,
Shall we find the true history of the ancestors, the pleasant culture,
once, ask the smoke which accompanies the bullet shot by the rifle's trigger,
will it say something?[73]

Beyond any specific ethnic claim, one feels the extent of the helplessness of the Magars when faced with the devalorization of a war-like ideology, military valour and, more generally, of the *kṣatra* vis-à-vis the *brahman*. This recent and brutal devalorization is not highlighted just by Magar authors; 'the Khukri,' says Surendra Singh K.C.,[74] 'began to lose its shine. The pen got mightier', and Brahmanocracy is its most manifest consequence. The situation in Nepal calls to mind, mutatis mutandis, Michel Foucault's

---

[71] Sushri Shiva Thapa, 2050 VS/1993, 'Gorkhali', *Gyavāt*, p. 51.
[72] Expression meaning faithful to the king, to the employer.
[73] Samjog Lapha Magar, 2053 VS/1996, 'The old pillar and me'.
[74] 'Politics of putrefaction', *The Kathmandu Post*, 3 June 1999.

remarks[75] on the end of the 'society of blood'. However, to the valourization of literacy and school, the Magars from rural areas still retort: 'What is the use of reading and writing, if you want to eat, plough?' The elite among the group is still composed of warriors, and moreover, it is a war-like ideology that shapes the Magars worldview: the most eminent among them are those who received the Victoria Cross; fidelity, the gift of oneself and the spirit of the body are the ultimate values; women appreciate necklaces of cartridges or even shoulder-belts, and many men don battledress on a daily basis. Even their relation to the earth is mediated by war: it is the spilled blood of the Magar warrior which, soaked in the earth forever, gives it value and makes a true organic Magar being out of it. The Magars, consequently, are the sons of the earth, the *Bhumi putra*.

On the other hand, as a consequence of their painful working life as ploughmen, the Magars also maintain a relation of paternity with the earth as they have fertilized it with their sweat. This relation is reinforced by the fact that they have also named it. For these two reasons they are also the fathers of the earth, *Bhumi pitra*.[76]

These inalienable bonds with the earth are reinforced in inverse proportion to their rejection of Hindu culture, which was brought in by mere colonists, notwithstanding the ancient presence of autochthons. Perhaps because it was borrowed, or because it is only a reformulation of ideas that never ceased to exist, many features of janajāti ideology brings to mind a decolonialization movement, and one consequently understands the important role of historical frescos: they provide a 'scientific' base to the construction of group identity, and legitimize the rejection of the oppressor group and those symbolizing it, the Brahmins (or Bahuns), who are literally accused of cultural genocide.

One can therefore conclude that while the Magars followed a process of sanskritization until 1990, they have since then embarked on an opposite trend that one may term 'desanskritization', in which upper castes no longer constitute the model to be aspired for, but form a kind of counter-model.

---

[75] Foucault, *Histoire de la sexualité 1*, pp. 194–5.
[76] On this topic, see G. Budhathoki Magar, 'Adibasi Magar ra Nepal bhumiko sambandha tatha namakaran'.

However, this new trend undoubtedly concerns the dominant fringe of the Magar society in the same way that sanskritization, too, was a more important concern for the dominant Magar lineages than it was for others. Indeed, at the time of my fieldwork in a village in central Nepal between 1986 and 1990, the distinction between the low-status Magar clans and the higher status ones (called *Bhaisi khāne* and *Bhaisi nakhāne* respectively, or the buffalo-eaters and non-eaters) was clearly reinforced by different degrees of sanskritization. It would not be improbable to suggest that sanskritization, which affected the dominant lineages more deeply than the others, had perhaps created this internal hierarchy. The dominant clans would not eat buffalo or pork, and used to call upon a Brahmin for birth and death rituals, whereas the lower-status clans were less puritan not only in regard to their diet, but also vis-à-vis Hindu rituals. If they did not call upon a Brahmin, it was not because of any opposition, but because of need. The essence of their argument amounted to: 'as for us, we are poor and we prefer to offer sacrificial gifts to our matrimonial allies (*celibeṭi*); we do not need Brahmans because we do not need to be prestigious. If we could afford goat and chicken, we would stop eating buffaloes...'.

However, the differences between the two groups relate to both their practices and their supposed territory of origin. The process of Sanskritization was certainly used to reinforce this distinction, but it is unlikely that it created it ex nihilo.

In less time than one might have imagined, these formerly low-status groups were accorded the status of 'authentic' and even 'pure' groups, that is, groups not contaminated by Hinduism, at least in the speeches made by activists. Observations in villages are not sufficient to measure the real effect of the ethnic discourse. However, the fact that the Magar Association had to impose fines in some regions shows that not all members of the group are enthusiastic about being 'educated'. The ethnic programme clearly gives rise to a new elitism, in which it is always advisable to be like the high castes, albeit in a new mode. Tribal minorities such as the Magars no longer have to be ontologically associated with the high castes, claim myths of origin stipulating a common origin, or adopt rituals, food practices and alliance rules according to their model; rather, they have to lay claim to the same 'weapons': an incomprehensible language and alphabet (the Akkha lipi, which replaces Sanskrit), specific handbooks of rituals written in Magar, collections of sacred texts, great men of the nation, etc. This process may be termed para-sanskritization. What will occur in this new context to those who will be unable, or unwilling, to follow the desanskritization process? Will they form, in their turn, a scorned and exploited group? Will they have to pay fines for not obeying the new ethnic authorities?

Here is an example of how ethnic action was perceived by an uneducated Magar villager: in April 2001, having received an invitation card meant for two persons to a conference on Buddhism organized by a Magar association, I suggested to a Magar friend from the village of Timal that he accompany me. Obviously not very interested, he declared that it was a meeting of Magars from Dolpo, a remote district where small Magar communities, who live in close contact with Tibetan groups, practice Buddhism. Surprised, and aware that this was not at all the case, I asked him why he said that. He answered, 'it is only in Dolpo that Magars are Buddhist'. Apparently unaware of the conversion preached by the Association, my friend had reasoned according to his own image of the Magar group, and relegated Buddhist Magars to the category that they corresponded to in his mind, and which did not at all relate to him.

However, the rate of literacy is growing rapidly, and the ethnic associations' publications have brought about a deep transformation in Magar identity in most regions.

6: Villagers of Bungkot, Gorkha, Showing the Remains of
Lakhan Thapa's Palace (Photo: M. Lecomte-Tilouine).

5

The Messianic and
Rebel King Lakhan Thapa
Utopia and Ideology among the Magars[*]

The Magars are scattered throughout the country, though their presence is strongest in their original territory, the Magarant. The majority of Magars are peasants, but many of them are enrolled in the Indian and Nepalese armies, and young men now often emigrate temporarily to India or 'the Gulf' to earn money. Since the 1990s, the Magars have been closely linked to Maobadi activism, both as victims and perpetrators, especially in the districts of Rolpa and Rukum. Despite the great number of publications on this subject, our knowledge is still far from satisfactory, as it often originates from biased sources such as the army, the leaders of the movement, journalists who have not done any lengthy fieldwork, or villagers going by hearsay. For the latter—perhaps the best source for understanding the sociological origin of the guerrillas—the majority of Maobadis are comparatively educated young men, who are unable to find paid work and unwilling to become farmers like their fathers.

* Originally published as 'The History of the Messianic and Rebel King Lakhan Thapa: Utopia and Ideology among the Magars', in D. Gellner (ed.), *Resistance and the State: Nepalese Experiences*, New Delhi: Social Science Press, 2003: 244–78.

They live in groups in the forests, where they hide during the day. Villagers often say, 'During the day the policemen walk, during the night the Maobadis walk'. In the first few years, armed Maobadi groups mainly attacked police stations and their aim, according to the people, was to get rid of the police as well as wealthy men.[1] While many wealthy families in the hills owned land both in the Terai and around their houses, they usually preferred to spend most of the year in the more temperate climate of the hills. In an attempt to flee the Maobadis, many have been forced to leave the hills and settle in the Terai. However, the simple peasants also feared the Maobadis during 1996–2001,[2] because burglars used the guerrilla war as a pretext to rob the common man. Villagers used to say that they could not distinguish the Maobadis from the Daubadis, the name they had given these opportunist thieves. Many also said that they preferred the Maobadis to the Khaubadis, 'the eaters' or corrupt politicians from the capital. The ideology of the Nepalese Maoist movement is strongly egalitarian and communalistic: these two features attract Magars because they have always emphasised the qualities of equality and mutual help that prevail among their group.

The question of status is also debated within the framework of the other major ideological movement that has emerged over the last decade in the Magar community: ethnic revivalism. Indeed, parallel to the Maoist war, ethnic associations, ethnic meetings, and ethnic

---

[1] Their target, as formulated in the text 'Strategy and Tactics of Armed Struggle in Nepal', was adopted by the central committee of the Maoist party of Nepal in March 1995, and is as follows:

...the target of armed struggle will be the confiscation of the lands of feudals and landlords and their distribution amongst the landless and poor peasants on the basis of the land-to-the-tiller principle, and in order to cut the roots of imperialist exploitation to attack projects such as industries, banks etc. which are in the hands of comprador and bureaucratic capitalists, and also projects run by government and non-government organizations.

The Maobadis' main allies tend to be farm workers, bonded labourers, landless peasants, porters and poor peasants, cart pullers, ricksaw pullers, and drivers of tempos and taxis. Their strategy is to make peasant revolution the backbone, and rely on and unite with peasants to surround the city from the countryside.

[2] From 2001, Maoist People's governments were established in several regions, and the situation changed.

publications have flourished. These two streams have developed at the same time. Though not closely connected, they do overlap to a certain extent,[3] and there are some striking examples of individuals who are activists in both movements, such as the Magar poet Jit Bahadur Sinjali, who is (or was) both an ethnic activist and a Maoist militant, or the more recent case of Suresh Ale Magar.

In many respects, these two movements appear as two distinct paths: one advocates peaceful changes within the law, the other the use of violence and revolution.[4] However, both preach something approaching a utopian ideology, that is, the building of an ideal society which will no longer be characterised by rich or poor, low or high, alcoholism, etc.

In this chapter I shall discuss and analyse the case of a Magar rebel of the nineteenth century, whose story has many features in common with those of the Maoist guerrillas. Interestingly, this rebel is a major figure in Magar ethnic activism, and is also recognized by Maoists as the first figure in the history of revolution in Nepal.[5] The Lakhan Thapa rebellion thus sheds light on current events by placing them within a historical line of revolutionary movements; in turn, the current situation will help to articulate the recent reinterpretation and instrumentalization of this old rebellion within the framework of ethnic and/or political Magar movements.

Lakhan Thapa was probably born in 1834. He joined the Magar battalion created by Prithvi Narayan Shah, but after reaching the rank of captain, he quit the army in 1869 and established himself

[3] On the links between Magar ethnic activism and Maobadism, see Marie Lecomte-Tilouine, 'Ethnic Demands within Maoism'.

[4] These two paths are also specifically related to each of the two major subgroups constituting the so-called Magar ethnic group. While ethnic activism is apparently more prevalent among the 'southern' Magars, Maoism is strongly linked to the 'northern' Magars. However, this occidental taxinomy is not used by Magars themselves, who distinguish between the eastern and western Magars on the basis of more accurate geographical observations.

[5] In 'Strategy and Tactics of Armed Struggle in Nepal', one reads,

Here, even after the development of the centralized Nepalese state, the Nepalese people have been fighting and opposing in their own way the atrocities let loose by the ruling classes, especially the Ranas and the Shahas. Notable among these are many clashes within the different ruling classes and the rebellion of Lakhan Thapa against the Ranas.

in the village of Bungkot, in Gorkha district. There he organized a rebellion against the government of Jang Bahadur, creating, in the process, a utopian kingdom. He built a palace which had an exercise ground for his 'soldiers', and in 1871 was crowned as local king by the population. He used to say:

Jagadamba Kalimata offered me this prediction, (*bardān*): 'Jang Bahadur has sold Nepal to the barbarians (*mleccha*), the people call for help. Displace Jang, relieve Mother Nepal of the burden of sin, re-establish the *satya yug* in Nepal!' Let's go, my brothers, be ready![6]

Although Lakhan Thapa was hanged before his house in 1876, he is believed to have used his tantric powers to bring about the death of Jang Bahadur seven days after his own.

In his well-known history of Nepal, Balchandra Sharma describes Lakhan Thapa as 'ridiculous'; the Ajanta dictionary goes further: the entry under his name reads, 'a worthless person; a good-for-nothing fellow'. Who was this 'ridiculous' and 'worthless' man in whom Magar ethnic activists have found a potent symbol for their movement? Indeed, official acknowledgement of the ill-treatment meted out to this Lakhan Thapa was the first of the ten claims the Nepal Magar Sangh set before the Nepalese government in the 1990s.[7]

In February 2000, the anniversary of Lakhan Thapa's death formed the occasion for a great meeting organized jointly by various Magar associations: the Magar Samaj Seva Kendra (Lalitpur), the Nepal Magar Sangh (Kathmandu), the Sorathi Kala Kendra, and the Central Magar Students' Union.[8] The *Rising Nepal* of 24 February

---

[6] Rana Magar, *Gorkha Magaraharu.*

[7] Interestingly, in a recent Nepali dictionary (Cataut, *Dotyali brihat sabdakos*, p. 708), there are two entries for Lakhan Thapa: the first defines the name as belonging to one of the first martyrs of Nepal, while the second calls him a ridiculous person. Somehow, the recent recognition of Lakhan Thapa as a martyr has not erased the ancient, derogatory meaning of his name.

[8] From *The Kathmandu Post*, 15 February 2000:

Lalitpur, Feb 14—People from different walks of life gathered here today to mark the 124th death anniversary of Lakhan Thapa, the first martyr of Nepal. Lakhan Thapa was born in 1834 in a remote village of Bungkot, Kaule VDC in Gorkha. He retired as army captain after 14 years of service

2000 announced that His Majesty's Government had decided to declare the late Lakhan Thapa as a 'first martyr', and to provide Rs 500,000 to erect his statue in the village of Bungkot in Gorkha district, where he led his action and died. An article in the same newspaper, dated 6 March 2000, reported that while the Magar association had expressed its appreciation of this decision, its members had gone further, asking the government to erect a statue of Lakhan Thapa in Thapathali, and rename it 'Place of the Martyr Lakhan Thapa', issue a stamp bearing his portrait, and rename the Manakamana cable car the 'Lakhan Thapa Cable Car'.

Numerous articles, and even some books, all by Magar authors, have recently been devoted to the life and deeds of Lakhan Thapa. Some older texts also mention him, but only in passing. I shall first sketch out his biography using these older documents, whose perspective is obviously different from the more recent ones. I shall then examine his new image as moulded by Magar scholars, and finally compare the differences between both views.[9]

Only the more recent writings debate the birthplace of Lakhan Thapa. According to Shivalal Thapa, one of his chief biographers,[10] he was born in Arghau, a village located in Kaski district, central

---

and later became a religious preacher. He started revolting the general public against the rule of Jang Bahadur. As a result, he was hanged to death in his own residence at the age of forty-two. The programme was jointly organized by Magar Samaj Sewa Kendra (Lalitpur), Nepal Magar Sangh (Kathmandu), Sorathi Kala Kendra and Central Magar Students' Union. On the occasion, Minister for Local Development Chiranjivi Wagle assured any kind of support to the task or plan related with martyr Lakhan Thapa. He said, 'We will soon include Lakhan Thapa in the school curriculum.' At the function, various other speakers highlighted on the role played by martyr Thapa. The programme was chaired by Nepal Magar Sangh district chairman Dharma Raj Thapa.

[9] The documents consulted for this chapter are as follows: military reports published in the *Regmi Research Series*; an undated chronicle published in Nepali by Gyanamani Nepal; and the biography of Jang Bahadur Rana written by his son. I contrast this corpus with recent Magar writings, which claim to be based on local oral traditions, and with the oral traditions I collected in the village of Bungkot.

[10] The most oft-quoted reference for Lakhan Thapa is Shivalal Guruchan Thapa Magar's book *Ojhelmā Parekā Magarharu*. It contains one chapter on Lakhan Thapa and one on his friend Jayasim Cumi Rana. The former chapter

Nepal. When he was four or five years old, his father, a soldier in the British Indian Army, took him away to Lucknow. According to this author, he was educated there. Other Magar writers have rejected this hypothesis. According to Rana Magar, Lakhan Thapa was probably born at Manakamana,[11] as he bears the name of the famous saint who founded the sanctuary of the goddess Manakamana. Why, argues this author, would he have gone from India to Bungkot, a village close to this sanctuary, and why would he have enrolled in the Nepalese army if his parents were in Lucknow and his father in the Indian army? Similarly, Ranamagar finds it difficult to believe that Lakhan Thapa's name derives from the city of Lucknow rather than from the saint Lakhan Thapa, as asserted by Shivalal Thapa. According to Harsa Bahadur Buda Magar,[12] Lakhan Thapa was born in 1891 (VS 1834) to a Magar family residing in Kaule, a hamlet located in Bungkot, in the Manakamana neighbourhood. This author also rejects Shivalal Thapa's version of Lakhan Thapa's birth and childhood. Why, he asks, would Lakhan's father have risked taking his family along the dangerous path, 'infested with tigers, bears and brigands', that led to India? Buda Magar also notes that the descendants of saint Lakhan Thapa's younger brother had inherited the priesthood at the Manakamana temple, and continued the custom of adding the founder's name, that is, Lakhan Thapa (the first), to their own. On the basis of his name, Budha Magar argues that Lakhan Thapa the second belonged to the same lineage.

In 1911 (VS 1854), aged twenty, Lakhan Thapa joined the Nepalese army and was attached to a Magar battalion, the Purano Gorkha Gana, created by Prithvi Narayan Shah. The history of this Magar battalion sheds some light on the participation of this ethnic group in the great geo-political changes that occurred in Nepal during the eighteenth and nineteenth centuries. The Purāno Gorkhā Gana had taken part in the 'unification' of Nepal, and played an important role in the successive annexations of the eastern

---

is reproduced in Shivalal Thapa ('Pratham Sahid Lakhan Thapamagar [dvitiya]').

[11] Rana Magar, *Gorkha Magaraharu*, p. 73. The Manakamana temple is located in Gorkha district.

[12] *Rastraka gaurav tatha Nepalka pratham sahid Lakhan Thapa Magar (dvitiya)*.

Chaubisia kingdoms, the Kathmandu valley, the western Chaubisia and Baisia kingdoms, and Kumaon and Garwhal.

This battalion of Magar recruits was first attached to the Shah Thakuris' cause and helped them in their conquests. Soon after their blitzkrieg, the battalion distinguished itself in 1815 during the Anglo-Nepalese war. When Lakhan Thapa joined its ranks, these exploits were still quite fresh in people's minds, and certainly contributed to the Purano Gorkha Gana's fame. Soon after he was recruited, however, the battalion, then under the command of Jang Bahadur, the usurping Prime Minister, was sent to rescue their previous enemies, the British, during the Sepoy mutiny. The Purāno Gorkhā Gana was one of 25 Nepalese battalions that were sent to Lucknow in 1857 to help quash the Sepoy mutiny. This event certainly upset the Nepalese order, and should be placed in its proper context if it is to be understood.

The Nepalese soldiers were in an obviously difficult position under these circumstances. In fact, it should be noted that Magar soldiers have often served causes that have not directly concerned either them or the defence of their territories. Leaving aside the feelings of the soldiers who 'unified' Nepal, it seems that during the reign of Jang Bahadur, rebellions arose among the tribal recruits of the Nepalese army.[13]

---

[13] According to an undated chronicle of the kingdom of Garh (Dabaral 'Charan', 'From the Yamuna to the Sutlej'), 'Ram (sic) Bahadur Shah gave orders for the conquest of the hill principalities. This order set off a wave of jubilation in...the army. Soldiers were paid full salaries during a campaign, and also expected to profit from plunder.'

Interestingly, the main thesis of the Maoist text 'Strategy...' states that the Nepalese people are violent in nature, and that '[t]he reactionary propaganda that the Nepalese people are peace-loving and that they don't like violence is absolutely false'. The text is an apologia for the use of violence. It states that 'Until today, whatever general reforms have been achieved by the Nepalese people have had behind them the force of the violent and illegal struggle of the people', but it severely criticizes the engagement of the Nepalese in other people's struggles: 'Foreign imperialism and its running dog, the domestic reactionary ruling class, have conspiratorially turned the brave Nepalese into mercenary soldiers.' Long before 'foreign imperialism', the Nepalese, and especially Magars, were engaged as mercenaries. Thus, B. Acharya ('Social Changes during the Early Shah Period', p. 169) writes of the Malla kings

The Ramsay narration[14] reports a rebellion that is surprisingly similar to the Lakhan Thapa case despite taking place twenty years earlier, in June 1857—just before Jang's decision, in July of the same year, to send 14,000 men to India to reinforce the British army:

On the 2nd of June a serious event was expected at Kathmandu, owing to the state of feeling which was supposed to exist in the sipahis of Gurung class, and the measures which the Darbar intended to adopt should they hesitate in pronouncing sentence of death upon a Gurung Jamadar, who had confessed being engaged in a conspiracy to assassinate Maharaja Jung Bahadur. It had been decided to attempt to annihilate 1700–1800 men, (52 guns had been placed in position for the purpose) should they not promptly pass the sentence of death that was required of them. Happily, the Resident succeeded in inducing the Minister to change his plans and a bloody struggle was averted, which, had it taken place, might have led to a revolution and a total change in the Nepalese policy towards the British Government.

Although we are not certain whether this rebellion was linked to the decision to send the Nepalese army against the sepoys, this affair set a precedent for the Lakhan Thapa rebellion. In addition, it highlights one aspect of the Nepalese government's policy vis-à-vis ethnic problems: as this case illustrates, this policy consistently induced the members of an ethnic group (here organized in a single battalion) to either punish their defecting member, or collectively receive the same punishment.[15] This perverse yet efficient totalitarian policy seems to have been adopted in the case of Lakhan Thapa as well, whose denunciation and arrest was the work of a group of soldiers comprising of, among others, several Magars, as attested by historical documents.[16]

The British Resident mentions yet another agitator whose politico-religious discourse may be viewed together with the

---

of the Kathmandu valley: 'They also used to invite Khas and Magars from Gorkha and Tanahu for military assistance'.

[14] Reproduced in Hasrat, *History of Nepal*, p. 334.

[15] While the Ramsay account appears to indicate that the Gurung rebel was not killed, a letter written by the same resident, quoted by Whelpton (*Kings, Soldiers and Priests: Nepalese Politics 1830–1857*, p. 211), reports that he was put to death by his own regiment at the Tundikhel.

[16] He was perhaps also executed by Magar soldiers, but no document mentions who hanged him.

allegations levelled against Lakhan Thapa. A man, whose identity remains unknown, is said to have wandered through Nepalese villages in 1852, claiming that Jang Bahadur was planning to sacrifice 150 children to the gods and that he himself was in charge of collecting them. The terrified mothers, it is said, offered him huge amounts of money in exchange for their children. This man was arrested and taken to the Tundikhel in Kathmandu, where he was forced to confess his crimes in front of the army.

Although there are no details, this case bears a striking similarity to Lakhan Thapa's. Indeed, Pudma Jung Bahadur Rana[17] states that before his rebellion, Lakhan Thapa had already once been arrested and judged by Jang Bahadur for having extorted money from villagers in the guise of a 'holy man':

He had for some time been in the habit of masquerading as a saint about the streets of Gorkha, and of extorting money from the simple-minded rustics who gave credence to his pretensions. He had been sent over for trial to the Maharaja, before whom he confessed that he was assuming that disguise merely for bread, and then he was let off as a silly fellow from whom no danger could be expected. He then used this pardon for the purpose of further cheating the people to whom he represented that he had won forgiveness from the Maharaja by virtue of his saintly qualities. The pardon had encouraged him in his malpractice, till he was arraigned of the charge of fomenting a rebellion and hanged....

This account does not mention the exact nature of Lakhan Thapa's early 'malpractice', for numerous holy men wander around and beg in Nepalese villages without being prosecuted. This first arrest may indicate that his speech was already subversive in tone, even before he took a decision to instigate an organized rebellion.

As for the man mentioned by the resident, he had his tongue cut out in front of the troops after confessing his crime. Why was this confession and torture organized before the army? Was this man a soldier? Or was the scene intended to edify the army?

Other historical details tend to indicate that under Jang Bahadur, the army was viewed as a reduced, idealized image of the whole society. Thus, it was before the army, for instance, that the king announced to his 'people' the nomination of Jang Bahadur as Raja

---

[17] *Life of Maharaja Sir Jung Bahadur of Nepal*, pp. 302–4.

of Kaski and Lamjung in 1856.[18] In fact, since its creation by Prithvi Narayan, the composition of the Nepalese army had consistently reflected the social structure. Prithvi Narayan had divided the army into four ethnic battalions, which corresponded to the division of society into the four classes to which he often alluded in his memoirs: Bahuns, Khas, Magars, Thakuris.[19] This initial ethnic organization of the army was retained (or recreated) under the Rana regime. However, each battalion had both artisan castes and high castes, presenting an image that paralleled the caste system: the head of the army was the king (or the prime minister), the highest positions were given to his family and high-caste individuals, the bulk of the troops comprised of mid-ranking groups (including all the tribal groups), and this entire ensemble was served by low castes, such as musicians or blacksmiths. This organization in a way mirrors the codification of groups as it appeared in the Jang Bahadur code,[20] dated 1854. Like in any dictator's dream, the army plays the role of an ideal society that is made real, organized and modelled at will, and where control and command are not obstructed by individuals.

Under Jang Bahadur Rana, the mise en scène of the execution of the rebels is particularly symbolic, and provides a striking example. It explicitly links an individual to the group to which he belongs as a reminder that from the king's point of view, it is only communities that can be seen, rewarded or punished when they, or any of their members, commit any crime.[21] Such was the case of the Gurung

---

[18] Hasrat, History of Nepal, p. 332.

[19] Naraharinath 2016VS/1959, p. 7.

[20] Whelpton (Kings, Soldiers and Priests, p. 210) writes that Jang Bahadur 'decided to segregate the different groups in their own regiments. The intention...was to minimize the danger of mutiny....'

[21] Whether mono-ethnic or not, the company formed a single body. Thus, when Bakhtwar Singh Thapa was dismissed and imprisoned by Bhimsen Thapa, the Samar Jung Company he had commanded was punished equally:

> Men of all other companies were given a weekly holiday on Saturdays, but the Samar Jung Company was denied this privilege. Even its flag, known as 'Devatā' was not spared, and was treated in an undignified manner. The flag-bearers...used to raise the flag above their shoulders, and install it on the ground when necessary. Bhimsen Thapa enforced rules requiring the flag of this company to be carried on the shoulders in a low position, instead of being raised, and to be thrown on the ground as occasion demands....

soldier mentioned by Ramsay, whom Jang Bahadur planned to have executed by the 1,700 men of his own battalion, who were themselves surrounded by 52 guns ready to fire. Equally symbolic was the case of the man who was forced to confess his crimes on the Tundikhel in front of the army, after which he had his tongue cut out and was then paraded in that condition through all the villages he had visited, as was the case of the five people who were beheaded at the five gates of Kathmandu for having plotted to assassinate Jang Bahadur. Lakhan Thapa's execution was symbolic as well, as we shall see.

As a leitmotif, the Magars tell of the military bravery of their ancestors, claiming that this has not been recognized by the state, not taking into account the fact that they thus helped high-caste leadership. For example, in the history of the unification of Nepal, Magars picture themselves as the heroes who built the country, without considering the possibility that they might have worked against their interests by annihilating the power they held in petty kingdoms such as Palpa, where they were numerically dominant and closely linked to the royal family. This is perhaps due to the fact that the petty kingdom, which grew into a nation by swallowing its numerous neighbours, was a former Magar territory, where the dominant Magars were closely related to the royal family through their cults. In a way, the Magars undoubtedly feel that Gorkha's victory is also their own. In current historical reconstruction, the Magars present themselves as the champions of the Thakuris, welcoming them to their territories, protecting them against the Muslims, consecrating them as kings in many places, offering them their princesses, and serving them faithfully in their temples and their armies.[22] In many ways, Lakhan Thapa's action, as recounted by Magar scholars, is in continuity with this relationship between the Magars and the power-holders.

These rules were strictly followed even by the Rana rulers and remained in force till democracy was proclaimed in Nepal (Acharya, 'General Bhimsen Thapa and the Samar Jung Company', pp. 66–7).

[22] On this subject, see Chapter 3.

LAKHAN THAPA'S REBELLION
AND THE 'KINGDOM' OF BUNGKOT

In 1869 or 1870, Lakhan Thapa and his faithful friend, Jaya Simha Cumi Rana, received three months' leave. They went together to Bungkot where his friend's family—and perhaps also his own—lived. Once there, they decided not to return to the army and began building a utopian and rebel kingdom. It is said that they constructed a palace and an exercise ground in which to train their 'soldiers' in Bungkot. Their army comprised of 1,500 men, described as Bhotes.[23] Shivalal Thapa presents it[24] as a huge army led by two heroic generals, Supati Gurung and Sukadeva Gurung, who were shot to death by Jang Bahadur's soldiers after Lakhan Thapa's arrest. A report on his arrest, dated March 1876, provides a precise description of this palace.[25] Written by soldiers sent to Bungkot by Jang Bahadur, it states, 'The house in which Lakhan Thapa lives is surrounded on all sides by a wall 8 cubits wide and 16 cubits high, like that of a fort'. The building boasted five floors, as indicated in an extract from a chronicle published by Joshi and Rose.[26] Lakhan went further and was consecrated as king by the local population, according to some sources.[27] The biography of Jang Bahadur, written by his son Pudma Jung Bahadur Rana, reports this fact, but in a more ambiguous way: '...a rebellion of a somewhat curious nature disturbed the peace of the country. A certain Gorkha, formerly a soldier in the army, set himself up as a king...'.[28]

This point seems to trouble some Magar scholars like Harsha Bahadur Buda Magar.[29] This author denies the reality of this consecration not on the basis of any historical reason, but simply because it seemed unthinkable to him that such a 'devotee of the

---

[23] Rana, *Life of Maharaja Sir Jung Bahadur of Nepal*; Regmi, 'The Lakhan Thapa Affair'.

[24] 2052VS/1995a, pp. 22–3.

[25] Regmi, 'The Lakhan Thapa Affair'.

[26] Joshi and Rose, *Democratic Innovations in Nepal*, pp. 43–4.

[27] For instance, in the works of Shivalal Thapa and B.K. Ranamagar.

[28] *Life of Maharaja Sir Jung Bahadur of Nepal*, p. 302.

[29] *Rastraka gaurav tatha Nepalka pratham sahid Lakhan Thapa Magar (dvitiya)*, p. 23.

king and the country' (*rājabhakta, deśabhakta*) could proclaim himself king. Portraying Lakhan Thapa in a light that, in his view, was more suitable under the circumstances, he states that Lakhan Thapa had merely declared himself Prime Minister. B.K. Ranamagar[30], while not denying the reality of the royal consecration, tries to excuse Lakhan Thapa's pretension, attributing it to the influence of the royal blood that flowed in the veins of the Gorkha Magars:

When he said, 'Having killed Jang Bahadur, I must reign', Lakhan Thapamagar was perhaps more motivated by his blue blood [in English in the Nepali text] than by anything else. Indeed, there was a time when the Magars were the kings of Gorkha. They were kings and their descendants acted in this way from the effect (*prabhāva*) of their blood. There is nothing ridiculous in this.

However, the royal consecration is not mentioned in all sources, and remains unconfirmed. Regardless of what actually happened, however, it fits in well with the political context of the time, when the seizure of power was usually marked by accession to the title of Raja.[31] Jang Bahadur himself felt it necessary to be crowned king of two provinces of Nepal (Kaski and Lamjung) by the king of the country or the 'king of kings', in order to legitimate and make permanent his ambiguous and fragile position as Prime Minister. In the same way, numerous rebel leaders of the Sepoy mutiny proclaimed themselves kings. These leaders are even said to have offered Jang Bahadur the kingship of Lucknow if he joined them, as reported by a British resident in Nepal:[32]

From the moment he reached Gorakhpur, on his march towards Lucknow, Maharaja Jung Bahadur, by his own account, was in communication with the

---

[30] *Gorkha Magaraharu*, p. 77.

[31] 'Human Rights Movement in Nepal' quotes other cases of self-proclaimed tribal kings among the Gurung group:

No sooner had Lakhan Thapa's revolt been suppressed than another rebellion by Gurungs in Lamjung broke out against the Rana regime. Shukdev Gurung, who proclaimed himself as the government and Baudh king and opposed the Ranaism, was immediately taken into custody. He... died in the prison [in] March/April 1876 because of inhuman torture. In the same connection, Supati Gurung of Gorkha also proclaimed himself the Baudh king....These movements started spontaneously as a reaction against depriving the tribals from their tribal rights.

[32] Hasrat, *History of Nepal*, p. 336.

rebel leaders, who offered to make him the king of Lucknow if he would join their cause and turn upon the British army. This had an ill-effect upon the Gorkha soldiery, many of whom openly gave out that they would return to the plains during the next cold season to annex certain of our districts.

Lakhan Thapa was among those Nepalese troops who were in contact with these rebels, and perhaps found in them a model for his own political programme.

Whatever the historical veracity of Lakhan Thapa's consecration, he did build a fort or palace and gathered weapons and men, thus creating a veritable utopian kingdom within a kingdom, that too at its most symbolic point, in the vicinity of Manakamana's temple. Obviously Lakhan Thapa did not merely provoke an unorganized and spontaneous revolt. On the contrary, he seems to have worked methodically according to a well-established schedule to build an alternative government, as witnessed by his fort, his army and his accumulated wealth. His proposition to the emissaries of Jang Bahadur is further evidence of the presence of a government within his 'kingdom'. In their report dated March 1876,[33] these emissaries noted:

Lakhan Thapa has promised to appoint some of us as generals, and others as colonels and captains. He designated Jahare Chumi as a general, and Biraj Thapa Magar, Juthya Thapa and Jitman Gurung as colonels.

This short extract is particularly interesting. Taken from a report by Major-Captain Shumshere Jung Thapa Chetri, who led the expedition, it shows Lakhan Thapa trying to enrol these men in his own army, offering them very prestigious positions. As a matter of fact, the proposition was made to Magars and Gurungs. Considering Lakhan Thapa's alleged attitude, one wonders about the circumstances under which this first expedition to arrest him was conducted. We may legitimately suppose that these soldiers were chosen strategically from among the Tibeto-Burman populations and that they acted as spies, pretending to adhere to Lakhan Thapa's cause so as to discredit him more easily.

Lakhan Thapa's utopian kingdom was centred around his palace, which combined a royal aspect with a military one as it

---

[33] 'The Lakhan Thapa Affair', p. 74.

served not only as a palace, but also as a fort surrounded by a thick high wall and an arms depot. In addition to these two aspects, and on the model of every Nepalese fortress, Lakhan Thapa's palace also had a marked religious dimension. It has been repeatedly mentioned that Lakhan Thapa claimed to be the reincarnation of Saint Lakhan Thapa, suffixing to his name the title 'Second'. We will never know for certain whether Lakhan Thapa the Second was actually a descendant of Lakhan Thapa the First, a fact that would have facilitated his pretensions. If his adoption of the saint's name suggests that he belonged to the lineage of the priests attached to the Manakamana temple, as noted by H.B. Buda Magar, other facts point to the contrary. First, he was recruited as 'Lakshman Thapa',[34] which shows that he adopted the name 'Lakhan' later, in keeping with his new pretensions.

More revealing is the fact that he founded a temple dedicated to Manakamana within his own fort. An extract from a chronicle[35] clearly relates how Lakhan established a new cult of Manakamana:

Again under the reign of this king, in the area of Gorkha, a plotter (lucā) of Magri caste declared: 'I am the avatar of Lakhan Thapa, it is not necessary to go to Srimanakamana to offer the pujā, I will do it here; I worship her by making the sandhyā pujā, having myself built a house with several floors and having placed a sacrificial post in it.' In this way he gained the confidence of people, who flocked from many villages to offer pañcabali and other sacrificial ceremonies. By doing this, the villagers ceased going to worship in Shri Mana Kamana's temple, causing the anger of the goddess.

This account shows that Lakhan Thapa made a point of separating the worship of the goddess from her famous temple, and consequently from her traditional priests. This fact still reinforces the assumption that not only was he not the legitimate priest of the goddess, but that he was even opposed to the latter, an opposition manifested in his diverting devotees from the path leading to the Manakamana temple, and inducing them to come to him instead.

---

[34] Buda Magar Rastraka gaurav tatha Nepalka pratham sahid Lakhan Thapa Magar (dvitiya), p. 13.

[35] Nepal, 'Siddha autariko rajain garne utkantha', p. 45.

As can be seen, this chronicle reproaches Lakhan Thapa for having founded a new cult to the goddess in an illegitimate place, thereby usurping a significant source of power.

The diversion of worship from an instituted temple to a private residence seems to have constituted a serious offence and an act of political bravado. A chronicle relating the history of the Newar kingdoms reports a similar case, which had resulted in severe punishment for the persons concerned.[36] During the reign of Jaya Prakash Malla (in the second half of the eighteenth century), a certain Sodhan, the head of the monastery of Bu Bahal in Patan, acquired control over his disciples through the tantric powers he had at his disposal when he sat on the body of a man sacrificed by a yogi. He then settled with them in a house where, having gathered the emblems of the gods, he proceeded to turn each of his disciples into the incarnation of a divinity. He diverted the devotees from temples to his place, where, he said, all the gods were. It was a serious enough offence for him to be executed on the king of Patan's command, along with his disciples, who were each offered in sacrifice to the divinity they were supposed to incarnate. The chronicle does not report any other crimes from the devotees.

In order to understand the significance of Lakhan Thapa the Second's diversion, it is necessary to emphasize the role played by Manakamana and her priest, Lakhan Thapa the First, in the history of the kingdom of Gorkha, and by extension that of the country (Nepal), which had been unified by the sovereigns of Gorkha. According to many legends, whether oral or contained in the chronicles of Gorkha (Gorkhā vaṃśāvalī), Manakamana is the form that the wife of Ram Shah, who reigned over Gorkha during the first half of the sixteenth century, had taken.

According to the chronicle of Gorkha, this queen had been venerated during her lifetime. She exhorted the Gorkha men to fight against the powerful army of Lamjung, telling them that they would be protected by their dharma. The Goddess and Gorakhnath are said to have marched before the men of Gorkha, who were not wounded by the enemy's weapons even when they hit them. After

[36] Wright, *History of Nepal*, pp. 250–1.

the battle was won, the chronicle says, offerings were brought to the queen.[37]

The queen maintained close relations with Lakhan Thapa, a Magar ascetic who was her servant and advisor. The significance of his political role in the kingdom can be gauged by a brief mention in the Gorkha chronicle, which records that it was Lakhan Thapa who took over the reins of government during the prolonged absence of King Ram Shah, who had gone away for several months in order to practise austerities.[38] Gorakhnath himself, in an audience he gave the king and Lakhan Thapa at the top of a wooded hill, entrusted the protection of the Gorkha royalty to Lakhan Thapa. Several episodes in this text refer to this ascetic, reporting his numerous feats, such as his ability to be in two places at the same time. One day the king asked him whether he could obtain for him the privilege of reigning over Nepal (which at the time meant the Kathmandu Valley), to which Lakhan Thapa answered, 'It is not for you, but for your descendants (santān); but why do you ask me this? Ask it of your wife who is an incarnation of Devi.' The text relates that one day, the Magar ascetic saw the queen in the palace courtyard, accompanied by her divine troops.

He then followed the divine queen who, mounted on a lion, went up to Beni, where Gorakhnath and the other gods were holding a meeting. That day, the queen revealed to Lakhan that she was the goddess Mankamana, and informed him of her wish to have him and his descendants worship her. Lakhan Thapa then spoke to the king, and suggested that he touch his wife's body in the middle of the night on certain dates. He would then see that it was cold. He also advised him to stay awake during the night of *Bhaumāstamī*, which is the day rituals are addressed to the goddess-queen. The king did as suggested, and saw the queen in her divine form, accompanied by Lakhan Thapa and Gorakhnath. On this occasion he obtained from her the promise that one of their descendants would rule Nepal.[39] According to the chronicle, when Ram Shah died, the queen threw herself onto her husband's burning pyre; and at that very instant,

---

[37] Naraharinath, *Gorkha Vamshavali*, p. 42.
[38] Hasrat, *History of Nepal*, p. 109.
[39] Naraharinath, *Gorkha Vamshavali*, pp. 33-9.

their bodies disappeared, much to the astonishment of the crowd. At the same time Lakhan Thapa, too, disappeared.[40] Lakhan Thapa's role, and his relations with the queen, are therefore seen to have been exceptional and enigmatic.

Another version of the origin myth of Goddess Manakamana relates that one night, the king discovered the queen missing from her room. He discovered her in the form of the Goddess, accompanied by Lakhan Thapa, who had assumed the form of the lion upon which she was mounted.[41] The prosaic reader of the chronicle, astonished at the queen's nocturnal escapades with this Magar, will perhaps suspect a more ordinary adventure, rendered extraordinary through this deification. Was the queen's infidelity unbelievable? Was it a precaution against the possible rise of the Magar community? Was the king weak? Or should one simply believe in wonders? Whatever the case may be, other queens of the Shah line of Gorkha, such as the wife of Krishna Shah, Ram Shah's grandson, were thereafter regarded as incarnations of Manakamana. More generally, this goddess provided the kingdom with her protection throughout its history. These stories show how the Thakuri kings' relationship with the goddess was mediated by this Magar ascetic and his descendants. This configuration is not unique; rather, it corresponds to a model prevalent in the old confederation of the twenty-four kingdoms of central Nepal.[42]

---

[40] Ibid., p. 54.

[41] These oral myths are reported by Unbescheid, 'Blood and Milk or the Manifestation of the Goddess Manakamana', and Shrestha, *Speaking Stones*.

[42] A comparison with Chapter 3 shows that the same mythic motives are present in both the Lasargha shrine dedicated to Alam Devi and the Manakamana temple. In both cases the goddess is most important for the royal Thakuris and is served by a Magar priest. Also, the *Buddleia asiatica* tree is venerated in both: as the tree on which the goddess's palanquin was placed in the middle of the Lasargha shrine, and as Lakhan Thapa's walking stick, which grew into a tree after his disappearance, in Manakamana. In both places, a hole is considered holy: this is a hole into which the goddess disappeared in Lasarga, and into which Lakhan Thapa disappeared in Manakamana. These two shrines appear to be variations on the themes of the Goddess, the Thakuri king, the Magar priest, the Buddleia tree, and the hole. This suggests a common underlying structure, which should be investigated in other similar places.

By presenting himself as an incarnation of this famous mediator, did Lakhan Thapa aim to restore the power of the Shah kings, which had been usurped by Jang Bahadur, or was this a mere act of self-promotion? He undoubtedly intended to get rid of Jang Bahadur. According to Pudma Jung Bahadur Rana,

His graceful manners and persuasive tone soon procured him an armed following of 1,500 men, at the head of whom he threatened to march to the capital, and after assassinating Jung Bahadur, to seize the reins of government, and inaugurate the golden age of Nepalese history. On receiving news of this insurrection, the Maharaja at once despatched a few companies of the Devi Dutt Regiment to put down the fanatic, instructing them not to use force unless they were met with force. Happily the rebels surrendered their arms after a brief resistance, and were soon caught and sent over to Kathmandu in chains. The ringleader 'Lakhan' and twelve of his firmest supporters, whom he probably called his 'apostles', were brought in bamboo cages, and the rest on foot. Subsequent investigation brought to light the details of the whole plot. They were then to march to the capital, where Lakhan was to be proclaimed king amidst the shouts of the whole population.[43]

The chronicle quoted by Gyanamani Nepal does not report any such assault on the part of Lakhan Thapa and his troops, and speaks of only one arrest on the charge of illegally collecting weapons.[44] However, the report by Major-Captain Shumshere Jung Thapa Chetri devotes a passage to the action:

On Falgun 26, 1932 (approx. March 9, 1876), Lakhan Thapa, accompanied by a large number of Bhotes armed with muskets and swords, proceeded toward

---

[43] This is the same text as that quoted by Joshi and Rose (*Democratic Innovations in Nepal*, p. 44):

According to a semi-official account, the leaders of the agitation had planned to kill Jang Bahadur at Deorali on his return from a hunting expedition with the Prince of Wales in the Terai and to 'march to the capital, where Lakhan was to be proclaimed king amidst the shouts of the whole population'.

[44] At this time, in the year 33, this cunning Magar having said, 'I am going to take my revenge against Shri 3 Maharaj', held a counsel with bad men who obeyed him. They gathered swords, rifles, bows and arrows. The people of Gorkha learned about this and having spied them and verified the facts, went to Nepal to bring the news to Shri 3 Maharaja who sent soldiers and officers to bring him back (Nepal, 'Siddha autariko rajain garne utkantha', p. 45).

the west pretending to join (Prime Minister Jung Bahadur's) entourage, but actually with the intention of making an attempt on his life.[45]

This report then discloses Lakhan Thapa's project:

He has announced that Prime Minister Jung will be assassinated, that the Second Prince (Upendra Bikram) will become king, and that he himself will succeed (Prince Upendra Bikram). He said he would assassinate (Prime Minister Jung Bahadur) at an opportune moment either at Tarku or Manang-Besi (in Lamjung district). If this was not possible, he would go to Tibet, secure the help of the Tibetans, accomplish his mission, and then become king.[46]

As reported here, Lakhan Thapa's project fits in perfectly with the context prevailing at the time, as it exploits the conflict between Nepal and Tibet, as well as the eternal competition between brothers for the throne. In this document, it looks more like a realistic political programme than a simple utopia born from the imagination of an isolated villager. Interestingly, his plan consisted not only of killing Jang Bahadur, but also in settling King Surendra's younger brother Upendra on the throne, and, in the longer term, of sitting on the royal throne himself.

This ambition does not fit in so well with his present status of a martyr, that is, with his supposedly disinterested sacrifice of his own self for his country; however, we should emphasize that the report quoted here may have blackened Lakhan Thapa's reputation intentionally.

Lakhan was arrested by the army, apparently while he was still inside his fort. This detail either contradicts the claim that he was marching westwards to lay an ambush, or it should be presumed that this attempt failed before his arrest. The chronicle published by Nepal states:

Having encircled the house of this conspiring Magar, near Gorkha, they put under iron all his henchmen and seized all the weapons they had gathered, then led them to Thapathali. The examination of the facts took place during a lawsuit and [Lakhan Thapa] was put in jail as well as his principal accomplices, while all the others were left free. Later, in the month of Paus of the year 33, this plotter Lakhan Thapa was hanged in front of his house as well as

---

[45] Regmi, 'The Lakhan Thapa Affair', p. 74.
[46] Ibid.

alongside his principal accomplices. His house and his temple were destroyed and razed to the ground.[47]

M.C. Regmi adds some interesting detail[48]:

The Prime Minister ordered Colonel Tek Bahadur Rana to reinforce the troops under his command with those in Palpa, if necessary, and capture Lakhan Thapa and his accomplices. Major-Captain Shumshere Jung Bahadur Thapa Chetri was ordered to render necessary help to Colonel Tek Bahadur Rana, capture Lakhan Thapa and his accomplices if they passed through Palpa, and send them to Kathmandu, and report the matter to Prime Minister Jung Bahadur through the Indrachok Police Station. In addition, he was ordered to take necessary security measures to protect Prime Minister Jung Bahadur from assassination in case he visited Palpa in the course of his tour.

Pudma Jung then indicates the type of sentence passed on Lakhan and his close relations:

Lakhan and six of his followers, who had taken an active part in the conspiracy, were sentenced to death; the others whose offence was merely that of passive participation were pardoned, and allowed to go back to their homes. Lakhan was hanged on a tree in front of the shrine of the goddess Manokamna who, as he alleged, had inspired him to the deed of blood.[49]

These 'historical' texts, produced rather soon after the event, dwell only briefly upon Lakhan Thapa's demise, but note that he was hanged on the site where he had led his action—beside his house or the temple of Manakamana—after being judged in Kathmandu.

It is significant that the execution took place there, as if to show his former partisans the particularly striking symbol of his defeat and his masquerade. The goddess herself was made a witness to the death of the devotee she had allegedly elected, in accordance with one of Jang Bahadur's humiliating and cruel ideas.

Before comparing these chronicles with Magar publications on Lakhan Thapa, it should be noted that in his book on the Josmani sect, Janakalal Sharma[50] offers another interpretation of Lakhan's political action. According to him, Lakhan Thapa was a *siddha* of the powerful Josmani sect, which developed under its sixth *santa*,

---

[47] Nepal, 'Siddha autariko rajain garne utkantha', pp. 45-6.

[48] Regmi, 'The Lakhan Thapa Affair'.

[49] Rana, *Life of Maharaja Sir Jung Bahadur of Nepal*, p. 303.

[50] *Josmani santa parampara ra sahitya*.

Shashidhar, during the reign of Prithvi Narayan. These ascetics provided initiation to many influential people at the court of this king, and later received several land grants from Jang Bahadur to establish monasteries in the Gulmi area. Shashidhar is known to have had eleven gurus and the Josmani sect, which developed in Nepal, seems to have been a mixture of different currents, such as Nathism and Hatha Yoga. This sect was not restricted to twice-born castes, and recruited many adepts from among the Nepalese tribal groups. Among the four famous disciples of Shashidhar whom he sent in four directions to preach, three were tribal: one was a Magar, one a Gurung, and another a Sunuwar. Lakhan Thapa is said to have been initiated by Mokshamandal, Shashidhar's Magar disciple.

The most famous among Lakhan Thapa's Josmani santa contemporaries was Gyanadil Das. He was born in Ilam and initiated in Okhaldhunga, and he founded a new monastery in the Gurung village of Rumjātar. Janakalal Sharma[51] reports that there were numerous Matwali (an ancient name for the janajāti or indigenous peoples) in his monastery, and that this provoked the local Brahmins' anger. Sharma describes Lakhan's fort as a Josmani monastery, and claims that Jang Bahadur arrested him because he considered this sect a threat. As a matter of fact, Gyanadil was arrested and led to Kathmandu at the same time as Lakhan. While the latter was sentenced to death because of his army and the weapons he had accumulated, no such charge could be levelled against Gyanadil, who spent six months in jail and soon became very influential in Jang's entourage. He initiated many prominent people including Ranaudip, Jang's younger brother. He finally left the Kathmandu Valley carrying a white flag and a nagarā drum offered him by Jang Bahadur Rana, which he set up in his monastery. In this account, Lakhan's political action is incorporated into a wider religious organization that had taken the revolutionary step of treating Twice-Born and Alcohol-Drinkers as equals. Lakhan's membership in the Josmani sect explains why he was 'parading disguised as a holy man', as Pudma Jung Rana put it. However, the different treatment meted out to the two adepts arrested at the same time shows that

[51] Ibid., pp. 87–8.

Lakhan Thapa was not sentenced for religious heresy, but rather for his political action.

We shall now compare this tentative reconstruction of Lakhan Thapa's life with the recent presentations of Magar scholars, which are apparently based on oral traditions.

I shall base my discussion mainly on an article by Shivalal Thapa Guruchan Magar, whose writings on Lakhan Thapa[52] are particularly significant because they are often reproduced in, summarized, or discussed by, other Magar authors. Furthermore, this author is Secretary, Central Committee of the Nepal Magar Sangh, a fact that lends some official weight to his writings. The psychological portrait of Lakhan Thapa is more developed here than in earlier writings, and it goes without saying that it is radically different in tone. Lakhan is described as 'small of size, but having much wisdom', 'solving problems quickly', 'skilful in combat, the handling of weapons, and horsemanship'; 'going everywhere himself during the combat', and as 'disciplined and friendly'. As a loyal son, says Shivalal Thapa, his project was to found a family on his return to Nepal and bring his parents back with him. Moreover, this author insists on his genuine friendliness, and repeatedly mentions the close friendship between Lakhan and Cyami, which led them together to the same death.

In this posthumous psychological portrait in his biography, Lakhan Thapa is presented as the very archetype of the Magar: a modest villager who emigrated to India, a valiant soldier and faithful friend moved by the suffering of his people, and, finally, a martyr. All these aspects associate him with the self-image of the Magars: their supposed 'rightness'[53] and their willingness to shed blood for the motherland, an aspect they have established as a symbol of their identity, and the insoluble print they have left on the country. Lakhan Thapa is described as an enterprising and very generous man. He not only took the initiative to build his palace, but, according to Shivalal Thapa, also built himself a temple fitted

---

[52] See, for instance, *Ojhelma pareka magarharu*, and 'Pratham Sahid Lakhan Thapamagar (dvitiya)'.

[53] The adjective *sojho* is often applied to the Magars. It means 'uncrooked, straightforward, open, frank, honest', but also has a negative connotation—of being 'simple-minded'.

with four gates, in which he placed a round stone icon and other stone statues, and set up various divinities with his tantric powers, including Gorakhnath and Gorakhkali. His palace housed great wealth, which was also attributed to his supernatural powers. Each day, says M.S. Thapa,[54] this extraordinary man, assumed the form of a child in the morning, an adult in the afternoon, and an old man in the evening. He displayed his powers spectacularly on one occasion, as reported by Shivalal Thapa:

When Jaya Simha Cumi decided to follow the example of his friend Lakhan Thapa and did not return to the army after their three months of leave, he was reprimanded by his grandmother who told him, 'Whence came this Lakhan Thapa to die here? He perverted our Jaya Simha. Our grandson, who was very well employed, is to become a good-for-nothing like him.' Having heard that, Lakhan Thapa addressed her. 'What do you need grandmother? Rice?' And he touched an empty basket and filled it with rice. Then he added, 'Do you need vegetables?' and he filled the house with the vegetables she desired. Having thrown sacrificial rice, he even made the stones and the wood move, and these came walking on their own. This is how he gathered wealth. After having filled up his great reserves of rice he distributed some. When they saw these acts, all were surprised.[55]

In this account by Shivalal Thapa, the intervention of the supernatural allows Lakhan Thapa to don the royal role of rich benefactor and spendthrift, concerned with ensuring, like Ram Shah or Henri IV, that none should suffer hunger in his 'kingdom'. As for the incredulous reader, he may wonder how Lakhan gathered the money to finance his rebellion. The speech credited to the grandmother is revealing. It offers an opposing view to the author's general presentation of events. This embedded counterpoint suggests from the very beginning the fate of Lakhan's rebellion.

According to Shivalal Thapa, negative reactions to Lakhan's revolutionary kingdom were initially voiced not by the government, but by the local high castes.[56] Given the present context of ethnic revivalism, he ascribes this reaction to a caste conflict:

[54] *Pracin Magar ra Akkha lipi.*
[55] S. Thapa Magar 2052VS/1996 b, pp. 6–7.
[56] The chronicle, quoted by Nepal, attests to the fact that Lakhan Thapa was denounced by the 'people of Gorkha'. Also see S. Thapa 2052VS/1996 b, p. 5.

All these acts [of Lakhan Thapa] displeased the local Bahun-Kshetris. They were jealous to see that those who were their herders and ploughmen had become kings and ministers.

To show the reader the extent to which the local Bahun-Chetris had subordinated the Magars even within the latter's own territories, Shivalal Thapa notes, 'They were so deeply established in Gorkha that even the place names consisted of their clan names (Devakota Gaun, Thapa Gaun, Vagle Gaun)'. Interestingly, Lakhan Thapa's arrest and even his death are now attributed by Magar authors to the high castes, and not directly to Jang Bahadur Rana. Shivalal Thapa recounts how the Thapa Chetris of Simudipani stole a box containing documents from Lakhan Thapa's palace:

On one of these documents was written 'I am a devotee of Gorakhkali. The goddess sent me here to become the king. Jang Bahadur governs the country tyrannically. I must raise my weapons against him. My faithful minister is Jaya Simha Cumi. We must prepare a good army.'[57]

The Chetris of Gorkha, he continues, went to Jang Bahadur with these documents. As a result, the latter sent his soldiers to Gorkha with orders to hang Lakhan Thapa. However, soon after that, reports Shivalal Thapa, Jang Bahadur's wife had a dream. She saw a man with white moustaches and a beard, who told her, 'If Lakhan Thapa is killed, your husband Jang Bahadur will die exactly seven days after. If you want to spare your husband, tell him not to kill Lakhan Thapa.' The queen, so the story goes, woke up and related her dream to Jang, who paid no attention. She then wrote eight letters to her husband, which he did not read. While she was bringing Jang Bahadur the ninth letter, she fell unconscious at his feet, and he finally asked one of his guards to read it. Having listened to the letter, he declared, 'I have made a serious mistake', and immediately despatched soldiers with new orders: 'Go and tell them that Lakhan Thapa should not be hanged'. The soldiers rushed to Gorkha, but when they reached the Budi Gandaki River, they were prevented from crossing by the felon Thapa Chetris.

Indeed, upon learning that soldiers were approaching with the order to spare Lakhan's life, the Thapa Chetris ran to the river, and

---

[57] S. Thapa Magar 2052VS/1996 b, p. 5.

for three days prevented the Bote and Majhi ferrymen from taking the soldiers across. Meanwhile, Jang Bahadur's army surrounded that of the rebels, and seized Lakhan Thapa as well as Jaya Simha Cumi. 'They could have escaped, but they were not fleeing death, and as heroes they were ready to die.' The soldiers read out the death sentence that had been pronounced by Jang Bahadur, and took the two men away to hang them from nearby trees.

These events are similarly reported by M.S. Thapa,[58] who states, however, that it was the Bhusal Jaisis of Bungkot who prevented the soldiers from crossing the river, adding that when the Magars of Bungkot came to know what they had done, they were expelled from the village.

The most striking parts in Magar writings on Lakhan Thapa pertain to his death. Most report the same facts, but I will again quote from Shivalal Thapa's account. Before his execution, Lakhan Thapa addressed the crowd thus:

If my body rots and falls to the ground after my hanging, know that Lakhan Thapa is dead. But if my body dries and shrinks, know that Lakhan Thapa is alive. Keep preciously the cord with which I was hung, I will come back one day.[59]

Even now, local people recount how Jaya Simha Cumi's body rotted and fell to pieces, whereas Lakhan Thapa's body dried up and remained tied to the tree, as he had predicted it would. In a similar account written by Samjog Lapha Magar,[60] Lakhan Thapa is also supposed to have said before his execution, 'Jang Bahadur will be my sati', thus predicting the event that is now attributed to him: the death of Jang Bahadur. Indeed, Lakhan died on the second day of the month of Phagun, and seven days later, as foretold, Jang himself died under suspicious circumstances. It is sometimes said that a tiger killed him, but for Shivalal Thapa Magar,[61] 'It is probably because it was difficult to write that Jang Bahadur was killed by the tantric powers of a Magar, that some historians say that he was killed by a

---

[58] *Pracin Magar ra Akkha lipi.*
[59] S. Thapa Magar 2052VS/1996 b, p. 6.
[60] 'Nepalko pratham sahid kaptan Lakhan Thapa Magar'.
[61] 2052VS/1996 b, p. 6.

tiger'. M.S. Thapa[62] reports that some people believe that Lakhan Thapa assumed the shape of another man after his death, and then killed Jang Bahadur. He mentions a story, according to which Jang was killed by a young Magar whose wife he had seduced.

Through his own death, followed by that of Jang, Lakhan became a prophet and a messiah. He announced the signs of his immortality that were to be read on his own corpse, which he intended to prevent from rotting. He conferred the status of a relic on the instrument of his death when he asked for it to be carefully preserved. And, finally, he presents his death as his final victory over Jang, whom he describes as his sati.

In this reversal, Jang's fate is thus closely associated with Lakhan's. But while Lakhan's death is an apotheosis, a grandiose victory of a victim transformed into a divinity, Jang's end reminds obscure forever.

However, in a way the current Magar presentation of Lakhan's life tends to exonerate Jang Bahadur, who is presented merely as a Pontius Pilate. He is shown to have been frightened by his own decision, and to have recognized that he had made a mistake. In fact, he is even said to have gone to Bungkot to beg Lakhan's corpse for forgiveness: 'When Jang learned [from his soldiers] the news [of Lakhan Thapa's execution], he no longer had any peace of mind. He jumped on a horse and, followed by his army, reached the spot where Lakhan Thapa had been hanged. He then asked for pardon from the hanged corpse of Lakhan Thapa'.[63]

In addition to the remarkable visit he received when dead, Lakhan thereafter became deified. Several Magar authors note that the villagers of Bungkot worship him every year during the month of *paus*, offering him animal sacrifices. He is said to be worshipped as a Bhayāri Devatā, a divinity related to the earth, and in the form in which people who have suffered violent deaths are worshipped. If the nineteenth-century texts specify that Lakhan's palace was destroyed by the army, the local tradition, as reported by Shivalal Thapa,[64]

---

[62] *Pracin Magar ra Akkha lipi.*
[63] Shivalal Thapa Magar 2052VS/1996 b, p. 6.
[64] Ibid.

states that it remained uninhabited for a long time because people thought that 'one day Lakhan Thapa will come back alive'.

I went to Bungkot's Kaule hamlet in April 2001. A primary school named after Lakhan Thapa had been built on the site of his palace, and a memorial was under construction. During the course of the construction, the villagers unearthed two inscribed pillars and three carved stones: one looks like a Shiva linga, another like a stone window, and the last one is a flat stone engraved with geometrical drawings. They are said to be the remains of Lakhan's palace. It is there that I heard from Jayasim Cumi Rana's great-grandson, who is now in charge of Lakhan Thapa's rituals, the story of his ancestor. While his story is similar to what is reported in recent Magar writings, it has a very different orientation:

Lakhan Thapa and Jayasing Rana were soldiers in the army. When Jang Bahadur was ruling, both of them were in the same company. Together they asked for leave and went to Jayasing Rana's place. After two months they did not wish to go to Kathmandu. Jayasing's mother reprimanded them both: 'Here there is no good food, there are no vegetables, you must go quickly to join your army,' she said.

The two men told her: 'mother what do you need?' The mother answered: 'we have no unhusked rice, no husked rice nor any vegetables.'

They responded: 'Don't worry, this will be ready this evening.' And one of them sowed rice in the rice field while the other planted vegetables. Then they both went about their occupations. After half an hour the rice was germinating in the rice field, as well as the vegetables. Around twelve the rice had flowered as well as the vegetables. Around one, the rice was ripe. They cut it to cook it the same evening, dried it, and husked it so that it was ready. They also prepared the vegetables in this manner.

The mother was astonished. Seeing that they had prepared rice and vegetables in a day, she told them: 'oho, what a wonder performed by you, my sons'. 'This is not so extraordinary, we can do many other things,' they answered. The mother added: 'If it is so, you can become kings.'. The two of them answered: 'yes, we can be the kings of this village, see', and so saying, they built a palace, a pond to raise fish, a temple to put the gods in. They also built a stone fountain. After having done all this they wrote on a paper: Lakhan Thapa the king and Jayasing Rana the minister, and put it in their pocket. But they lost the written paper, which was found by Siracan Thapa Kshetri who had come to their place of worship to offer a cult.

After having found the paper he went to King Jang Bahadur and made a report. He gave the paper to Jang Bahadur who said: 'eh, someone has established a kingdom inside my kingdom', and ordered his soldiers to go and arrest them. From Bungkot they took them to Kathmandu. During the inquiry, they confessed that what was written on the paper was true. 'We have conquered all the villages and possessions of the Bhure raja and since then we have been reigning. Now you are trying to push me off the throne,' Jang said. 'No, we are not trying to push you off, we are only displaying the improvement of our condition *(pargati dekhāune),* we won't take the royal throne,' they answered. King Jang Bahadur said: 'take them to the place whence you have fetched them and kill them there.' The soldiers took them to the palace of Kaule, in Bungkot, Gorkha: to its right side they hanged Lakhan Thapa from a Khirra tree, to its left side they hanged Jayasing Rana from a peach tree. Since the time Jang Bahadur had given this order, his queen had started to have bad dreams: she saw an old man who told her that her husband would die soon after their death. She went several times to warn him, saying that they were like gods and should not be killed, but until her ninth attempt the king did not agree. When she came the ninth time, he thought that one should listen even to the words of women and sent to Bungkot the order to spare their lives, an order which he gave to some soldiers. But when they reached the Budhi Gandaki, they met Lakhan Thapa and Jayasin's enemy: Siracan Thapa Kshetri. He gave the order to the Majhis to not lead anyone across the river before the execution of Lakhan Thapa and Jayasing Rana, and to not even bring the news that there was anyone wanting to cross. For three days, they refused to allow the soldiers sent from Kathmandu by Jang Bahadur to cross. When they finally reached Bungkot, Lakhan Thapa and Jayasing Rana had already been executed. Seven days after their death, Jang Bahadur was killed by a tiger while hunting in a forest. Hence the Magars used to quote this saying: Lakhan Thapa the corpse, Jang Bahadur Rana the sati.

Lakhan Thapa dried on his rope, he flew up into the sky but Jayasing's body rotted, people say. The soldiers searched for Jayasing's son, but he had been hidden and was spared. Because the blood of Lakhan Thapa was mixed in with the blood of Jayasing, we performed his death rituals, took his belongings and his gods. Because their blood was mixed, we had to perform his death ritual in the same way as if somebody's blood touches me, I must perform his death ritual. Every year, in the first pancami (fifth lunar day) of Pus (February–March), be it the bright or the dark fortnight, we perform a cult to five gods. I have been the priest since 2014 VS (1957). The five gods are Kalināg, Bhuyar, Bahra Barāha, Caunta Bairahi and Bhairavi.

Question: Is this cult addressed to Lakhan Thapa? Is Bhuyar a form of Lakhan Thapa?

No, these five gods were worshipped by Lakhan Thapa. I perform the cult he was performing. We offer rice to Kāli Nāg and Bhumi first. For these two I must choose a virgin boy, a grandson or someone else, since only a virgin boy can worship them. Then a sheep is offered to Bahra Barāha. Chicken, roosters, goats, whatever people bring is offered to Bairahi, and finally a rooster is killed for Bhairavi.

Q: And what is the relationship between Lakhan Thapa and Manakamana's Lakhan Thapa?

There's no relation, they are different. Manakamana is also an important goddess, we worship her.

Jayasing's great-grandson's version of the events reveals some peculiarities. He insists on Lakhan's magical deeds, and makes no mention of a political aim or will, apart from a desire for 'improvement'. This narrative suggests that Jang Bahadur died because he had killed holy men. The priest even seems to view Jang as the legitimate king, when not dissociating him from the dynasty that unified Nepal. Similarly, he does not link Lakhan Thapa the First with Lakhan Thapa the Rebel. The priest also refers to a *personal* animosity between Siracan Thapa Kshetri and Lakhan, and makes no reference to any ethnic or caste antagonism. The Kshetri who denounced Lakhan is even presented as a devotee at Lakhan's shrine, a point that complicates the scenario. In addition, the priest clearly denies the traditional existence of a cult addressed to Lakhan, but notes that 'the Sangh [that is, The Nepal Magar Association] had recently established a ceremony, a worship of his statue'.

However, the association made by some Magar writers between the cult addressed to Bhayāri and Lakhan, who had suffered a violent death, is not surprising since Bhayari, the earth-god, is often related to violent death among this group. In fact, what was left locally were the gods worshipped by Lakhan, and his mode of worship. We must note, though, that as this set of gods is very commonly worshipped in this region, Lakhan's worship should not be taken to reveal any specific customs that he may have founded; rather, it shows his deep integration in local Magar traditions. His opposition to the Hindu order was nevertheless conveyed to me by an old Newar from a neighbouring hamlet, who told me that he had not heard much about Lakhan Thapa from his elders apart from one of his sayings: 'one must eat everything, be it chilly, be it beef'.

Lakhan Thapa's rebellion was obviously a messianic movement. It is significant that local tradition remembers the leader's charisma and supernatural powers much more than his strategic or political programme. Jhum Bahadur Roka Magar[65] goes as far as attributing a pre-natal will to Lakhan, who is described as a kind of avatar: 'Great

---

[65] 'Pratham sahid Lakhan Thapa Magarko mulyankan ojhelma', p. 8.

men such as the hero (*vir*) Lakhan Thapamagar are obliged to take birth on this earth because tyranny, oppression and despair prevail in this country'. Numerous parallels can be drawn between this rebellion and the revolts organized during the same period among tribal groups in India. The leaders of these revolts were ascetics, holy men, gods' reincarnations. They were endowed with magical powers, notably the ability to transform bullets into water. They promised their followers a return to a Golden Age, when tribes were not dispossessed of their lands.[66] All these attempts met a bloody end.

These messianic and utopian rebellions took no account of the reality of the structures they would have to fight, or the difference between the two sides' weapons and organization. As Fuchs emphasizes,[67] the tribal groups 'had no material and political resources to defend themselves, and thus were forced to take refuge in religious and magical means to find redress'. This is Mannheim's famous thesis, according to which the non-consideration of reality is characteristic of utopia, and typical of the dominated classes. Should we then consider a utopian movement a still-born form of rebellion, the desperate and final reflex of an oppressed group, which has no effect? I shall answer in the negative, because if utopia does not take reality into account,[68] it is then by nature revolutionary. Now, as Polack and Bloch have shown, utopia is also an anticipation of the future.[69] What is utopian in the nineteenth century may well become a realistic ideology in the following centuries, because utopia shakes up reality. Thus, the messianic utopian revolts ended in blood are not mere failures, but models. They are in fact sacrificial models, and are similar in nature to those which, in the Hindu world, are at the foundation of the

---

[66] On this subject, see, for example, Fuchs, *Godmen on the Warpath: A Study of Messianic Movements in India.*

[67] Ibid., p. 22.

[68] It would be more exact to say that utopia does take reality into account, but on a different register. Thus, the leaders of Indian tribal messianic rebellions used to say that they would transform British bullets into water. Reality was known, but fought with a different kind of weapon: that of magic versus technique.

[69] On the history of utopia, see Tower Sargent and Schaer, *Utopie, la quête de la société idéale en occident.*

universe and royalty (see Chapter 6). As such, they confer power, they are generative.

Several recent Magar writings express this dimension, such as Sagar Thapamagar's poem:

Go ahead Magar tribe,
Looking at the pages of history!
Let Lakhan Thapa's dream come true
Working all together!!

Or the role attributed to Lakhan's rebellion by Balkrishna Kauca Magar:[70]

Even if the kingdom [of Bungkot] did not last long, it was followed by opposition all over the country and it is Lakhan Thapa who brought new ideas and a new kind of kingdom to the people.

It is said that through his 'sacrifice', Lakhan was able to get rid of Jang Bahadur Rana. More importantly, however, the initial sacrificial model confers another type of power: it becomes, for future generations, the founding myth and model upon which new types of political action, more realistic or less idealistic this time around, can stand.

In his story, as presented by Shivalal Guruchan Thapa or M.S. Thapa, Lakhan Thapa appears to have been martyred more because of caste conflict than the Rana regime, which is his official position as 'First Martyr' of Nepal. Jhum Bahadur Roka's article[71] reinforces this link: according to this author, Lakhan was executed because the Ranas could not tolerate tribal claims for justice and autonomy. The demand that the government nominate Lakhan Thapa as the 'first martyr' was therefore not a neutral one from the Nepal Magar Association's point of view. Rather than being just another condemnation of the already much-blackened Rana regime, it was a political act aimed at competing with the high castes on their own ground and outside the traditional political game, since, as stated by Balkrishna Kauca Magar,[72] 'Lakhan Thapa is a partyless martyr'.

---

[70] 'Pratham sahid Lakhan Thapa Magarprati apaman ki irsya', p. 9.
[71] 'Pratham sahid Lakhan Thapa Magarko mulyankan ojhelma'.
[72] 'Pratham sahid Lakhan Thapa Magarprati apaman ki irsya', p. 10.

Indeed, martyrdom became a new form of political legitimacy after the fall of the Rana regime in Nepal, just as the 'résistants' had filled all the political positions in France after World War II. The martyrs, and the individuals associated with them, have acquired an almost symbolic right as compensation for what they have endured. Interestingly, each party has its own martyrs, and is also seen by opposing groups to be creating new martyrs when it comes to power.

Thus, the Congress or Communist parties, whose members were martyred under the Rana period and later on, then created martyrs in the Maoist party when they were in power.[73] Political leaders transform their deaths—even the non-violent, natural ones—into the gift of their selves by offering their corpses to the country, in a political act that consists of offering one's eyes. This gift is highly visible: for instance (in spite of his old age), the removal of Man Mohan Adhikari's eyes featured in large colour photographs on the front pages of Nepalese newspapers. Although political parties founded on ethnic or caste grounds are denied a legal existence, ethnic activists have noticed that most martyrs come from high castes. M.S. Thapa[74] thus writes in the prelude to his article on Lakhan Thapa: 'Whereas Tanka Acarya, who was not executed because he was a Bahun, was called a "living martyr" and paraded on a cart, the Nepalese make fun of Lakhan Thapa Magar, Thiravam Malla, Bhimadatta Pant, Laldhvag Gurung, Cokabahadur Gurung, Ramprasad Rai, Ratna Bahadur Bantava (Rai)...'. Jhum Bahadur Roka[75] states that had Lakhan Thapa belonged to a high caste, he would have received the greatest honours.

In their different versions on Lakhan Thapa's life, Magar ethnic activists reveal their political positions. They include both individuals trying to promote the dignity of the Magar group, such as Harsa Bahadur Buda Magar, who plays down Lakhan Thapa's personal ambition in order to raise him to the level of defender

---

[73] On martyrdom in Nepalese communist ideologies, see Ramirez (Pour une anthropologie religieuse du maoïsme népalais), and for a more recent article on the subject, based on Maoist poetry, see Chapter 8, this volume.

[74] *Pracin Magar ra Akkha lipi.*

[75] 'Pratham sahid Lakhan Thapa Magarko mulyankan ojhelma'.

of the country, and individuals of a more revolutionary bent of mind, who aim to fuel communal conflict on an ethnic basis by interpreting their history as a simple and unidirectional subjection. This may lead to the identification of one group as the oppressive ruling class, and the others as the oppressed proletariat.[76] As if to illustrate Mao's writing, as quoted by the Nepalese Maoist party,[77] Magar scholars aim to change their current status by revising history as written by the dominant castes. This idea is expressed by numerous authors, such as Samjog Lapha Magar[78]:

[76] An article published in the *Kathmandu Post*, 12 January 1999, suggests a close link between ethnic and political activism among the Magars:

Kathmandu, Jan 11. Nepal Magar Association (NMA), member of the Nepal Nationalities Federation, today announced that they have no affiliation with the underground Nepal Communist Party (Maoist). The association announced this at a press conference organized today. Addressing the press conference, Gore Bahadur Khapangi Magar, chairperson of the association, said though the association has no affiliation with the Maoists, the Magars are being victimized. He said most of the victims of the Maoist Movement have been Magars. 'If you look at the number of those who've died in the police-Maoist clash you'll see that most of them were Magars', he said. In a press release distributed today, the association has condemned the government for arresting its members on false charges. The association has demanded that the government release those who were arrested on charges of being Maoists, resettle those who were displaced by the conflict and compensate those who have lost their family members. Khapangi said the association had submitted a memorandum to this effect to the government three months back. He added that none of the successive governments have been serious about the nationalities movement. Citing one such example, he said, 'When the association apprised the then Home Minister Khum Bahadur Khadka about the high incidence of Magar killing he said in a place where Magars are the majority who do you expect to die? Certainly not the Brahmins.'

In the same way the *Kathmandu Post* of 10 January reports a similar suspicion voiced to the chairman of the All Nepal Nationalities Association: 'Newly elected Chairman Ale Magar, when asked if his group was associated with communist parties, denied any such link. But he admitted that "though the association shares beliefs with leftist parties, we have no affiliation with any political party"'.

[77] '...The only intention of the proletariat to know the world is to change it' (sic). See 'Strategy...'.

[78] 'Nepalko pratham sahid kaptan Lakhan Thapa Magar'.

'What is called the history of Nepal is a partisan and illusory history, which we reject. History is the writing down of that what is dead, but history itself never dies. This is why it is time now for all the Magars to write down their history.' However, the history they have chosen to dig up is the story of a popular (and ethnic) rebellion, as if they were recounting the present situation through recourse to the past. The parallel is obvious in some recent writings on Lakhan Thapa, such as those of Balkrishna Kauca Magar:[79] 'At that time it was not possible to resist Jang Bahadur's power after having established a new kingdom, just as the present government look for those who oppose its politics, like the Maobadis, and kill them'. The recent declaration of an independent government, the 'People's local government',[80] in the tiny village of Bhawang, Rolpa, led by Santosh Budha and Khim Bahadur Thapa, may be viewed as a re-enactment of Lakhan's dream, albeit one supported by a much wider organization.

I would like to end with a poem written by Lakshman Alemagar,[81] in which the suffering of a group deprived of its own history is beautifully rendered. When nothing else is left, an attachment to the land becomes the major link with identity, described through the striking image of the soil imbued by the blood of the ancestors, thereby combining the two basic forms of identity distinguished in Europe. This image returns as a leitmotif in Magar writings and sheds new light on the importance of martyrdom and violent action: on the dire necessity that perhaps compels them to 'write history with warm blood'.

WE ARE WRITING HISTORY OURSELVES

We are the priests of this country,
It is we who were the kings here,
History was given to be ours,
Why is it now out of our reach?

If we look and search in history
Our name is in the first place.

[79] 'Pratham sahid Lakhan Thapa Magarprati apaman ki irsya', p. 9.

[80] *The Kathmandu Post*, 20 May 2001.

[81] This poem, entitled 'Lekhnu cha itihās hāmīle', was published in *Gyāvaṭ*, Baisakh 2050, p. 69.

We are the protectors of this country,
Nobody should think that we are weak.
We are the original inhabitants of this land.
We know everything over here,
We take care of them all.
History brings us its help.
Our power is boundless,
Equal to the heroes and valiant warriors.
History, we write it with warm blood,
As did our immortal ancestors.

...

Look, all these hills, all these fields,
All are imbued with our ancestors' blood,
Saying: 'Where is the karma of our descendants here?'
Today they are worrying...

7: King Birendra's Double Crossing the Symbolic Border of the Kingdom
(Photo: Franck Bernède).

6

The Transgressive Nature of Hindu Kingship in Nepal[*]

A great deal of ink has been expended on detailing the paradoxes inherent in monarchy. Plato and the medieval jurists had already noticed that the king alone had the power to transcend the law, and had the legal power to break the Law. Various astute solutions have been found worldwide down the ages that allow one person to reach the supreme position of king, without acknowledging the superiority of the actors conferring kingship upon him. In addition to these universal problems, kingship poses specific questions in relation to its particular social and cultural context. Within the Hindu caste organization, the uniqueness of the king and his need to be in a permanent state of purity require particular resolutions. In fact, the very idea of Hindu kingship can be viewed as a paradox. The Hindu king is consecrated by the four varṇas during his coronation, and therefore is privy to a uniqueness that is by definition antinomic to the functioning principles of the caste structure, which is based on distinction and complementarity. And kingship appears to challenge the pre-eminence of the Brahman, a pre-eminence that many commentators consider one of the hallmarks of caste.

* Originally published as 'The Transgressive Nature of Kingship in Caste Organization: Monstrous Royal Doubles in Nepal', in D. Quigley (ed.), *The Character of Kingship*, Oxford: Berg Publishers, 2005: 101–22.

Hindu mythology shows that the uniqueness of the primordial being, Purusha, was broken at the creation of the universe, when his body was dismembered to create, from its different parts the classes of human beings. These classes are ranked in a hierarchy according to their correspondence to various parts of Purusha's anatomy enumerated in vertical order: thus, Brahmins, who emerged from his month, form the highest category, Kshatriyas, who came from his chest, are ranked second, Vaishyas, who originated from his thighs, are ranked third, and last come the Shudras, who emerged from his feet. During the coronation of a Hindu king, however, this process is reversed, as the four classes of society collaborate to consecrate the single body of the king. Hindu kingship is therefore antithetical to the functioning principles of the caste system: distinction and complementarity. While the king belongs to the second of the four classes, the Kshatriyas, his consecration sets him apart from, and above, his own class, as well as the entire social system he commands. He thus becomes a divine being. Nevertheless, the king possesses a human body, which is inevitably connected to impurity, and this is incompatible with his divine status. I shall show that in the Nepalese context, the king perforce has to depend on producing monstrous doubles of himself. These doubles allow him to remain detached from the groups to which he belongs, and to deal with the impurity inherent in mundane life. It is as if the royal function had the peculiar ability to create a miniature internal caste system, reproducing the principles of distinction and complementarity, but via transgressions.

Nepal was created through the military 'unification' of about fifty kingdoms during the second half of the eighteenth century. The history of the royal dynasty of the Shah is marked by three stages: its obscure origin in India, its establishment in the hills of central Nepal during the fifteenth century, and the rapid conquest undertaken by them in the east and the west in the second half of the eighteenth century. During the course of this conquest, the Shah moved their capital from Gorkha, in the hills, to Kathmandu in the valley of Nepal (now normally referred to as the Kathmandu Valley), where the Malla kings had been reigning since the medieval period. From this time onwards, the Shah kingship had to adjust to the Malla kingdoms, and any study of the former would be incomplete without taking the latter into account. The distinctive characteristics of both the Shah and Malla kingships may be examined by looking at three modes through which their principles were conveyed: royal chronicles, the morphology of the royal palace, and the main rituals of royalty.

Contrasting Malla kingship with the Shah kingship, which succeeded it on the same throne but over a much wider territory, helps to show how elements were separated or recombined to create a new composite form of kingship, one that maximized the legitimacy of the newly extended Crown. This opposition also highlights the specific features of each kingship, showing in passing that it is possible for Hinduism and caste systems to be associated with very different forms of royalty, even within a similar context in terms of scale, location and period.

If we first consider the chronicles of the Malla and Shah dynasties, it is clear that they differ in their composition and subject matter. The Gorkhali chronicles recall the history of *a line* and follow it in its displacements, while the chronicles of the Malla dynasty are included in the history of *a place*: the Kathmandu Valley. Royalty is thus conceived of differently in the two cases: in one it is associated with a territory, and in the other, with a dynasty.[1] Another related difference is that in the chronicles of the Kathmandu Valley, kingship is not primordial, but is preceded by the sacralization of the area through the appearance of gods, the arrival of famous saints, and the establishment of great sanctuaries. By contrast, the chronicles of Gorkha take the geographical context into account only when it relates to the Shah dynasty and its conquests. We are thus dealing with two different types of kingship: a warlike and mobile form in the case of the Shah, and a territorialized form among the Malla.

In the chronicles, the arrival of these two great medieval dynasties in this area of the Himalayas provides an astonishing parallel. I will not take into account the opinion of several historians, which state

[1] To qualify this remark somewhat, it should be said that the chronicles of Kathmandu Valley follow the history of some dynasties, recounting how such and such a king came to settle in 'Nepal' (that is, the Kathmandu Valley). In the same manner, following the division of the Valley into three kingdoms, the text deals with each line and kingdom independently until their conquest by the Shah of Gorkha.

that the mythical founder of the Malla dynasty never reigned in Nepal, or that the Shah of Gorkha are not Rajputs. I am dealing here with representations, and from this point of view, the embellished or modified history contained in the chronicles is relevant, since this is what the rulers wanted to retain of their imaginary or real pasts. The Malla and the Shah shaped their origins in similar fashions, linking them to an escape from India and the barbaric Muslims.[2] More generally, all the historical dynasties of the kingdoms included in present-day Nepal claim Indian origins, but none relates its arrival to a military operation. The event is either presented as fortuitous, occurring on the way back from a pilgrimage, or as an escape from India at the time of the Muslim invasion.

The Himalayan zone is thus not presented as a territory of Hindu military conquest, but as a holy area where Hindu kings settled for the purpose of devotion, or to protect their endangered religion. The ancestors of both the Malla and the Shah would have fled towards the mountain wilderness, carrying their tutelary deity with them. In both cases, the goddess requested the king to carry her to the mountains in order to protect her from the Muslims; both royal families also face similar episodes when they confront the wilderness, which leads to the degradation of one of its members. Fleeing with his tutelary goddess, Harasimhadeva, the founder of the Malla dynasty, spends the night in a terrifying forest. There, his deity directs him to a sword concealed beneath a large stone and asks him to stand on the stone with the sword in his hands, ready to kill the snake that lives under it. The king kills the snake and empties the pits surrounding the stone of their riches. However, next morning the goddess compels the king to designate his own son as the one to sacrifice a buffalo to her. Through the sacrifice of this impure animal, the king relegates his heir to the low rank of butcher, forming a new caste that was henceforth to be in charge of impure royal sacrifices.

The founding princes of the Shah dynasty of Gorkha are also said to have fled their Indian kingdom after being attacked by Muslims, carrying their tutelary goddess with them. On the way, they are

---

[2] For an Indian parallel, see Gell, 'Exalting the King and Obstructing the State', p. 437.

forced to offer a local goddess another type of impure sacrifice, that of a pig, which enables them to cross the river separating them from the mountainous territory where they plan to settle. At the first crest located beyond this limit, one of the princes falls asleep on a large flat stone. While he sleeps, the stone lifts up and his tutelary goddess sinks into the soil beneath. The princes continued their quest, leaving their goddess and their degraded brother, who had performed the pig sacrifice for their sake, to perform the duties of the priest of this enigmatic shrine (see Chapter 3). Magar priests, who claim to have descended from this degraded prince, still honour the goddess there, in the form of a hole in the ground.

The similarity between the events in both stories suggests that this is an archetypical model of the origin of kingship. We are not presented with an origin ex nihilo. A royal person, surrounded by other members of the royal family and carrying his tutelary divinity with him, is forced to move towards a wild region in order to save his life and religion. There, a divine test leads to a transformation of the royal into the impure, and the royal but impure sacrificer forever remains the mediator between the king and his tutelary divinity, who embodies his power. In these two myths, royal transgression is thus presented as a prerequisite of kingship: the new site of royalty does not result from an alliance or military conquest, but from the degradation of a potential king. It is significant to note that in the case of the Shah, it is one of the royal brothers who is degraded, while in the Malla myth it is the king's son. Indeed, the history of these two dynasties reveals a major difference concerning the main group of kinsmen competing for the throne. Among the Shah, there are many more conflicts reported among brothers than between fathers and sons. Among the Malla, however, the reverse is the case.[3]

---

[3] The difference in persons who may legitimately compete for the throne is illustrated in other ways as well. For instance, King Pratap Malla is represented at the centre of four of his sons, whereas the Shah king is ideally surrounded by his four brothers who represent his 'limbs', or his 'cautara', his four protectors, who hold the positions of ministers and advisers and lead the army at his side. In both cases, the king is at the centre of a group of princes (be they his sons or brothers), who surround him on four sides, representing, through their formation, the four directions of the universe. The Rana ministers, who originate from the same area of central Nepal as the

THE ANCHORING OF KINGSHIP IN SPACE

In Shah kingship, the place where the king is established forms, quite naturally, the heart of his kingdom. The royal person creates a sacred territory around himself, which is supplemented by the installation of his tutelary goddess. Thus, the Shah dynasty, which had originally settled in Kaski, spread out on two successive occasions when a royal junior brother founded a new neighbouring kingdom. Yasobrahma became king of Lamjung in this way, and later another junior member of the royal family, Drabya Shah, was crowned in Gorkha. In both cases, oral traditions and written genealogies describe how the new sovereign was consecrated. He was seated on a large stone where a ṭikā mark was placed on his forehead, and he was covered with vermilion powder. In the next stage, a part of the family goddess is removed from the original kingdom and established within the new palace. Kingship is thus associated with the person of the sovereign and the place of his coronation, a summit or a stone, and is reinforced by the presence of the family goddess.

This schema underlines the extent to which the Shah royalty focused on the person of the king. It is not surprising, then, that the Shah sovereigns' palace was a very modest one, comprising of a small building housing the royal quarters and a temple to the goddess. The palace was constructed as an extension of a natural fortress, that is, on top of a steep, almost inaccessible slope. As Inden[4] and others had shown, the king, his throne and his palace were miniature representations of the whole kingdom. It is significant that the minimal representation of kingship for the Shah of Gorkha is a stone, the one that their mythical founder

---

Shah, developed this principle, which places the royal brothers on a relatively equal footing vis-à-vis access to the throne. The Rana prime ministers usurped political power between 1849 and 1951. They were made the kings of the Nepalese provinces of Kaski and Lamjung by the king of Nepal in 1856, and instituted a particularly interesting type of kingship, since succession was not from father to son but from one brother to the next eldest. This model is perhaps a development of the Shah's mythical and symbolic representations of kingship.

[4] 'Hierarchies of Kings in Early Medieval India'.

had spent his first night, and upon which they were crowned. They employed the term *dhuṅgo* (Nepali for 'stone') to indicate the whole of their kingdom. According to M.C. Regmi,[5] it was much later—in the eighteenth century—that this term came to refer to the kingdom, and the fact that it underlines the royal territory's indivisibility contrasts with earlier practices. However, it seems to me that the indivisibility of the kingdom was not a new idea for the Shah, though it was extended to a much greater territory once Prithvi Narayan Shah and his territorial conquests appeared on the scene in the eighteenth century. Indeed, the history of this dynasty reveals no territorial division between brothers or sons, unlike most cases in the Kathmandu valley and the kingdoms of western Nepal. On the contrary, from the very beginning of the Shah history, the eldest son inherited the whole of his father's territory. The younger brother might create a new kingdom, but this had to lie outside his brother's territory. As soon as a new kingdom was established, it displayed its independence by declaring war on its kingdom of origin. The new Shah kings even broke one of the most fundamental rules of Hindu identity, gotra membership, in order to display their independence and uniqueness.[6]

A modern example of this fundamental idea of the unit formed by the kingdom can be found in the remark made by Kirtinidhi Bista,[7] former Prime Minister, who presented a reversed vision of history when he wrote that before the advent of Prithvi Narayan Shah, 'The kingdom had remained divided into tiny principalities', as if the entity that was the 'kingdom' of Nepal had somehow pre-existed its creation.

The unitary conception of Shah kingship, aptly symbolized by the stone, contrasts sharply with the complexity of the Malla

---

[5] 'Preliminary Notes on the Nature of the Gorkhali State and Administration'.

[6] This is documented in the two stages of expansion of the Shah of Gorkha. It is well known that Prithvi Narayan Shah changed his gotra from Bharadwaj to Kasyapa. In addition, Dharmaraj Thapa (*Lok samskritiko gherama Lamjung*, p. 71) writes that King Narahari Shah of Lamjung, who was Kasyapa, had already changed his gotra in order to attack his younger brother, the king of Gorkha.

[7] 'The Crown and Nepal', p. 57.

kingdoms of Kathmandu Valley, defined by M.C. Regmi as corporatist. In the Malla kingdoms, the noblemen had the ability to dismiss a king or even seize power (as in Patan), thus limiting the power of the sovereign.[8] The complexity of a State that revolved around the person of the king is embodied strikingly in the form the Malla palaces took. A city within the city and a fortress within the fortress, Malla palaces had nothing in common with the modest reinforced dwellings of the Shah and other Thakuris of central Nepal. This disparity cannot be ascribed simply to their differences in topography or wealth, though these were significant. The oldest Malla palace, that of Bhaktapur, is the most complex because each king made his own additions: it included ninety-nine courtyards. The Kathmandu palace, which became the royal palace of the modern state of Nepal following the Shah conquest, had a total of thirty-five courtyards before the 1933 earthquake, which damaged it.

Each courtyard had its own function and was dedicated to a particular divinity. The numerous courtyards were connected to each other by narrow passages. The most significant courtyard for the Malla kings of Kathmandu was without doubt the Mul Chowk or 'main courtyard', built by Ratna Malla shortly after the foundation of the Kathmandu dynasty in the sixteenth century. It was in this courtyard that the Mallas' tutelary goddess, Taleju, was (and continues to be) brought down to the human world for three days during the Dasain festival to bestow her blessing on the king. It was also there that the Malla kings were consecrated. Although we do not possess a detailed description of this ritual, some of its features can be captured by combining the major elements specific to the Mul Chowk: that is, Taleju's temporal descent to the earth from her high temple, and the coronation of the king.

[8] Father Cassino, a rare witness of the Malla institutions, described one of them in these terms:

Therefore, (Ranjit Malla) called a general council of his people on the 26th of April, 1742. In the meeting they were to freely express train to their feeling and give to their opinion....All of them had their faces covered to hide their identity and spoke in affected tone not to be recognised. Some scolded the king, even called his names; others threatened him with dire consequences.... (quoted in D.R. Regmi, *Medieval Nepal, Part II*, p. 247).

The Taleju goddess has a well-known feature: no dwelling in the city is allowed to reach or exceed the height of her temple as a mark of devotion on the part of the king towards his goddess and the Malla kings confered a monumental character on this temple in order to allow their city to develop. King Pratap Malla, in particular, constructed a temple in Kathmandu that exceeded the height of her original temple located in Bhaktapur. However, this well-known fact[9] assumes greater significance when we consider that this vertical measurement was supplemented by yet another measurement: the horizontal one, represented by the size of the main courtyard. Hodgson[10] noted that the Mul Chowk corresponds to a *ropani*, the common Nepalese measure for a unit of land. This unit differs according to the quality of the land, and corresponds to three surfaces associated with four different qualities. The better the quality of the land, the smaller the unit. The ropani unit, with its specific variable geometry, manifests itself in the different contours of the main courtyard. Steps define the smallest surfaces, while the walls of the buildings that frame this courtyard form the largest surface. Located in the heart of the palace (which itself forms the heart of the kingdom), the Malla kings' main courtyard was thus the measuring standard of the kingdom. The vertical measurement of the world, the space between the ground and the sky that was legitimately occupied by the king and his subjects, was set in accordance with the goddess' temple, while the horizontal standard was defined by the royal courtyard. Created within these two axes of order, the Malla sovereign was the focal point of this sacred geometry and the Master of the measuring unit of the Earth and Sky.[11] In contrast, the Shah

---

[9] This rule is sometimes applied to divinities other than Taleju: to the chariot of Matsyendranath in Patan, for example.

[10] *Hodgson Papers*, Vol. 14.

[11] However, this essential detail concerning the dimensions of the main courtyard has never been published to my knowledge; neither is it mentioned by the Nepalese nowadays. Admittedly, many elements relating to the Malla kingdoms were forgotten and not recorded. But in 1792, when Bahadur Shah, Prithvi Narayan's youngest son, who continued the fabulous conquest undertaken by his father, ordered a land register of the new kingdom to be drawn up in his role as regent during the reign of his young nephew Ran

dynasty believes that the king's territory is unbounded, but radiates from a centre, defined by the famous stone.

It appears that the Shah sovereigns had sought, at various stages, to reconstitute this symbol of the royal stone within the complex Malla palace that they seized. The Shah had even shifted the site of the royal consecration from the main courtyard to another, the Nasal Chowk, because, according to Vajracarya,[12] this was much larger than the previous one.

The Nasal Chowk courtyard had a platform at its centre, used for sacred dances during the reign of the Mallas. The whole courtyard was dedicated to the god of dance, Nasah dyah. During the time of the Mallas, a golden statue of Indra, the king of gods, would be placed on this platform during the annual festival in his honour. It was perhaps this association that led the Shah kings to seat themselves on this dais. Alternately, it could be that they found a base corresponding to their usual symbol of royalty in this platform: that is, a focal, elevated and strong point on which the king would stand. This idea was reinforced when King Rajendra Bikram Shah ordered the Nasal chowk and its dais, originally made of bricks according to Newar fashion, to be covered with black stones, giving it 'a permanent and impressive look'.[13]

Interestingly, while the Shah established their kingship within the Malla palace, they always distanced themselves from this symbolic centre. The first conqueror of the Kathmandu Valley, Prithvi Narayan Shah, rarely lived there. During the nineteenth century, the Shah constructed another palace for their residence, though the royal rituals continued at the old Malla palace. The new palace at Narayanhiti, located just outside the old city of Kathmandu, has frequently been modified, and, with each room named after a district in the country, stands as a symbol of the kingdom's modernity. The

---

Bahadur Shah, the chronicle states that he died 'on account of this sin of ascertaining the limits of the earth' (Wright, *History of Nepal*, p. 261). Despite the prosaic interpretation advanced by Sylvain Lévi (*Le Népal*, Vol. 1, p. 299), who documented people's suspicious attitude towards the sovereign's action, we may wonder whether the regent had usurped a royal prerogative or imported a Malla tool of governance sooner than necessary.

[12] *Hanuman Dhoka rajadarabar.*

[13] Ramjham, *The Rising Nepal*, p. 12.

throne is located on a dais in the room named Gorkha, an ambiguous appellation as it refers not only to one of the seventy-five districts of Nepal, but also to the original kingdom of the Shah dynasty. In a way, the Shah still appears to reign from Gorkha, albeit a Gorkha transplanted to the Kathmandu Valley.[14]

During the eighteenth century, both these contrasting conceptions of kingship were confronted with a choice they had to make between two possible kings. In Kathmandu, the absence of an heir to the throne led to a distant relative—who already had sons—being crowned in the palace. When he died, his eldest son, Jayaprakash Malla, was enthroned. However, the chronicles report that the people rapidly replaced him with his own young son as the young prince had been born in the royal palace's Mohan Chowk courtyard, while his father had not. Here, we come across the element I had outlined earlier vis-à-vis Malla kingship: the rivalry between father and son and the immanent nature of the royal power, which seems to emerge literally from the different courtyards of the royal palace. Malla kingship seems to be conferred upon birth in the specific courtyard dedicated to maternity, the Mohan Chowk.

As for the Shah, the chronicles relate how Prithvi Narayan's father had had several wives. The third queen had been pregnant for two months when the second queen became pregnant, and dreamed that she had swallowed the sun. As this dream predicted, her child was born prematurely, before the third queen could give birth. Wishing to abide by the rules of primogeniture, the noblemen and the king organized a council to debate a problem that highlighted the strength of the patrilineal transmission of kingship: at which point is royalty transmitted, at the time of conception, or at the time of birth?[15] The

---

[14] Nevertheless, to this day, 'tradition requires the King to spend at least the auspicious coronation night in the old palace...' (Shrestha *The Rising Nepal*: 35).

[15] The universal problem concerning the transmission of monarchy was further complicated by the specific difficulties connected with polygamy. However, the problem remained even within a monogamic context. For instance, M. Bloch (*Les rois thaumaturges*, p. 85) showed that in medieval Europe, the strength of monarchic ideas led some to consider not the eldest son, but the first son born after the coronation of his father as the king. The king had to be the son of a king and not of a prince for a perfect transmission.

latter was finally taken to be the decisive moment. But the noblemen probably stuck to a transcendental conception of kingship in making this decision. Indeed, the Shah dynasty considers the sun its ancestor and superior father: with the rising of the sun, the king and his people experience the monarch's divinity, and reciprocally people say that when the king goes out, the sun shines. The dream had prophesied the link between the heavenly body and the child, a link manifested in his early birth. The message was all the more acute given that birth was conceived as the first encounter with the sun. Thus, while the Malla king is seen to emerge from the grounds of the palace, the Shah king emanates from the sun.

ROYAL INSTALLATION AND FUNERALS

The chronicles do not provide details of the Malla kings' installation ceremony. They do, however, state that the mark placed on the king's forehead during his consecration as the new sovereign of Kathmandu was given to him in the presence of the two other Malla kings (of Bhaktapur and Patan) in the Kathmandu Valley. The elder of these sovereigns, both of whom were from the same dynasty as the king of Kathmandu, was the one to place the mark on the new monarch's forehead. Seniority in terms of age, as opposed to kinship, is specific to the Newars, and is also found in their kinship and political relations. For the Shah and the hill population of Nepal on the other hand, authority is conferred on the one who holds the most senior rank in the patriline, whatever his age might be.

The principle of co-consecration among Malla kings recalls some forms of royalty that had existed in the Kathmandu Valley during an earlier era. From the thirteenth to the fifteenth centuries, the Nepal Valley formed a single kingdom. During this time, two royal dynasties occupied the throne alternately: when a member of one dynasty was on the throne, the crown prince of the other was elected to succeed him, and vice versa. This associative principle provided for the consecration of the king by an elder of royal status.

In contrast to the complexity of their society and administration, the Malla coronation ritual appears as a simple delegation of the kingship embodied in the kin kings, especially the oldest of them. The collegial Malla kingship appears to be an independent institution, ruled internally on the basis of a precarious criterion, age. While the collegial kings were not the only actors in the Malla royal coronation, they were certainly the most important ones, since historical documents have mentioned them only. On the other hand, the Shah king, the centre of a far less complex organization, is consecrated through lengthy rituals in which the whole society is represented. Even the shortest and earliest descriptions of the Shah kings' installation highlight its collective and social aspects. In the chronicles, the king is said to be consecrated through a mark placed made on his forehead by a group of people, who include Brahmins and noblemen.

In recent times, the Shah king has initially been coronated before the cremation of the preceding sovereign. However, the complete crowning ceremony took place only a year or later in order to avoid the paradoxical combination of joy and sorrow, auspiciousness and inauspiciousness. The Nepalese distinguish three principal stages in the long ceremony of coronation: the *snāna*, or royal bath; the *abhiśeka*, or sprinkling ceremony; and the *āsanarohaṇa*, ascent to the throne. During the snāna, the king's body is rubbed with twelve different kinds of earth. This earth is not taken from different places in the king's domain, however; rather, it is associated with different qualities. The sanctified king's body is thus not transformed into a delimited territory, but into an ideal ground representing his kingdom. The king is then anointed by four people belonging to the four varṇas of the Hindus: with clarified butter carried by a Brahmin in a gold pot, with milk brought by a Kshatriya in a silver container, with curdled milk brought in a copper vessel by a Vaishya, and by a Shudra, who brings honey in a wooden pot. After this, eighteen different kinds of water are sprinkled over the king's body. Again, these do not represent territories but categories, as they are taken 'from a tributary, a stream, a lake, a whirlpool, from a river flowing towards the north, from dew drops, water warmed by the sun...etc. Besides, various...fruits, flowers, leaves and herbs are placed on the head of the sovereign, one by one.'[16] During the rituals, the king is first transformed into an ideal terrestrial body, then consecrated by the whole society represented by its four castes, and finally associated with sanctified waters and plants.

[16] Poudyal, 'The Coronation—Some Interesting Rituals', p. 84.

Afterwards, the sovereign sits on a throne covered with the skins of various predatory animals and the royal priest, *rāj guru*, ties a gold band around his forehead and places the crown over it. The Shah king thus appears as the master of the earth, water, vegetation, and animals at the time of his installation; however, it is significant that nothing links these elements to a territorialized space. Instead, through this ideal representation of the world, the king is settled as master of the whole universe, that is, of an unbounded kingdom. This is clearly in opposition to the Malla depiction of the sovereign as the master of his circumscribed kingdom.

The entire Shah coronation ritual is interpreted as a sacrifice of the person of the king to the sacrificial ceremony, *yagya*, which represents the nation. The platform on which the throne is placed is described as a sacrificial surface, the *vedī*. The king is said to have died as far as he himself and his family are concerned, and have acquired a collective and cosmic dimension in the process instead.

After the completion of snāna, the king is considered to be born of a national womb, and as such he belongs to the entire nation, not just to the initial places and family of birth. Soil and water used in the snāna are considered to constitute the newly evolved physical system of national magnitude. By requiring the king to accept such inanimates as part and parcel of his system, the king is expected to inject his own consciousness into them so that they can be invigorated with life. With the completion of this part of the ritual, the king belongs to all and all belongs to him.[17]

Sharma further states that because the king is anointed by the four varṇas, he becomes a symbol of unity and equality. In fact, this 'equality' is characteristically Hindu in nature. While there is indeed equal participation in the anointing of the king's body by the four varṇas, the inequality between their natures is attested by the order in which they perform, and the substances associated with each of them. This aspect is underlined by the same author when he writes:

With the king seated on the throne, representatives of all sections of the population profess their loyalty and pledge their support to the king so that

[17] Sharma, 'Coronation: The Indigenous Way to Ideal Government', p. 98. As can be understood from this statement, it is the universe that benefits from contact with the King, rather than the reverse.

the king may have at his command the knowledge of the intellectuals, bravery of the strong, and sweat and toil of those who labour.[18]

This tripartition brings to mind the three great functions distinguished by Dumézil. It does in fact correspond to the reality of the Nepalese caste organization, which is ternary despite its ideal Hindu quadripartite presentation. It places the king both above and at the centre of the caste system—the very system that creates him and endows him with power. The creation of the king can simultaneously be seen as a counter-creation, a restoration of the primordial being (Purusha) by its different 'members', since he is put together by the same four varṇas that are said to have emerged when Purusha was dismembered by the gods during the first sacrifice.

If the Malla coronation ritual seemed to be a private affair between kings, their death and funerary rituals, by contrast, concerned all of society. At the time of his death, the Malla king had to impart the *mantra* of Taleju to his son. The 'four classes and the thirty-six castes', as they were called, were then obliged to attend the funeral and perform a specific ritual function, which chiefly involved their playing different kinds of musical instruments. The neighbouring Malla sovereigns used to install the new king quickly before the cremation of the previous one, after which all of them could be said to have been present at the cremation. Royal mourning subsequently took place inside the palace, and at the end of the mourning period a more elaborate form of coronation was held.[19] Thus, the society headed by Malla kings used to display its unity and organization not at the time of coronation, but on the occasion of his death, during this second sacrifice of the king's person. Perhaps because kingship was not considered unique but was shared by different branches of the same dynasty, the Malla king apparently did not behave in any specific way during the royal mourning period.

This, however, was not the case among the Shah. The chronicles of Gorkha provide very little information concerning royal funerals. We do learn, though, that the great king Ram Shah had had a premonition of his death, after which he began educating his son about his new role. He walked himself up to the cremation place, followed

[18] Ibid., p. 99.
[19] D.R. Regmi, *Medieval Nepal, Part II*, pp. 400–4.

by all his noblemen, and died there, while piously listening to the recitation of a holy text. Alerted by noblemen, the queen arrived at the cremation site, placed a ṭikā mark on her son's forehead, and jumped onto the burning pyre of her husband. The two royal bodies immediately disappeared, much to the crowd's astonishment.

This unique and brief description underlines the essential point behind Hindu funerals, that is, the radical manner in which the dead disappear. Ideally, like any Hindu, the dying king leaves the world before his death through his journey to a holy place of cremation (which is believed to be detached from this world), or when he leaves the mundane world to become a renouncer.

The Malla king used to transmit an essential part of the kingship to his heir through the Taleju mantra, before the confirmation of this kingship by neighbouring and related kings. Shah kingship, however, possesses no such mechanism of continuity. In their current rituals, the break is avoided by negating the interval between two reigns.[20] Death becomes formal only upon its announcement, and the death of the king is announced at the same time as the proclamation of the new king's name. This double and simultaneous public announcement holds the two generations together, and provides the necessary continuity in kingship within the same dynasty in much the same way that the French used to shout: 'Le roi est mort, vive le roi!', that is, 'The king is dead, long live the king'. A very short coronation ceremony takes place before the previous king is cremated, after which the new king is forbidden to participate in his predecessor's funerary rituals.

The Shah kings' funerary rituals comprise two central features that distinguish them from ordinary men. First, as we have just seen, they are not led by the eldest son, who is the conventional head mourner. Second, they include a ceremony to expulse the dead king. These two characteristics can be read as transgressions allowing for the establishment of the new kingship.

The king openly breaks the family rules of the patriline during his initial installation by not leading the funerary duties for his father (or elder brother). This initial transgression is particularly striking, since

---

[20] A. Mayer ('The King's Two Thrones') showed that this negation is characteristic of numerous Hindu kingships.

not only does the king not fulfil his filial duty, the main purpose behind producing a son as far as Hindus are concerned, but he also displays no signs of mourning. He does not shave his head and is not prohibited from taking salt. What is more, he is the main figure in an auspicious ceremony that takes place while impurity prevails in the whole kingdom. To minimize the danger arising from this situation, the first coronation ceremony is kept short and is performed before the cremation of the royal body since the latter causes greater impurity to prevail throughout the kingdom than the death itself. Following the royal cremation, the kingdom remains closed for three days, after which it goes into a declining state of mourning for another ten days. The argument often used to explain why the king does not appear to mourn his father is that the king should never be in an impure state. However, this argument contradicts the widespread belief that the king, like fire, can never be soiled. The king is not polluted by contact with low castes, for instance, since he is partly created by one of them and since he himself places ṭikā marks on the foreheads of all his subjects during the Dasain ritual, irrespective of their caste or creed. He is, in fact, the only one who is capable of doing so without being polluted himself or polluting others—another sign of his externality.[21]

In fact, in a more general way, it is said that whoever carries the crown should not look upon death. His participation in any funerary ritual is prohibited, regardless of whether the ritual concerns a member of his own family. Therefore, it is not about the king not seeing the dead king; rather, he should not look upon death in general.[22] Whatever the reasons behind this prohibition, the Shah kingship displays this paradox. It is presented as an uninterrupted line of descent, yet the continuity of the line is not guaranteed by the

[21] The king shares these characteristics with other humans who are also incarnations of divinity: the dhāmī oracles of western Nepal, who may not perform death rituals, even for their own parents, and may apply the ṭikā mark on the foreheads of impure castes without being polluted (see Shrestha-Schipper 2003).

[22] Perhaps we witness here a conflict between kings, since it is well-known that the god of death, Yama, is himself royal. He is the king of Dharma, who calls the living to his own kingdom when his time has come. See Malamoud, Le jumeau solaire.

succeeding eldest son, but by a younger son. As a rule, in Nepalese society the continuity of the patriline is ensured by joining together the dead father and the surviving eldest son. The son is literally superimposed on his dead father. He is said to take upon himself his pain and suffering through the avoidance of certain foods, salt and clothes; any wrongdoing on his part directly affects his dead father's fate. Through the royal mechanism of delegated mourning, the king is somehow detached from his patriline, and the succession of kings appears almost as a parallel line, held together with its natal line through the intervention of the young. The king is also detached from his subjects during the royal mourning, since they are all polluted by it while he is not. On the other hand, his own death brings about his re-attachment, since three generations of dead kings, together with the three generations of one's own ancestors, are worshipped during the *śrāddha* rituals.

Royal funerals have a second notable characteristic: they pollute Brahmans and degrade one of them. Indeed, unlike ordinary people, the royal corpse is not carried by close kinsmen, but by Brahmins enlisted in the army. The army plays a crucial role in the Shah kings' funerals.[23] During a particularly problematic royal funeral, such as the one that took place in 2001 when Crown Prince Dipendra committed regicide, patricide and matricide before taking his own life, a Brahmin can replace even the kinsman who normally lights the pyre.

The second extraordinary characteristic is seen on the eleventh day following the cremation. Over the previous ten days, like any ordinary man, the kinsman who takes on the role of mourner for the sovereign constructs a 'subtle body' of the dead king from an offering comprising ten rice balls. This is a dangerous body that should be sent to the ancestors' resting place. For the Hindus from the hills of central Nepal (which is where the Shah come from), this stage is usually symbolized by the destruction of a small mound of earth representing the body of the dead, while gifts are offered to the family priest in the name of the deceased. These gifts are

---

[23] All actors in Shah royal funerals are recruited from within the army, underlying the warlike character of these kings.

not accompanied by food offerings, and are not considered particularly polluting.

The modern royal ceremony, however, is very different. On the eleventh day following the cremation, a Brahmin is invited to consume a dish called *kāṭṭo*, the consumption of which transgresses conventional boundaries in an extreme manner. Different sources differ on the exact composition of this dish: according to some, it contains some brain tissue of the dead king, or the powdered bone of his forehead; others state that it is sprinkled with ashes from his pyre, or that it contains two products that should not be consumed at the same time—milk and meat. Whatever the real ingredients, the majority believe that the kāṭṭo contains part of the dead sovereign's body. In addition, it also flouts the conventional prohibition against eating anything at the site of funerary rituals on the eleventh day after cremation.

Immediately after this meal, the Brahmin (in this context referred to as *kāṭṭe* Bahun) is dressed as the dead sovereign. He is made to wear brocaded clothes, a replica of the royal crown, and some personal objects of the deceased sovereign, in particular his shoes and glasses. These last two are important symbols of sovereignty since the king must never walk barefoot on the ground, and because his glasses serve the function of reinforcing his 'holy vision', which confers merit on those upon whom it falls. The kāṭṭe Bahun is then perched upon an elephant, sheltered under a royal umbrella. Astride the elephant, he crosses a river that marks the symbolic border of the kingdom. Theoretically, he is supposed to then be expelled from the kingdom forever,[24] but, again theoretically, he also receives whatever he asks for in exchange.[25]

[24] The fact that the king's double is expelled from the Kathmandu Valley is perhaps revealing, pointing to the possibility of the Shah kings having retained something of the specific nature of the Malla kingdoms when they established their capital there.

[25] To my knowledge, there is no mention of this ritual among the Shah before their conquest of Kathmandu Valley. Shortly after the conquest, however, full-status Brahmins participated in the funerals of the Shah king of Gulmi kingdom (in central Nepal). On the other hand, the Malla sovereigns as well their subjects practised this ritual, for which they employed a local Brahmin of low status or certain Brahmins from Vaijanathdham, that is,

CONCLUSION

Full-status Brahmins are regarded as terrestrial gods or *bhū-deva*. In the Shah kings' funerals, one such Brahmin is made to commit the most odious of crimes – that of consuming the dead king's body. This Brahmin dies in order to allow the new sovereign to reign over his kingdom. The procedure can be linked to the installation ritual, during which Brahmins create ex nihilo a terrestrial divinity, an avatar of Vishnu, who is embodied in the person of the king.[26] This creature can be destroyed only by the degradation and subsequent exile of its creator, at whom the people throw stones and shout abuse.[27]

Jagannath in Orissa. These Brahmins, called *pātra brahman, mahāpātra brahman* or *mahābrahman*, are not allowed to enter any house, and nobody drinks the water they have touched. Additional research is necessary to document the Shahs' former practices, but we know that in the case of Ran Bahadur, the first Shah king to be crowned on the throne of Kathmandu, a Mahabrahman of central India, who lived across the Narmada river, was used. It was apparently only recently, since the return of the Shah monarchy following the demise of the Rana in 1951, that Brahmins of high status began to be used again. Bhatta Brahmins of Indian origin acted as kāṭṭe Bahun for Tribhuvan and Mahendra, while Nepalese Upadhyaya Brahmins were selected for the last two monarchs, Birendra and Dipendra, in June 2001 (see Bhattarai, 'Kāṭṭe khanekhvaune itihas'). With time, and perhaps because it corresponds particularly to their transgressive nature, the Shah kings committed an increasing sacrilege by using a full status Brahman or they may have returned to their former traditional sacrilege after having adopted a more institutionalized form of ritual (by using a low status Mahabrahman) for some decades following their conquest of the Kathmandu Valley. The Shah adopted the convention of returning a Mahabrahman, a ritual specialist who is already marginalized, to the other world after they established their dynasty in Kathmandu in the late eighteenth century. This was perhaps borrowed from the Malla kings' tradition. However, the recent practice of using a high-status Brahmin at royal funerals shocked many Nepalese, particularly Brahmins (see Timsina, 'Ridiculing Brahmanism').

[26] On this procedure, see Witzel, 'The Coronation Rituals of Nepal, with Special Reference to the Coronation of King Birendra (1975)'.

[27] This practice had not been observed for the last two kings, probably because of the great shock accompanying their violent deaths. It had been documented for King Mahendra, as the report by the French ambassador to Nepal, dated 23 February 1972, shows: '...il fut obligé de quitter la vallée sous

This ceremony only concerns the sovereign, since the gifts made on behalf of the queen, or a prince who is not heir to the crown, go to the palace priests as usual.

As soon as he consumes the sacrilegious meal of the king's body, the Brahmin becomes a monstrous figure, an untouchable Brahmanic king, as if the destruction of kingship meant the symbolic destruction of the caste hierarchy and, subsequently, its whole order. The representatives of the two great powers, spiritual and temporal, are merged into one figure, which is in turn relegated to the lower end of society and then expelled by the population. As in many African cases, the Hindu king is thus ritually expelled from his kingdom. Considering the stoning and the degradation, which, for a Brahmin, is a punishment equivalent to death, capital punishment of Brahmins being prohibited, one might safely presume that through this ritual, the king is even symbolically put to death.

This revival of the king after his death nullifies the concept of interregnum. This empty space is filled by a kind of double royalty, which lasts till the end of the funerary rites. While the untouchable Brahmin king is paraded before the kingdom,[28] the new king remains hidden, except on two occasions that frame the crucial moment of the cremation of his predecessor's body. He appears in public during his ascent to the throne and during the subsequent short parade in the city that precedes the cremation, and he delivers an official speech at the end of the cremation.

Like the coronation, the king's expulsion from his kingdom underlines the sovereign's close relationship with the earth, whose husband, or *Bhu-pati*, he is considered to be. While his vital principle is expelled in the form of the monstrous Brahmin who ate it, another part of his person, the material remains, is scattered in various holy places, so as to return it to the elements from which he originates, and thereby to regenerate them.

---

les huées et les lapidations de la foule' or 'he was forced to leave the valley under the hoots and stoning of the crowd' (Toussaint, 'Mort et crémation du roi').

[28] In addition, an auspicious form of the dead king is highly visible on the altars set up in his memory everywhere in the kingdom during the mourning period, particularly in front of his palace.

The three transgressions linked to Shah kingship may be understood as manifestations of the ambiguous nature of kingship in general, and analysed using the model of sacred kingship defined first by Frazer, and then refined by Luc de Heusch within the African context. This exercise in decontextualization and comparison allows for an original reading of Hindu kingship in Nepal by casting its internal logic to one side. De Heusch[29] showed that during their installation, the kings of Kongo are set radically apart from normal kinship rules through an act of incest, or through the consumption of a newborn from their own lineage, that is, through an incestuous form of cannibalism.

Incest is not absent from Shah kingship since the Thakuri caste, from within which all kings of Nepal are recruited, is noted for their marriage preference with the matrilateral cross-cousin. This alliance is considered incestuous by all other high-status groups as they view the matrilateral cross-cousin as a classificatory sister. The Thakuris themselves endorse this view with regard to other groups since, as kings, they have fined and punished groups other than theirs who practised this form of marriage. Moreover, the Shah dynasty has imposed this incestuous rule on a group which traditionally did not practise it—the Rana, who have been their matrimonial allies since 1850. As members of the Chetri caste group, the Rana regard the father's sister's son as a brother.

Vis-à-vis marriage, however, nothing distinguishes the king from other members of the Thakuri caste. Still, it is noteworthy that the king comes from a group which practises a form of marriage that others regard as incestuous, and does so with impunity.[30] This discrepancy is viewed by the common man as stemming from the Thakuris' foreign origin, another point that may be compared with the African instance, where 'the king comes from elsewhere'.[31]

We have seen how the Shah king undergoes a cultural demise. This does not necessitate, as it does in many African cases, ending his term of office (or killing him) when he shows signs of ageing and

[29] *Les rois de Kongo et les monstres sacrés*, p. 31.

[30] This type of alliance is usually said to have been borrowed from the Muslims, or from the Nepalese tribal groups.

[31] *Les rois de Kongo et les monstres sacrés*, p. 49.

ill health. On the contrary, the Nepalese king's cultural end takes place after his natural death, but it performs a similar function of leaving the field free for the new sovereign.

Moreover, as is common in African kingship, the Shah king is dependent on the presence of abnormal or monstrous figures: the king-eating Brahmin, the degraded royal sacrificer, and the younger brother as mourner. In contrast to the African cases, however, the monstrosity of these figures is not physical, but wholly cultural: kingship compels them to transgress kinship and caste rules, while not sparing them the consequences of this transgression.

The first transgression we examined involved the degradation of a royal heir by the king. It is presented as a disinterested act, a self-sacrifice on the part of the royal figure in order to tame the local wild forces by means of an impure sacrifice. This forms the preliminary to the establishment of kingship in a new territory. It is an initial condition that is not repeated, but is perpetuated by members of the new group it gives rise to (the butchers in the Malla kingships), or the existing group with which the degraded heir has merged (the tribal Magar group in the case of the Shah). The two groups are ascribed a low but pure status, falling into the strange Nepalese class of 'pure Shudras'.

The second transgression goes against the normal rules of kinship at the time of funerals. It temporarily pollutes the younger brother of the king, and allows the latter to be detached from his family for the duration of the impure mourning period as well as his coronation, which takes place at the same time.

The third transgression is aimed at expelling the dead king from his kingdom. It can be considered the last step in the detachment process that characterizes kingship. This transgression differs from the first two in that it has consequences for others besides the royal family. In this instance, the double comes not from the royal family, but from the Brahmin caste. And while the other transgressions appear to somehow possess noble (or royal) characteristics, the motivation behind the king-eating kāṭṭe Bahun is as monstrous as can be, since it involves the voluntary self-desacralization of a Brahmin for money. Through these complex mechanisms of transgression, the king masters both categories of pure and impure while remaining, by definition, pure himself.

We have seen how the ritual procedures of the royal installation recall elements in the creation of the social order. However, this mirroring of social diversity through the sacrifice of a unique male body, and the creation of yet another male body by the various social classes does not constitute transgression, despite the fundamental role it plays in the Shah dynasty's myths of origin, and the royal funerary rituals. The transgressive dimension, on the other hand, is quite central to the Hindu myth concerning the origin of kingship. Rather chaotic, this myth proceeds in stages. Yama, the king of Death (and a Kshatriya by birth), has a daughter who marries Anga, a king with no offspring who cannot offer sacrifices. Anga's wife conceives a boy from the food offered her by a being born from a sacrificial fire. She gives birth to Vena, an evil king who, inheriting his maternal grandfather's qualities, hunted men as if they were deers. Vena demands all the offerings, claiming to represent all the gods, thereby angering the Brahmins, who kill him with sacrificial grass blades. Disorder then spreads over the earth, which is deprived of a king, and hordes of poor people attack the rich. So the sages decide to create a new king from Vena's corpse. From his thigh, they first extract a black and evil being, a Nishada or tribal man, who they send to the jungle, and then Prithu, the first mortal king, who goes on to marry the earth.

This myth recalls that Hindu kingship is not created ex-nihilo, but from pre-existing forms of kingship that may be qualified as 'impossible'. It is a last successful attempt in a series of inauspicious, excessive, or dangerous forms of kingship: the lord of death with no male offspring, Anga with no children, Vena the terrible, and finally the black and wild Nishada. The last, Brahmin-approved king, Prithu, does not erase the previous ones, which coexist in different realms (the world of death, the forest) or planes of reality (as each king possesses a dark and terrible side). This myth brings to mind the story of the Shah or the Malla of Nepal, fleeing bloody and terrible Muslim rulers, their establishment becoming possible only after they drive away one of their own, exiling him in the wild and/or impure sphere, an act each generation repeats through the symbolic exile of the Brahmin embodying the dead king, who is also made part of the impure sphere by being rendered untouchable.

Of the three great models concerning the origin of kingship—the magical origin, conquest, and the contract—none truly corresponds to the Himalayan case, which combines elements of all three models, but lays most emphasis on the initial transgression preceding the establishment of kingship. This transgression can certainly not be placed within the blurred category of 'magical origin', since a very precise process leads to the symbolic death of a potential king embodied in the person of the closest heir to the throne, who then gives birth of an impure ritual specialist linked to royalty. This transgression plunges a potential king into a particular low caste—that of a sacrificer. Now, the king is the supreme sacrifier (and sacrificer)[32] of the kingdom, and the transgression results in splitting the royal function into its pure and impure aspects. This sequence, whereby a royal impure sacrifice – which is also the sacrifice of a royal person—precedes the establishment of kingship, may be interpreted as one answer to the paradoxical position of the king in Nepalese Hindu society. He is a member of a specific group (a lineage of a sub-caste of Kshatriyas known as Thakuris) whose members are all somehow set apart from the rest of society, and yet he stays detached from this group during coronation. In fact, the detachment resulting from the coronation rituals is usually described as a sacrifice and a rebirth. The king is said to die both for himself and the interest of his group in order to adopt a universal role. The royal function bifurcates the king's initial Kshatriya status—elevating it to his divine aspect on the one hand, and degrading it in the form of his impure doubles on the other. Both are necessary for the prosperity and smooth running of the kingdom.

The transgressive character of Shah kingship is particularly apparent in their use of a high-status Brahmin in place of the Mahabrahman traditionally entrusted with taking the impurity of death upon himself. The splitting of the ritual function between impurity and purity specialists, considered by Hocart to be constitutive of the caste system, cannot be called fully transgressive. This splitting was indeed institutionalized among the Mallas, as

---

[32] A sacrifier is the person who commands, or patronizes a sacrifice, and a sacrificer, the person who performs the sacrifice.

well as in several regions of India. In Malla kingship, the king's two primary impure doubles were recruited from specific castes—the Butchers[33] (who, as we saw, were created through the requirements of kingship), and the Mahabrahmans (a low caste in charge of funerary rituals).

Shah kingship, on the other hand, is linked to transgressions that are less institutionalized as they are repeated with each generation. Degradation strikes a single individual chosen among the group, and thus affects all Brahmins, who are viewed as potential eaters of dead kings. In the same way, the initial degradation of the royal heir still affects the Magar group into which the royal pig sacrificer was assimilated (or which he created) through his degradation.[34] This in turn influences the perception of the Shah royal dynasty, which is often said to have originated from the Magar tribe.

The Brahmin acquires an eminently paradoxical status vis-à-vis the caste system he heads, and the king who rules over it. He forms both ends of the caste system; he both makes and eats the king. From occupying the highest position, he transforms into the most repulsive creature.

The tribal groups, particularly Magars, have just as ambiguous a role to play with regard to the Shah kingship, since, through the degraded royal/tribal sacrificer, they are made to offer sacrifices to their own chthonic gods for the sake of their conquerors.

Somehow, it seems that the caste system allows every group and individual to deal with impurity according to their respective rank, with the exception of the king. The external and paradoxical position of the king, as one embodying all the castes while always remaining pure, leads to a ritual decomposition of the royal function, creating a parallel caste system within kingship itself.

---

[33] In Nepali this caste is known as the Kasai, in Newari the Khadgi.
[34] This particularly concerns the Magars. On this subject, see the previous chapter.

8. Back Cover of the Maoist Journal *Naulo Bihani*, Showing the Maoist Leaders as the Successors of the Shah Kings of Nepal (Photo: M. Lecomte-Tilouine).

7

Regicide and Maoist Revolutionary Warfare in Nepal
Modern Incarnations of a Warrior Kingdom[*]

On 1 June 2001 the drunken Crown Prince of Nepal, Dipendra, killed his parents, King Birendra and Queen Aishwarya, and seven other close relatives in a shooting spree, after which—according to the official report—he shot himself. By 4 June the assassin, having been declared king in the interim, had died, and his uncle Prince Gyanendra, Birendra's only surviving brother, succeeded him to the throne. To make matters worse, the leaders of the Maoist insurgency attempted to exploit the occasion to spark uprisings in the cities. These failed to take off, but after a ceasefire in the summer, the Maoists began launching direct attacks on the Nepalese army for the first time, which resulted in the declaration of a state of emergency and led to what, in effect, could be considered a civil war throughout the country. US Secretary of State Colin Powell visited Nepal in January 2002 to offer the government support against the Maoist 'terrorists'. Although a second ceasefire was negotiated in January

[*] Originally published as 'The Modern Incarnations of a Warrior Kingdom: Regicide and Maoist Revolutionary Warfare in Nepal' (translated by David N. Gellner), *Anthropology Today*, vol. 20, no. 1, 2004. 'Massacre royal et révolution au Népal', in B. Steinmann (ed.), *Le Maoïsme au Népal. Lectures d'une révolution*, Paris: CNRS éditions, 2006: 113–45.

2003, this too broke down by September, leading to renewed violence and spiralling human rights abuses.

In spite of the worldwide media attention that the royal massacre generated, and in spite of its detailed coverage in Kathmandu at least, the intricacies of Nepalese politics and the symbolism utilized by both sides—the king and the Maoists—has remained largely unexplored. In this chapter, I reflect specifically on the relationship between the development of the Maoist movement and the royal massacre. Though the so-called People's War was launched by the Nepalese Maoist Party (CPN-Maoist) as early as 1996, the royal massacre marked a new phase, both in the development of its rhetoric and in its confrontation with the king. I interpret the emergence of the Maoist movement as reflecting the gradual weakening of royal power in Nepal, while at the same time noting how it ensures a significant continuity with the royal past, despite its communist ideology.

WARRIOR KINGS IN A CASTE SOCIETY

Nepal is a warrior kingdom. It might seem clichéd to present the country thus, since every Hindu king is, by definition, a member of the Kshatriya or warrior caste. During the second half of the eighteenth century, the kingdom of Gorkha forcibly unified more than fifty independent kingdoms and imposed its own character on the new state of Nepal that emerged from this campaign.[1] Created by the sword in this manner, Nepal has managed to remain an independent kingdom, and has neither been colonized by Westerners nor experienced civil war.

Moreover, it is well-known in the outside world for its export of soldiers renowned for their ferocity in battle, the Gurkhas.[2] The apparently gratuitous acts of regicide on 1 June 2001 and the violence of the Maoist movement, both before and after June 2001, cannot be comprehended without taking into account the manner in which the Nepalese state, the very basis of which lies in warfare, emerged.

---

[1] Stiller, *The Rise of the House of Gorkha: A Study of the Unification of Nepal, 1768–1816.*

[2] Caplan, *Warrior Gentleman: 'Gurkhas' in the Western Imagination.*

The Thakuris began seizing power in central Nepal as early as the fifteenth century. Over a period of two or three centuries these numerous small Himalayan kingdoms, led by kings from the same or related clans, fought incessant wars that may be characterized as 'ritual' or 'honour' conflicts, since they were aimed more at establishing a supremacy of status than seizing land or resources from the neighbouring kingdoms. The present kingdom of Nepal emerged from one such small kingdom, that of Gorkha in central Nepal. In sixteenth-century Gorkha, a junior line of the neighbouring kingdom of Lamjung, headed by the Shah lineage, became the centre of the dynasty that was to rule Nepal. At that time Gorkha was led by two figures committed to overthrowing established powers. Drabya Shah (reigned 1559–70) was a junior prince, but he was assisted—according to myth and dynastic histories—by the god-cum-saint Gorakhnath, a disciple of the tutelary deity of Kathmandu Valley. It is said that Gorakhnath was humiliated in the Valley and then he left for Gorkha where he manifested himself before the young prince Drabya Shah, and told him that he would become king and that his dynasty would subsequently conquer the Kathmandu valley. This explains much of the kingdom's atypically aggressive and expansionist conduct in the years that followed.

The unification campaign of Prithvi Narayan Shah (1723–75), the tenth king of the small kingdom of Gorkha, represents a major break from the formalized rules of war that the Thakuris had followed until then, which also partly explains his success. Instead of compelling the defeated kings to pay tribute and accept other obvious signs of inferiority, Prithvi Narayan waged an expansionist war, aiming to establish not an empire of vassal kings on the received Hindu kingship model, but a large centralized kingdom that would have no overlord, but an ultimate sovereign. The caste system, as practised by Prithvi Narayan and his successors, depended on kings in a very specific sense. As Hocart has emphasized, the holistic coherence of the caste system becomes apparent only in ritual contexts. According to Hocart, it is above all the treatment of impurity that gave rise to ritual specialists and the hierarchy of priests, from which, by extension, the hierarchy of castes derived. However, among the Hindus of the Nepalese hills, rites of purification such as cremation or shaving the head are not dependent on caste. Caste-based ritual services structure the entire society in a very specific context: when the whole population gathers around a royal centre and each caste carries out a specific task during the celebration of war through the worship of the patron goddess and sacred weapons.

WARFARE IN THE MEDIEVAL KINGDOMS OF NEPAL

Warfare played an essential and catalysing role in the little kingdoms of west and central Nepal. The ritual services of the different castes comprised of predominantly war-related functions: the Damai drummers and bell-ringers, the Sarki cobblers and scabbard-makers, the blacksmith-gunsmith Kamis, the tribal and Kshatriya soldiers, and the Brahmin priests and astrologers, who propitiate the gods of war and determine the auspicious moment at which to start the fighting, or mobilize troops. The various caste groups, whose activities are focused upon the king, are called upon each year to assist in the bloody sacrifices on behalf of the sovereign during the annual celebration of war, the Nepali Dasain or Durga Puja.[3] This cosmological order, which today survives only in such rituals, was in the past evoked in ritualized warfare. Warfare was the only activity that centred the entire society around its sovereign, with each individual, according to his specialization and rank, participating in a common project. Rituals of war often preceded a period of real warfare.

Social and political relationships were constantly open to contestation; this included not only the relationships of subordination or supremacy between kingdoms, but also structural relationships within kingdoms, since positions of honour and status were redistributed on the basis of conduct in combat. Thus bravery, even on the part of an Untouchable, could lead to a change in caste status, which affected not just the individual concerned, but his entire group as well.

Often, the person being rewarded for bravery was granted a position of confidence close to the king, as well as a certain amount

[3] Krauskopff and Lecomte-Tilouine, *Célébrer le pouvoir. Dasai, une fête royale au Népal.*

of land corresponding to that position. Those who performed badly on these occasions were punished accordingly. In this way, the warrior king ordered both the world and his society by means of his sword, which today is still used to represent the king, and, by extension, is taken as a metonym for royal power itself.

War offered a chance to rise in society, an opportunity no other institution could provide. Furthermore, every adult male was a potential warrior, since it was the rule that one man from each house had to take part in armed conflicts. The Maoists have revived this rule in certain places with respect to participation in their meetings and contributions to forced labour, and recently for participation in battle as well.

All men were thus provided with an equal opportunity to distinguish themselves before the sovereign in times of war. War thus represented a quasi-egalitarian context, a counterpoint of sorts to the hierarchical and exclusivist logic that governed all other activities. It is true that opportunities to shine came more frequently to warriors or priests than to those who served them, such as musicians and armourers. But in the chaos that followed a setback or a defeat, anyone of any rank could seize their chance.

More generally, war is structurally placed outside Hindu law because it triggers the notion of 'the dharma of dire straits' (*āpat dharma*), which allows all rules of caste to be broken in times of mortal danger. This has an important consequence: if the king's duty is to enforce respect for the law, as a warrior king he has an additional right, and even duty, to plunge his kingdom periodically into a state of temporary lawlessness.

One finds concrete traces of this aspect in the rule laid down by Prithvi Narayan Shah following an attack, which took his soldiers, who were undressed for a meal as per the tradition, by surprise. The king declared that henceforth, soldiers would no longer be required to respect the rules of purity while eating. Later on in the history of Nepal, a decree was passed stipulating that yaks were akin to deer, so that Nepalese soldiers could freely consume its meat during the war with Tibet. The leaders of the People's War have renewed this tradition by abrogating fundamental Hindu laws (traditionally, the great Hindu crimes were the murder of a Brahmin, a woman, a child, or a cow). Women, who traditionally do not have the right to kill even a chicken, are recruited in great numbers by the Maoists, though until recently their recruitment in the Royal Nepalese Army (RNA) was forbidden. Apparently children, who are similarly supposed to be kept out of conflict, have also found a place within Maoist ranks; however, this is denied by Maoist leaders, who are highly sensitive to the international condemnation of this practice. Lastly, the cows and Brahmins whom the Hindu king must particularly protect and who may not be put to death are rarely spared by Maoists: many Brahmin teachers were publicly tortured to death, and the Maoists, who eat beef, would at times even force the population to do so in order to destroy their 'superstitions'.

The kingdoms of the central Himalayas were not just geographically close. They were also similar in size, population, army, armaments and, above all, cultural values. Thus, the medieval period was characterized by war within and between groups that were sociologically alike. The People's War appears to have preserved this characteristic, since the fighters on each side are very similar: 'Ram Bahadur kills Shyam Bahadur', as the Nepalese put it—village neighbours kill one another.

Medieval Himalayan warfare seemed to have been a ritual contest that barely disturbed the social order, and perhaps even worked towards preserving it. Later, from the nineteenth century, the army, and war in particular, have offered peasants of modest means a chance for social mobility: those who managed to join the British Gurkhas, for example, were able to earn salaries that others could only dream of, travel the world, and, particularly during World Wars I and II, win the highest military honours.

In recent years, this fundamental role that war and the army played in regulating society, and even more so in people's dreams of social mobility, has eroded as a consequence of the rising levels of education—and the advocates of the People's War have skilfully used this to their advantage. For several years before the war began, in most districts the RNA did not recruit anyone who had not obtained his School Leaving Certificate. As failure rates in rural areas are extremely high, a large number of young men whose senior relatives were retired soldiers found themselves categorically excluded from a military career.

WAR = SACRIFICE: BRAHMINS AS RULERS
AND WARRIORS

The notion of taking up arms is very attractive and offers the chance of sovereignty, as Michel Foucault[4] has remarked. A Maoist battle report[5] illustrates this strikingly: 'As they examined the weapons, comrades showed how much they loved these weapons that were won with the blood of their comrades and that the capture of these weapons was an important factor in the victory'. The sacrificial function of the king's sword revivifies his sovereignty: at regular intervals the king is required to carry out blood sacrifices, and this blood regenerates his power. Beheading an enemy in war was itself a kind of sacrifice, a pure death; thus, when a warrior dies in war, his relatives suffer no impurity.[6] As a form of sacrifice, then, war constitutes a very particular context that falls outside the usual norms of purity and impurity. Through the performance of his role, the warrior is directly linked to the divine, since his very engagement is described as a self-sacrifice, a *bali dān*. Every warrior is thus potentially both a sacrificer and a willing sacrificial victim. In either case, the warrior performs a direct sacrifice without the intercession of a priest.

This conflation of war with the ritual of sacrifice had long been used by warrior kings to reduce their dependence on Brahmins. Now, as Maoists, Brahmins fight back against the king. This new challenge represents an unprecedented reversal in the traditional Hindu world order, a supplementary version of the classic antagonism that existed between Brahmins and Kshatriyas. Now it is the rebel Brahmin chiefs who challenge the sovereign Kshatriya with warfare in order to seize temporal power.

The caste status of the two leaders of the Maoist movement, who are both Brahmins, certainly stands in opposition to their

[4] Foucault, *Dits et écrits 1, De la nature humaine, justice contre pouvoir*.

[5] Dipak, 'Rukumkot Raid: A Live Broadcasting'.

[6] According to Dhakal Sharma (*Jutho sutak nirnaya*), there is no period of impurity following a death on the battlefield. If one dies from a war wound, the number of days of impurity is calculated against the number of days that have passed since the battle. Once seven nights have elapsed, relatives have to observe the usual ten days of impurity.

ideology, which is summed up quite simply in the name of their movement—the People's War.

Neither warriors nor emerging from the people, Brahmins are by definition an elite category, traditionally presented as 'gods on earth' and entirely separated from both death and sovereignty, since they have no right to kill (even an animal) and may not be killed themselves. The transition that these Brahmin leaders have been trying to effect, from thinkers—which on its own would not be enough to seize power—to sovereign warriors, seems to have involved a rather uneasy trial of strength. It is particularly revealing that the only internal conflict to be reported, or constructed in an attempt to destabilize the movement, concerned the principal Brahmin leader's desire to control every aspect of the Maoist organization, including its ideology as well as military actions. The existence of any internal conflict is, however, vigorously denied by the Maoists themselves (see below).

MAOIST BRAHMIN WARRIOR-KINGS?

The sociology of the Nepalese Maoist movement is still little understood. Today it has nothing to do with China: the Chinese government condemns the movement, saying it has nothing to do with Mao, while on their part the Nepalese Maoists have long regarded the Chinese regime as renegade revisionists. The Nepalese movement is not restricted to a single region, caste group, ethnic group or religious community, or even to a particular economic class. The strategy of the CPN (M) has been to drive away the political and economic elite from villages in the middle hill region, put an end to all local arms of the state, and finally, to replace state structures by those of their own party, while also instituting elections for 'people's governments'. The very nature of the movement continues to remain undefined. Its leaders proclaim Maoism to be a purely political movement, while the government labels the Maoists 'terrorists' (except when negotiating a ceasefire with them). The Maoists, who certainly fall outside the legal political field, aim to reform it through the use of force; their violence does not primarily target the general population, but rather those who represent the government—the police, the army, elected representatives, and members of well-known political parties. They thus align themselves with revolutionary movements that use terror to achieve their aims.

The Maoists' People's War has elaborated a new symbolic system, whose romanticism has attracted large numbers. Followers are offered a whole new way of life resembling an enormous Boy Scout organization, where young people in uniform go off to camp in the forest, and undertake good deeds in villages with the support of villagers. In this bohemian life of adventure, discussions on how to rebuild the world alternate with revolutionary songs and games of hide-and-seek played with security forces—though obviously with a degree of realism that goes far beyond the purely ludic and symbolic.

A striking feature of the movement is its remarkable logistical organization, which involves the movement of arms, the infiltration of areas controlled by the enemy, setting up meetings, and the publication and distribution of revolutionary tracts. The movement's ideology offers its members, especially those not particularly successful educationally or economically, a new interpretation of their circumstances; in particular, it gives them the opportunity to struggle against their situation and develop a new understanding of their oppression and exploitation. The Maoists have been able to develop a genuine mystique (to borrow an expression from Sanjeev Pokharel),[7] which combines violence and the bonds of brotherhood; this produces a high degree of cohesion within the movement, and terror outside it.

In 1951, when the present king's grandfather, Tribhuvan, returned to power after a century of governance with the Rana prime ministers at the helm (the Rana ministers having usurped military leadership), he immediately reclaimed his role as commander-in chief of the army. King Birendra had retained this role even under the 'democratic' constitution of 1990. Lacking other powers (though permitted by the notorious Article 127 to 'remove difficulties' in the functioning of the constitution), the role of the king under the present constitution has been reduced to its most basic aspect, that of warrior.

How far does the People's War build on the model of warrior kingship, and how far has it progressively attempted to replace it,

---

[7] Sanjeev Pokharel, 'Maoist War: Violence Between Hope and Sorrow'.

particularly through the behaviour of its two leaders since the royal massacre of June 2001?

When Maoist leaders launched their People's War in February 1996, this very initiative placed them in the position of sovereigns, since the first instance of sovereignty resides, as we have seen, in the declaration of war, which is an exaggerated form of the power over death. The publications of the CPN (M) illustrate this perfectly: the Maoist leaders speak to warriors, are surrounded by warriors, reply to the government by means of military actions, which speak for them just as much as their words do. Their victories are, above all, military ones. However, they are not themselves warriors: they never carry arms and never wear military uniforms or headgear.

By contrast, their troops sport a red headscarf, the kaphan, which, as the symbol of mourning, is said to convey their willingness to accept their own death.

Like conquering kings, Maoist leaders abrogate the legitimate right of the sovereign and his government to raise taxes on the land; the hitherto accepted Hindu view of land as belonging to the king is substituted by the precept, which states that appropriating 'surplus' revenues is illegitimate. Since schoolteachers 'do not work on Saturdays' and the Maoists consider Saturday a working day, in many places the former have to hand over one-seventh of their salary to the Maoists. One should note, though, that Maoist opposition to taxes on land is primarily symbolic, since the current level of taxation on land is insignificant. The Maoists also organize local elections and have set up people's tribunals, supplanting the royal prerogative of administering justice.

MAOIST LEADERS AS SUCCESSORS TO SHAH KINGS

The Maoists confronted the king and the monarchy only after the assassination of the royal family in June 2001. During the days immediately following the massacre, Maoist leaders concluded that the monarchy had effectively been abolished or, as supreme leader Prachanda put it, 'In the present circumstances, when objectively the monarchical system has ceased to exist...'. The Maoists had in fact claimed common ground with King Birendra. In Prachanda's words: 'As for those genuine patriots who saw in the king and the monarchy the means of safeguarding the country, there is no reason why they should feel terrified by the Maoist movement, towards which King Birendra had a liberal view'.[8]

Taking advantage of a popular rumour, which is fast becoming a widespread conviction and which claims that Gyanendra must have organized the massacre since he was absent at the time, apart from being the principal beneficiary, Maoist leaders have openly called him a murderer and an illegitimate king. In an unexpected reversal, these leaders have taken it upon themselves to uphold the values that the Shah kings supported, presenting themselves before the world as the natural successors to the Shah dynasty which, they claim, is now extinct. In a photomontage published in the pro-Maoist journal *Naulo Bihani* (2001), Maoist leaders are portrayed as maintaining a continuity with the Shah dynasty, which is shown to begin with Prithvi Narayan, the great warrior king who 'unified' Nepal. There are other indications of the Maoist strategy appropriating the glorious image of the Nepalese royal dynasty: Baburam Bhattarai, the other leader of the party, ends his press statement on the 'new Kot massacre' by citing Prithvi Narayan's famous injunction in his book of advice, the *Divya Upadeś*, to which the Nepalese ascribe an almost sacred status: 'Let everyone be alert'. The analogy between the Kot massacre and the royal massacre is itself rich in allusions, since the former event is perceived as having ushered in the autocratic and authoritarian rule of the Rana prime ministers, to the detriment of the legitimate rulers, who were reduced to mere puppets.

The People's War is repeatedly presented in Maoist writings as replicating Prithvi Narayan's unification, but on a 'voluntary' basis, in order to build a new state. To provide a concrete image of this future state, revolutionary meetings end with cultural shows that ostensibly represent the whole of Nepal, and demonstrate the voluntary association of different nationalities.

Since the assassination of King Birendra, the conflict has escalated into a direct confrontation between the Maoists and the king, each supported by their own army. The foremost slogan of the party has become: 'Down with the feudal-murderer Gyanendra clique'. The RNA is referred to as 'the hired asses of Gyanendra that go by the name of royal army', the Prime Minister is the 'king's vile lackey',

---

[8] Prachanda, 'On the Massacre of the Royal Family in Nepal'.

Gyanendra is the 'self-proclaimed "king"', the 'butcher', 'murderer', or 'puppet', the 'five times naked king'. Thus, the whole revolution has evolved into a civil war directed against the monarchy.

Henceforth, the army of the people will be opposed to the army of the king, which is no longer called 'royal' because it defends the kingdom, but merely because it defends the king.[9] In a recent statement, Baburam Bhattarai goes so far as to say that the Maoists are not seeking to establish a communist republic; nor are they seeking to share power with the current monarch:

...bourgeois (capitalistic) democratic revolution is the immediate political agenda and abolition of monarchy is the core issue of the entire project.... Whereas the one motivated (or ill-informed?) section prefers to believe the ultimate goal of this war to be nothing short of a communistic republic, the other keeps on harping it to be mere pressure tactics to get a larger share of loaf within the present monarchical dispensation. Both the views are...wide of the mark of the objective reality.[10]

The autocratic and feudal monarchy is a particular target, Bhattarai explains, because it combines in itself every different form of oppression: religious, regional and national. Furthermore, the monarchy dangles 'a Damocles sword over the parliament'. Thus, the monarchy is the target that needs to be destroyed.

Shortly after Gyanendra's dismissal of the prime minister on 4 October 2002, a move perceived as a 'coup', Prachanda directly defied the king, calling on him to sacrifice himself for the sake of the people and the nation by participating in a constituent assembly, which would draw up the new constitution.

In order to present himself as an alternative to the king, the principal leader of the CPN (M) had no choice but to adopt a warrior-like image, which he had only recently begun to cultivate.

PRACHANDA BECOMES A MILITARY LEADER

When the People's Liberation Army (PLA) held its first convention in September 2001, the arrival of Comrade Prachanda was greeted

---

[9] *Revolutionary Worker*, 1112, 29 July 2001.

[10] Bhattarai, 'A Communication from the Revolutionaries in Nepal on the Current (September 2002) Situation in the Civil War'.

with volleys of gunfire, in a manner similar to the arrival of the king at a military parade. Prachanda had himself proclaimed Supreme Commander of the People's Army on this occasion, thereby becoming the veritable alter ego of the king. There is a further parallel: just as the sovereign retained command over the army under the new constitution of 1990, the secretary of the Maoist party took over the official command of the armed forces just when rumours were rife about his conflict with the man who had until then been described as the head of the PLA. I am referring to Badal, a Magar rebel who had started a revolutionary movement called Sija, which the CPN (M) had managed to incorporate into their own. The rumour was widely put about, especially by army press organs. For example, the *Voice of the Army*, a mainstream publication, maintains:

> Frightened by the popularity of Comrade Badal, Prachanda...shivering and fearing to be killed by Badal...has dismissed him from the party. Having stopped the Sija campaign [led by Badal], he closed up the source of the 'Sija fountain of thought' and...created the Prachanda path.[11]

The Maoist answer to this rumour can be found in *Maoist Information Bulletin* 1:

> ...the reactionary rulers...tried to create the impression that a so-called military wing headed by Com. Badal [Ram Bahadur Thapa] was responsible for pressurizing the Party leadership to take the current course of action.... The actual reality is that our Party has developed a unified and centralized leadership under the supreme command of Chairman Prachanda and all the major decisions have been taken unanimously....Com. Prachanda is the Chairman of the Party and the Supreme Commander of the PLA....Certainly Com. Badal is not the 'Military Chief'....

By combining both executive and legislative powers, Prachanda has succeeded in gaining complete control over the movement, and, at least for the moment, in preventing the Magars from emancipating themselves and gaining access to the centre of power. Comrade Prachanda's speeches demonstrate that his new title of commander-in-chief of the army has required some adjustments: he declares it necessary 'to politicize the PLA', hinting at his intention to bring it under the stricter control of the party (and himself).

---

[11] Sampang, 'Janakrantidekhi janayuddhasamma'.

Henceforth, it is no longer about a popular movement struggling against oppressive reactionaries, but about the confrontation between two rival armies. The PLA is opposed to the RNA just as the leader of the party is opposed to the king, and the People's Council is presented as 'an alternative structure to the monarchical structure'. Like the monarch, the Maoist leader only expresses himself in the first person plural and retains control over his public image. There were only three known photos of him available in 2003, which have become veritable icons, and lend themselves to all kinds of photomontages. (It must be mentioned that the second photo already resembles a montage, with the head and the neck appearing much thicker than the arm and body of 'Prachanda'. It looks as if Prachanda's head has been superimposed on a body dressed as a Maoist.) Very few have seen him in the flesh, and his person is shrouded in mystery for villagers. However, they usually reject the possibility of his being an imaginary personage created by Bhattarai, as well as the more reasonable assertion that he is someone the latter uses for political purposes.

The invisible leader's speech and aura are certainly reinforced by his physical absence, which has raised him to the level of the 'terrible' legend that his name suggests (*prachanda*, in Nepali, means 'terrible').

SACRIFICE AND POWER

The rise of Maoist leaders to heights never previously attained, and the evolution of their movement can only be understood in relation to the image and behaviour of King Gyanendra. Steeped in the sea of blood that marked the occasion of his accession to the throne, and as the father of a prince infamous for alleged hit-and-run manslaughter offences, the king is described by Maoists with bloody imagery:

As if to fulfil a predetermined quota of human sacrifice every day, on an average more than two dozen persons per day have been brutally massacred by the RNA... [also called 'the royal butchers' in the same text].[12]

[12] *Maoist Information Bulletin*, 3, 2002.

However, far from dissociating himself from this bloodthirsty image, King Gyanendra has evidently opted to embrace it. His record so far is stamped with blood sacrifices and forceful actions, which have reverted to the wholly traditional models of the seizure and deployment of royal power in Nepal. At his first Dasain as king, Gyanendra set off on a pilgrimage of worship and sacrifice, visiting every temple on Nepalese territory that had a link to his dynasty. He went right back to the dynasty's origins—Lasargha, Gorkha, Nuwakot. Dasain, as we recall, is the great warrior festival, which reaffirms the sovereign in his position. During his first official visit to India, Gyanendra offered a total of five blood sacrifices to Kamakhya, the great Tantric goddess of Assam, an action that kept him in the news.[13] He then dismissed the prime minister and formed a new government, making use of a rather vague clause in the constitution to do so. Despite the fact that a large section of the royal family had been wiped out, the new king considerably augmented the annual allowance given him by the state.

Most of the king's actions, therefore, can be deemed repugnant, including his constant appeals to the gods, and demands for blood to flow. He has placed himself in a long tradition that might eventually end in the sacrifice—as the Maoists perceive it—of his own person, in either symbolic or real terms. An appeal for the sacrifice of the Butcher King at the Maoist movement's altar is made in a Nepali poem by Samir Yatri, published in the Maoist journal *Janaawaj*:

... swimming in a thick sea of blood
Which intoxicates and excites the gambler on his throne,
He staked all on the bloody tragedy of wiping out the
family of his own elder brother and killed him,
And calls himself the legitimate inheritor of the crown;
He killed him by drowning him in an ocean of blood,
And tasting blood, he feels exquisite pleasure.
He has become the puppet of the White House,
The butcher raised up in Narayan Hiti palace,
Has transformed a beautiful country into a charnel house,
He has made himself the Great King of slaughter.
This is the moment to burn the emperor on his funeral pyre,

---

[13] See, for example, 'Nepal King Leaves Bloody Trail Behind', *The Indian Express*, 28 June 2002.

This is the moment to throw the emperor in his tomb...
Let us wipe this emperor out with torture,
Let us turn his throne into his bed of thorns...

The figure of the king has quite possibly regained its catalytic role and even been reinvigorated in the context of the People's War, and in the aftermath of the royal massacre. This renewal of monarchy through the murder of the father (and/or the brother in popular imagination) and the assumption of power by the junior line takes us back to the origins of the Gorkha dynasty. Once again, the sovereign has allied himself with the Magar ethnic group which predominates in the western hill districts where the Maoists have their stronghold—just as his ancestors had done on numerous occasions in order to strengthen the king's power (his sword). After dismissing the elected prime minister in October 2002, Gyanendra appointed the president of the Magar ethnic association, Gore Bahadur Khapangi, as minister. Shortly afterwards, by some mysterious process, Lok Bahadur Thapa, the leader and founder of the Magar National Liberation Front, which had been an important ally of the Maoist movement, surrendered to the authorities. Soon after, the king, without consultation with any of the political parties, appointed another Magar, Narayan Singh Pun, the Minister of Works and Physical Planning, to lead the negotiations with the revolutionary leaders. This return to ancient forms of authority is not without its difficulties in the present context, and is likely to appear anachronistic to the growing urban elite.

On the other hand, the initial Maoist call for the sacrifice of (or by) the king has spread among the other political parties, particularly the Nepali Congress, as indicated by a recent newspaper headline: 'King's sacrifice needed for political stability: Experts'.[14] Among the experts quoted is Lok Raj Baral, professor of political science at Tribhuvan University, who declares: 'The more the king sacrifices, the easier will be the outlet'. Laxman Aryal, former Supreme Court judge and a member of the committee that had drafted the 1990 Constitution, adds: 'It is high time the king should express his sacrifice for the country'.

[14] G. Ojha, 'King's "Sacrifice" Needed for Political Stability: Experts', *The Kathmandu Post*, 2 June 2003.

CONCLUSION

I have argued that there is a connection between the emergence of the People's War and the gradual weakening of royal power in Nepal. Prachanda has increasingly represented himself as the king's alter ego, and, furthermore, as a legitimate ruler in opposition to a king who has been relegated to the rank of 'butcher', and thereby transformed into an unworthy version of the warrior king. The king has attempted to reinforce his role as sacrifier/sacrificer; however, the notion can be understood in manifold ways. While the king does indeed sacrifice to the gods, from the point of view of many he is sacrificing his subjects; the Maoists believe he should be the one to be sacrificed; and the main political parties proclaim that he should sacrifice his privileges for the welfare of the nation and for their own benefit. Kingly sacrifice is thus a matter of political consensus in present-day Nepal, and is perhaps the only political symbol on which everyone agrees. However, being a complex and highly contested notion, it is impossible to predict how it will apply to political developments in the future.

EPILOGUE

The Nepalese monarchy was abolished when Nepal became a republic on 28 May 2008.

9: A Young Magar Maoist Met on the Trail among a Hundred PLA Soldiers, Gulmi District (Photo: M. Lecomte-Tilouine).

8

'Kill one, he becomes one hundred'
Martyrdom as Generative Sacrifice in the Nepal People's War*

Launched in February 1996, the People's War has, over the course of ten years, caused at least 13,000 deaths. The Nepalese Maoists have a dual organization, comprising a political wing the CPN [M] and a military wing, the PLA, both under the leadership of Chairman Prachanda, a Nepalese Brahmin who lent his name to a local adaptation of Marxism-Leninism-Maoism called the Prachandapath, or Path of Prachanda.[1] Although it attaches significance to dialectics, on a theoretical level the Prachandapath often appears as a simplification of Marxism, using as it does binary oppositions such as oppressed-oppressor, proletariat-feudal and reactionary-revolutionary. In the military realm, the same binary view has been developed by one of the highest-ranking officers within the PLA, who believes there is only two types of war: just wars and unjust wars.[2]

---

* Originally published as '"Kill one, he becomes one hundred": Martyrdom as Generative Sacrifice in Nepal People's War', Special issue on 'Noble Death', Michael Roberts (ed.), *Social Analysis*, vol. 50, no. 1, 2006: 51–72.

[1] On the philosophy of the Prachandapath (in English), see, for instance, *Problems & Prospects of Revolution in Nepal*.

[2] Pasang, 'Yuddhako ek tippani'. Pasang is the commander of the PLA's western division (by far the most active division). In this text, Pasang considers war the initial state of humanity, and states that 90 per cent of the history of

Furthermore, these categories are not well-defined and cannot be easily applied to the multi-ethnic, multi-caste, and rather homogeneously poor society of Nepal (if we consider only the hilly part of the country).[3] However, it seems that the Nepalese Maoist movement combines Marxist ideology, from which it borrows its vocabulary and many of its ideas (in particular the scientific nature of its thought and methods and the historic nature of its actions), with a mystic theory that stresses the thaumaturgic effect of sacrifice, and its ability to effect political and social transformation. These two combined components provide a means through which to produce great men—on the first register, the thinkers of the movement, and on the second, any anonymous peasant who can attain posthumous and eternal glory through martyrdom or self-sacrifice.

In Nepal, in the past, war was equated with sacrifice. This was made explicit in the various practices reported, such as the conventional understanding that death on the battlefield does not pollute the relatives as death is normally supposed to do,[4] or the act of offering the bodies of slain enemies to a temple, which was observed by a Capucin father in the eighteenth century. The warrior's engagement is still described in present-day Nepal as a sacrificial gift of his own person, or *bali dān*. The warrior's sacrifice is not a substitution, as stated in Brahmanic theory, but an alternative: to offer the sacrifice (to kill) or to be offered in sacrifice (to die). The unknown presides over this alternative, which in both cases leads to glory. The relationship between them is symmetrical and, as such, close to the idea of substitution (by which the victims are interchangeable). But in the Maoist ideology, death loses its character of reciprocity: one's own warriors are noble and heroic, while the valour of one's opponents is denied or scorned. The rebel meets a 'glorious death' and becomes an 'eternal martyr'; however, the RNA soldier or oppressor is 'eliminated' or 'cleansed', or meets 'an infamous death'.

---

humanity was occupied by war, while the remaining 10 per cent was devoted to its preparation.

[3] Some aspects of this question are dealt with in M. Lecomte-Tilouine, 'Ethnic Demands within Maoism. Questions of Magar Territorial Autonomy, Nationality and Class'.

[4] Sharma, *Jutho sutak nirnaya*.

The one-sided sacrificial nature of the People's War (that is, the asymmetry of death) is a striking feature that distinguishes it from previous warfare. However, I argue that although this asymmetry is actively promoted by both sides as a condition that allows civil war or fraternal killing,[5] the conflict is perceived in a confused manner, even among the Maoists. Although they demonize the 'enemy' outrageously in their weekly publications, the Maoists also depict themselves through demonic imagery. Thus, they often portray themselves as the well-known demon killed by the Goddess: every drop of his blood that touches the ground gives birth to another demon. Similarly, the Maoist martyr's blood forms blood-seeds (*raktabīj*) that germinate in the land, giving birth to 100 warriors. Death and destruction are seen as creative.

Within the People's War, sacrifice aims at creating a better world on earth through its generative power, which will help realize the 'dreams of the martyrs'. This expectation contrasts with the celestial paradise promised to those who offered their lives as martyrs within Muslim or Christian traditions. In many ways, Nepalese revolutionary warriors appear as renouncers. They detach themselves (*tyāggarna*) from all selfish components of life, even from their material bodies, which they offer to the war as sacrifice 'on the altar (*vedī*) of the revolution'. Their renouncement is motivated by altruism. They act for the liberation of the people and the advent of a better world in a future that they will probably not enjoy. However, Maoist journals also stress the benefits accruing those who accept voluntary death. Self-sacrifice confers grandeur, shining glory and an abstract immortality on the fallen. It transforms them into stars that light up the dark world.

At present, we do not have a clear picture of the principal motivations behind individuals' desire to join the PLA; however, several Maoist authors state that 'a real culture of the martyrs has been created' by the People's War.[6] In fact, this 'culture' is

---

[5] Indeed, the government also denies the rebels an honorable status by referring to them as terrorists.

[6] The February 2003 editorial of *Janaawaji*, (50–1) reads as follows: 'The people who commemorate the martyrs have developped a new culture (*nayā saṁskṛti*) in which martyrs' doors and pillars are created, martyrs' photos are

also understood with reference to the agricultural meaning of 'cultivation', as the blood of the martyrs is said to 'irrigate the culture (*khetī*) of the People's War'.[7] The idea is sometimes presented as an imperative: the Path of Prachanda, which has been planted in Nepalese soil, needs to be irrigated with the martyrs' blood in order to grow.[8] This culture (in both senses of the term) is both constructed and fuelled by the abundant Maoist literature, as well as through ceremonies, memorial parks, songs and poems. I have particularly explored the poetry in order to understand the symbolic constructions that lead individuals to offer their lives in sacrifice, and to grasp the way a transformation has been effected from the figure of the hero (*bīr*), traditionally associated with the military realm, to that of a new figure, the martyr (*śahīd*).

Without valorizing military sacrifice, few wars could be undertaken. Its instrumentalization obviously depends on the form of the combat, and, in particular, on the mode of recruitment. In the Nepalese revolutionary movement—which has lasted for more than ten years—without the prospect of seizing power through weapons, victory and a possible rebuilding of society based on an order provided by the war seemed a utopian dream. This victory has been portrayed as 'a remote and luminous horizon', or 'a mountain' which, despite its difficulty, one endeavours to climb. Indeed, the People's War has evolved into guerrilla warfare, which has settled into a kind of durable balance of power status quo. The Maoists could mobilize the masses only after forming an alliance with the seven political parties;[9] however, the government forces were still unable to get rid of them. Since enlisting in the People's Liberation Army was based on free will, there must have been strong symbolic motivations at work to induce recruits to sacrifice themselves for a cause that was not likely to prove successful in the immediate future.

---

exhibited and villages, hamlets, companies, battalions and brigades are named with martyrs' names.'

[7] Rajesh, 'Melagairile punah tesro patak ragat bagaundako kshan'.

[8] B. Sharma, 'Bhalukholama shahadat prapta garnu hune mahan sahidharuprati hardik sraddhasuman'.

[9] On 31 August 2004, the CPN (M) announced the opening of a strategic offensive in the People's War. This followed the first period of 'strategic defensive', and a second one on 'strategic equilibrium'.

One can hardly give credence to the alternative notion which stated that the rebels were very naïve, or mere suicidal villagers, or were seeking monetary recompense.[10]

While the Maoist writings that could help decipher these inspirations are part of underground literature, significant portions are available on the Internet.[11] The two main Nepali newspapers follow the same model, with the first part focusing on current events, followed by theoretical pieces on Malema (Marxism-Leninism-Maoism), and finally a more popular section, including reports from battlefields, extracts from revolutionary soldiers' diaries, homage to the martyrs, and, invariably, poetry. This last category, through which ordinary individuals express themselves, provides most of the material studied here. Particular importance is accorded to poetry because of its perceived role in propagating the revolutionary movement. These revolutionary poems are 'written with the blood of martyrs', and are 'born from the ignited torch of the revolution', as Pandav Thapa explains. He then adds: 'literature has a rapid influence on the people. This is why the feelings conveyed in poetry fill people's life. If it were not thus, as our Chairman says, this type of literature would be poisonous.' Stanzas selected by Thapa for their 'vivifying' effect include the following lines, addressed by the poet to her martyred sister:[12]

The bullets that riddled your chest
made me swear to become bloodthirsty,
and I am focused while waiting on shortening the life of the butchers
who put you to death.

Prominence is given to poems written by close relatives of martyrs, more so to those composed by those who fell in battle. Poetry is understood as a mode of communication between the living

---

[10] The situation changed radically after the peace agreement, and several observers witnessed massive enrolment in the PLA in November 2006 after the official annoucement of a contingent of 35,000 soldiers. In the city of Pokhara, for instance, one observer estimates that 200 to 250 individuals were recruited in the Lake-side area with the offer of a monthly salary of Rs 5,000.

[11] Maoist writings ceased to be clandestine after the April 2006 movement. All the texts quoted in the present chapter can be read at http://www.cpnm.org.

[12] Pandava Thapa, 'Agoka muslobat umrieka kavitaharu. Dui'.

and the dead: the messages of (or to) the martyred dead acquire a supernatural force comparable to the glory of their death.

More than any other form of artistic expression, poetry is a vehicle of emotion in Nepal. In the villages, youngsters frequently open a diary containing this treasury in a very touching manner. Though the practice of penning poetry is widespread, I do not exclude the possibility that the 'popular' register recorded within Maoist journals might just be propaganda, written by a small number of leaders entusted with this moulding role. The homage addressed to beloved close kin who have died or gone missing displays the same noticeable determination, and always finishes in a very stereotypical fashion—with the solemn promise of revenge, which can be executed only by enrolling in the People's Army. Likewise, most of the published letters written by warriors before leaving for combat display an astonishing determination, and not the least sign of fear in the face of death.

Alternately, one wonders whether members of the Maoist movement have been conditioned so thoroughly that they all produce the same type of writing professing the same convictions in the same terms. It is likely that no one will ever know for certain. Yet, given the emphasis the chairman of the CPN (M) and Supreme commander of the PLA lays on the role of poetry, it is probable that control is exercised on the personnel's public outpourings.

However, this issue is secondary to the exploration of the impact of such publications. A newspaper such as *Janadesh* is widely distributed today, its sheets covering the walls of many peasant homes in rural Nepal, even those of households that do not seem all that revolutionary. One can thus be sure that its contents have a significant effect on its readers. The mystical cosmology of the Nepalese revolutionary universe is manifested in these printed artefacts, and we can reasonably consider its message to reflect—and influence—the spirit that leads to 'the gift of oneself'.

THE MARTYRED BODY

Violence and martyrdom occupy a large place in this literature, which defines both the nature of a human being and the history of humanity as violent, and war as the only means of obtaining political power. Although the Maoists present themselves as fundamentally superior to their 'enemies' in terms of military ability, they also view themselves as martyred people. Their hostility is seen as a legitimate response to the long history of violence inflicted by the state on the people, who are perceived as a broad suffering mass of people set suddenly ablaze. Thus, the martyred body is exalted as the image of revolutionaries and forms the image of those who revolt. Also, in a metaphorical way it symbolizes the revolution, the motherland, the truth.

Within the deepest darkness,
Truth is screaming,
Truth is crying,
But from its eyes it is no more tears but powder which has started to flow.
Those who seek to stop it, in the name of the supposed affront,
Each day assassinate people,
So that there is now no river or valley,
Which is not soaked with the blood of Truth, and strewn with its bones.
But,
The pools of Truth's blood, the pieces of its bones,
Having turned into bombs, here and there are exploding.[13]

This 'body of the revolution', of which each member forms a part, manifests itself in the large popular assemblies that pay homage to martyrs. These gatherings—which include relatives of martyred soldiers, as well as wounded soldiers and their close relations—are organized by the 'family of martyrs' (śahid parivār) or by the 'association of self sacrifice' (balidān sangh). On these occasions everyone listens to the speeches and appreciates the honourable attitude displayed by this core of afflicted people, who are placed in the front row, their faces covered with vermilion powder symbolizing the blood of the martyrs. These living martyrs call for revenge and ask for blood, reinforcing the anger of those assembled. The mothers of the martyrs are particularly placed in the role of pasionaria. The mother of the martyr Vinita (alias Mandhu Bhattarai) addressed the revolutionary warriors in these terms: 'My sons must bring the hot blood of the enemies to me, because it is necessary that I drink some before dying'.[14]

---

[13] Svalok, 'Yad gar Narayanhiti'.
[14] Anonymous, 'Janayuddha balidan sangh bankeko bhela sampanna'.

FAMILY TIES

The embryonic martyr is inexorably propagated and extended because of the fact that each drop of the martyr's blood is a 'blood seed' that give birth to a new warrior. Within the family of martyrs, as many texts testify, real kinship links are first activated to perpetuate the movement. A poem by Simana Sharma (2003), addressed to her martyred younger sister, reveals this theme.

Comrade Shyam,
Your unfulfilled great ambitions,
We will carry them out surely.
We will carry the rifle of your shoulder,
The red flag that you raised with your arm,
We will hold it up,
On the bloody way that you traced,
We will walk...
All the engagements that you were yet to achieve,
We will carry them out,
And even if it is necessary to die for the country and the people,
We will die.

Interestingly, the sibling ties between the poet and the martyr is absent in the poem, and is only revealed to the reader by the journalist introducing the poem. This subtle mechanism, designed to mark out the family tie while highlighting the lack of emphasis on the same, is part of a strategy of depersonalization.

Depersonalization helps to widen fraternal bonds to include the entire revolutionary family, and induces all members to share their deepest and innermost emotions. At the same time, it encourages the individual to not personalize the loss of a close relation, but to resituate the loss within a wider context. Thus, when faced with the question, 'What were your feelings when you learned the news of the martyrdom of your life companion and central member of the party?', posed by a journalist from *Janadesh*, Niru answered:

It is certain that we are social and material beings and one cannot deny that we have feelings, emotions and aversions. But rather than considering individually my life companion as a close relation of mine, he was an activist cherished by the proletariat....I do not deny that separation with his material form caused me sorrow...but when learning the news of his martyrdom, I remembered the 10,000 heroes and heroines who spilled their blood in the People war...and I told myself that without the overflowing of these million drops of blood the Prachanda Path could not have developed.[15]

Like many Maoists questioned under similar circumstances, Comrade Niru does not indulge in any sentimentalism. In their poems or farewell letters, the soldiers themselves often request their kinfolk to refrain from tearful lament; instead, the latter are asked to continue their action as a sign of homage. In his 'Message from the battlefield', Ksitij[16] says:

Father, whatever happens at the end,
do not let tears flow in front of the enemy,
sorrow is our friend...
rather than tears, anger should come out of your eyes.

At the same time, however, another narrative strand focuses closely on the sorrow experienced by close kin on the occasion of a martyr's death.

The rhetoric in this case is also very stereotyped, with sorrow being described at length in order to show how it transmutes into energy, anger, and the determination for revenge. In this way, martyrdom is considered to bring energy (urjā) to the revolution. Let us take the wounded Kalpana's account of her reaction to the news of the death of her comrade, who had fought with another brigade in the same battle.

When this brother told me that my friend had received martyrdom with the face of a kitten, I received a blow in the chest twice as painful as the one I had received in the hand. During sleeping time...I had the impression that an enormous weight was crushing me. I could not know if it was a dream or reality. Seeking to escape from this state, I started to have convulsions, I tried to shake my body, but it was not a dream, it was reality. In spite of my convulsions, I heard this news in truth. Out of our two hearts, we had formed one in the last year, so I had the impression that a large stone had struck my head, that my legs were trapped in mud, and that the sky was filled by enormous black clouds. Was I then asleep or did I walk? Did my friends carry me? I do not know anything of it, but I found myself at the last place where we had spoken, my friend and I. There I searched all around me, but this time was quite completed....Even if I better understood then the meaning of life and of the world and how self-sacrifice is the very energy of revolt, the separation with

---

[15] Darlami, 'Kamared Vishal lagayatko shahadatle krantilai ajhai ucaima puryaune cha'.

[16] Ksitij, 'Ranabhumibata sandesh'.

my friend for life, this treasure of thought and honest commander, burned me atrociously. Even if the martyrdom is inevitable, the eyes roll when considering the way by which it comes. But I made his death run into my being and finding myself as a member of the family of the martyrs, I experienced pride. By his death, his physical body was offered, but it made him survive. This is why...having transformed my tears into anger, having glued the pieces of my heart with the help of the Thought, I am now walking on the path which he showed....I will fulfil the dream that he left unfinished....Having offered my body, like comrade Yoddha, I'll know this moment and to mix my blood with his, on this path, bearing bag and rifle, the spirit embellished by the Great Thought, I've joined another war expedition.[17]

The family of martyrs is much wider than the circle of kinsmen. It includes every comrade, and thus the whole of the Maoist Party and Army, composing an assembly of 'comrades'. One mother of a martyr therefore addressed all the fighters as 'sons'—a pronouncement that shows how kinship ties are formed by the spilling of blood. Again, a top leader in the PLA, Badal, placed the martyrs (and possibly their families) in a generation that stood above the living comrades when he considered the latter 'the progeny (*santān*) of the martyrs'.[18] No differentiation is made between the living comrades: it is difficult to draw a clear distinction between friendship relations, marital relations or kinship relations, for they all address each other as comrade or life companions. Furthermore, they bear *noms de guerre*, which are often neutral or abstract, sometimes keeping even their gender ambiguous.

Not only is the martyrs' blood believed to give rise to new soldiers, but it is also elevated to the status of a holy, creative substance, one generating new social or political structures. It imbues the revolutionary movement with strength and energy, solidifies the earth or ground upon which the revolution takes place, and forms the foundation for new revolutionary orders.[19] As the martyrs are immortal, their blood, which contains their vital energy, is 'a never

[17] Kalpana, 'Benima jivansathi Ka. Yoddhako sahadatpachi sangalo anubhutiharu'.

[18] Ram Bahadur Thapa, 'Hami cunautiharuko mukabila garna jastosukai mulya cukauna pani tayar chaun'.

[19] Thus, the People's government of the district of Jajarkot is said to have been built on a foundation created by the blood of the sixty-five martyrs of the district. This holds true for the PLA battalions as well (blood foundation = *ragatko jag*).

drying blood'.[20] Those enlisted in the armed struggle incorporate this vital substance by collecting the martyr's blood (or a handful of earth mixed with it, or a symbolic red powder), and placing it on the forehead as a visible sign of this unification. At this moment, too, one swears an oath to carry the martyr's weapons and fulfil his or her 'dreams'.

The martyr thus survives not only in a spiritual form, but is also physically replaced with other warriors. These new recruits adopt new names, signifying the change their identities undergo joining the party. They no longer belong to themselves after this 'gift'. Despite such symbolic readjustments, upon a party member's death, his or her familial links are reiterated in a complicated manner. The martyr's family is granted a central place while paying homage, though the mourning rituals are not usually performed by relatives. This innovation stems from two aspects of former practices: first, death on the battlefield was traditionally credited with purity; and second, that martyrs are likened to ascetics, figures who are supposed to have burned their normal lives away and secured immortality.

CAMARADERIE

Due to the strong friendship ties, and perhaps because it prefigures one's own fate, the loss of a comrade is evoked in extremely touching terms, giving rise to similar expressions of determination and revenge. The commemoration texts (*śahid gāthā*) give the impression that the sentiment invoked by an alter ego's death is one way in which to transform loss and sorrow into destructive energy. At the same time, the publication of these intimate texts communicates this transformation and energy to others.

The terms and images used are similar in all the texts: the 'fire of sorrow burns in the spirit (*man*)', on the chest (*chātti*) 'weighs the heavy stone of pain', the 'soul (*ātmā*) is besieged by separation', 'the cloud of the feelings, burst by the sorrow, makes a rain of tears fall'. All these impressions spark the flames of fury, generate a desire for revenge, and create or reinforce a feeling of 'disgust' vis-à-vis the enemy.

[20] Regmi, 'Bīr sahid Ka. Ayamlai samjhada'.

How to start to describe the reality of the event? I am besieged by sorrow. In front of my eyes whirl the black clouds of emotion. They make a downpour of tears rain from my eyes. I have difficulties dealing with myself. I remember the remark of comrade Prachanda: 'war is science, art and also feeling'. In truth, for us the revolutionaries, the feelings are quite related to the science and the art of war. It is perhaps for this reason that it is difficult to manage the sorrow. Physical separation with my friend for life, my partner of war, comrade Rejina, did not only pain me, it also gave birth to anger in me. Flames burn in my eyes. The tears which run from my eyes act as oil in [the fire of] my thought. Her heroic martyrdom brings energy to the People's War. It gives birth to the feeling of fury. I am now disgusted by the enemy and full of a feeling of revenge. The physical body of comrade Rejina is no more in front of us, we will not see her ever again in her material form, it left this earth. But if her physical body fell, her thought did not fall, rather, by giving her life in sacrifice for the people and the country, she obtained the privilege of inscribing her name in the pages of history.[21]

The image of a burning fire within, one that is used repeatedly to describe the sentiments of a soldier ready for sacrifices in war, recalls the interiorization of fire on the part of the ascetic, who incorporates the sacrificial fire at the time of initiation, the ultimate cremation fire that forever detaches the individual from normal, mundane life. However, the Maoist warrior's internal fire completely destroys not only the selfish components of the individual, but also its enemies, the rotten regime. As such, it represents the fire at the end of time, or the ultimate war-like chaos before the Golden Age.

Human Weapons, Cast Indestructible

We are the volcano ready to explode,
We are the fire holders, the fire collectors,
Those who have nothing to lose,
But the wide world and all the rights to conquer...
In us occur the tremors of a daring earthquake,
Our heart is filled with the powder of sorrow and fever
Which presses our spirit and causes the insurrection,
We have a bomb in place of the head.[22]

At the same time that the body is offered in sacrifice, it is transformed into a terrible, explosive weapon, one forged in anger and set in iron. Such a martyr is Krishna Sen:

[21] Rima, 'Mero manaspatalma Ka. Rejina'.
[22] Isvarcandra Gyawali, 'Hami ra uniharu'.

When I
Saw him
I saw iron.
As iron
I saw him hot
I saw him red
I saw him strong
I saw him
Effective as
A bullet.[23]

The most effective and simplest kind of iron weapon of death is evoked in the poem's incisive form. Contrary to the 'heroes', the red soldiers are not just equipped with weapons, they are themselves the human weapons of apocalypse.[24] In this perception, nothing can affect the revolutionary soldier, whose destructive capacity is increased by his mutilation,[25] in the same way that the revolutionary army emanates from the repression directed against it.

Cut my hands, break my legs
Pull out my tongue, extract my eyes
I won't stop speaking, I won't stop walking
I'll write ever and ever,
I'll rather see better...
Destroy villages

[23] Sushanta, 'Sahid Krishna Sen! Lalsalam!!'

[24] Though the red soldiers are ready to die, martyrdom does not result from personal desire; rather, it responds to a necessity, a request formulated by the country, by Mother Nepal or by History:

My dear friend fell.
His spilled blood tinted the sky and the earth,
The top of Everest bowed as a sign of respect,
The rifle shot...
More blood must run,
The country requires ours,
If the earth asks for it,
We will offer it here in sacrifice (Sangkalpa, Untitled Song).

It is not by desire or wish,
His sacrifice was required by the country and by History (Ranabir, 'Jivan').

[25] The body is hardened by martyrdom (of oneself or others), the feelings are transmuted into anger, and the iron body is sometimes no mere image, as the bullets in the body are said to bring strength—as reported by a wounded soldier who kept several bullets in his body.

Make a river of blood flow...
Blood seeds will germinate.[26]

The revolution cannot be attacked, for 'the soldiers can have their eyes burst, their legs broken, the eyes and the legs of the revolution remain intact'.[27]

BEAUTIFUL DEATH

In the Nepalese Maoist philosophy, the meaning of human life is principally focused on death: achievements during one's lifetime and the value of life are considered negligible. Time after time, the reader of Maoist literature is taught that birth means death, and that self-sacrifice brings meaning to this inescapable event. It is death that distinguishes immortals from those whose fate, quite simply, is to be 'cleaned' (saphāya).

Human beings are born and then die. It is the law of Nature. No one can divert or stop it....The only difference in death is for what purpose one dies, how one dies and which death brings honour. The one who considers that his personal interest is meaningless and...who offers himself in sacrifice in the People's War, to this one death confers splendour of honour. Or the one who understood the definition of life and death and who understood that once born, it is necessary to die, only this one can know a splendid (ojilo) and high (uccā) death. In the class struggle for the liberation of the members of the oppressed class, more than 8,000 heroic sons and daughters of Mother Nepal offered their life in sacrifice. The sacrifice and the renunciation of these sacrificed soldiers made it possible to reach the top of Everest....The great warrior Comrade Rejina, having given up her pleasure and her material well-being, having understood that birth means death, is known by her death in the Great People's War, a death heavier than a mountain, higher than the top of Everest.[28]

Thus, as part of their mobilizing strategies, Maoist leaders propagate the idea that to die right now is ultimately not such a terrible thing.

---

[26] Vivash Yatri, 'Marne chaina kadapi jantako astha'. Many texts reporting the last moments of martyred soldiers echo this poem:
'The assassins broke his arms and legs and poured boiling water on his face....All his flesh fell from his head and face but Ayam continued to defy the enemy' (Sudha Regmi, 'Bīr sahid Ka. Ayamlai samjhada').

[27] Anonymous, 'Ghaite shivirma cahalpahal'.

[28] Rima, 'Mero manaspatalma Ka. Rejina'.

The grandeur of a splendid death through martyrdom are hence offered to even the humblest peasants in the People's War.

Since February 1996, the CPN(M) has been annually celebrating, in a highly symbolic manner, the 'week of the martyrs', which begins each year on the day the first official martyr of the People's War was killed. This great figure happens to be a young schoolboy, who was a Dalit (an 'untouchable'), and fourteen years old at the time of his death. The youthfulness of this icon and his traditionally depressed caste status contributes significantly to the popularity of martyrs' life stories. The following homage to Ka. Gopi (Dhanraj Gurung), an Indian citizen of Nepalese origin, written by his superior officer in the Maoist army, shows how martyrdom confers instantaneous fame and reverses hierarchy inside the PLA:

I want to speak of someone whose material life is no more, but whose life history remains alive. Who is he, who was he? How has he inscribed his name in history in such a short time? I will make this young person who survives whereas he is dead stand up right in front of you....He who respected me, now I hold him in respect, calling him my venerable martyr.[29]

In Nepal, the concept of martyrdom clearly depends on rebelling against an established power and thus on the imbalance embodied in the conflict, one that pits the weak against the mighty. In PLA representations, the first martyrs of Nepal are those who fought against the powerful Rana government, which they helped overthrow in 1951. In fact, the Maoists seek to federate all revolutionary movements under their own banner. Thus, the last day in the 'week of the martyrs' commemorates the peasant revolt of Jhapa, which occurred in 1972, well before the Maoists' own movement was born. In the context of the ongoing People's War, any person killed by governmental forces is given the status of martyr, even if he or she was not a member of the CPN (M). As for members of the CPN (M), they are considered martyrs and worshipped as such even if their death resulted from an accident.[30]

---

[29] Budha Magar, 'Nepali janayuddhama sahadat ek bharatiya Ka. Gopi'.

[30] As I saw in April 2003 in Dailekh district, where the CPN(M) had organized a meeting in memory of the district in charge who had died in a motorcycle accident.

DEMONIC ENEMIES

The development of a martyrology was made possible through the construction of an asymmetry between revolutionary and government forces, an asymmetry engineered through an emphasis on the enemy's radical alterity, and his dehumanization. Thus, one strand of representation denigrates state soldiers by depicting them as cowards who run away,[31] denying them the honourable status of warriors in contrast to revolutionary soldiers, who are ready to face the enemy and embrace death. Another strand of imagery portrays the government forces as mad assassins who kill everyone, from newborn babies to grandmothers, just for pleasure.[32] They are 'butchers' who have turned Nepal into a lake of blood.[33]

Mixing human blood with alcohol,
They drink it avidly...
The butchers who trade human flesh...
Captured 21 hopeful heroes
And,
Having bound their hands behind their back,
With their M16 bought by selling human blood,
They placed them in a line
And shot bullets in their temples.
In Doramba and Dandakateri they made a flood of blood run...
And performed a dance of demons. [34]

The government forces are denied even human status through such disparaging references to forces of ill-omen, such as bloodthirsty lions,[35] vultures,[36] dogs, or jackals.

The dehumanization of state forces is hammered in by constant reference to them as 'demons' (rakshas or *dānava*) who drink blood, imbibe intoxicating alcohol, and eat human flesh. They are said to indulge in man-hunting,[37] throwing little children into the fire, and

[31] Or who capture defenceless isolated red soldiers by encircling them, and then execute them.

[32] Rajesh, 'Melagairile punah tesro patak ragat bagaundako kshan'.

[33] Sitalkumar, 'Dhvans ra nirmanko dvandvatmak visleshana'.

[34] Vikas, 'Pyara pyara kamaredharuko samjhanama'.

[35] Anu, 'Muktiko nisvas pherne cahancha—svatantra'.

[36] Rima, 'Mero manaspatalma Ka. Rejina'.

[37] Rajesh, 'Melagairile punah tesro patak ragat bagaundako kshan'.

torturing their prisoners in abominable ways. In this manner, the People's War is cast as a re-enactment of the war between human beings (*mānava*) and demons (*dānava*).[38]

All these demonic attributes peak and coalesce within the persona of the opposing side's supreme commander, the king. Since the royal massacre of June 2001 and the coronation of King Gyanendra (Gyane, for the Maoists), the conflict has become more acute. The king is the object of the most derisive practices and discourse: his effigy is regularly burned, with the mise en scène sometimes including a collective round of spitting and shooting at his image, after which he is symbolically cremated.[39]

While singing the song of devotion to the nation,
To use a dagger to kill her,
To divert the cultural and natural goods,
While posing as the guardian of nature
Hey, king of the sale of our country!
Even the vultures which will walk on your corpse will be foreigners.
To give the title of heroism to slaughter,
To stamp on people, perched on Pashupati's bull,
To rape history
And drown truth in the Seti River to get rid of it
Hey, king of the landed properties!
Even the vultures which will walk on your corpse will be foreigners.
To destroy the beautiful villages,
To have killed those who one envies and to sell their flesh.
While making offerings to the rivers Koshi, Gandaki and Karnali,
To sell their water and to drink blood
Hey, king of the butchers!
Even the vultures which will walk on your corpse will be foreigners.
In the country of the red men, to display the black snakes' play,
To be delighted by the deaths which occur
In the poor and exploited villages,
Hey, king of the palaces!
Even the dog which will pour tears on your corpse will be a foreigner.
To go hunting in the villages with automatic weapons
And American helicopters

---

[38] Bhagat, 'Nepalma madhesko varga-samgharsa: Ek samksipta adhyayan'.

[39] These practices were, for instance, reported in Doti, western Nepal, in spring 2004. Anonymous, 'Hatyara Gyanendra ...'

To make economic blockades of the remote and hungry villages
Hey, king of the oppressors!
Even the vultures which will walk on your corpse will be foreigners.
Automatic weapons will not be able to save your government.
The assembled people will not be able to forgive you
Through the malediction of the bluebottles on your corpse,
Your cadaver will not die.
This is why if you have some honour,
For your country, come with a machine-gun,
Come with a Nepal made night vision helicopter,
As for us, we will place a stone of the country on your grave!
We will make the vultures of our woods fly on your cadaver.[40]

This complete negation of the enemy's humanity is a way of asserting that 'to clean' does not translate into 'to kill'. As in the sacrificial context, murder is denied. Though in both contexts (Brahmanic sacrifice and the People's War) violence is directed at the unification of the collective and towards creating a better world, the treatment of the victims stands out in stark contrast. In the sacrificial context, the animal is treated as a human (or conscious) being, and its consent is asked for before it is killed. The victim is fated to obtain a better status through its death. In the People's War, by contrast, the human victim is treated as an animal or demon that is doomed to be eliminated, or, like the king in the above poem, to remain forever a decaying corpse, trampled and defiled by the most horrific of creatures: foreign vultures, dogs and bluebottles.

With the construction of the king as the scapegoat of the nation, several approaches have been made to government soldiers to entice them to change camps. Captured soldiers were released after some lecturing, and wounded enemies were even treated. By assuming absolute power on 1 February 2005, the king may finally have adopted the role attributed to him by the Maoists since his coronation, and led to a form of unity in the country, that is, the alliance of all political parties against him.

INVERTED VALUES

The asymmetry elaborated within the People's War relies more generally on a global inversion of values, which is expressed in

[40] Chavi Subedi, 'Tera lashmathi gumne...'

strikingly through poetry and contributes to the morbidity of the Maoist universe. The poems contain detailed descriptions of the bloodiest events, invoking forceful images and delighting in the contemplation of announced, violent death. Voluntary immersion in this universe hardens the revolutionary soldier, who consequently fears nothing. Once the inversion of values is complete and the plunge into the ocean of revolution has been taken, no hold over the individual is possible, as illustrated in this poem by the woman soldier Laksmi Gurung:[41]

I have embraced death
O enemies do not try to set fire to my head,
As I am already ablaze by the sparks of the fire (of revolution)
Do not laugh, by spreading out in front of me thousands of corpses,
Because I am the traveller who crosses the ocean of blood,
Having made a bridge of these corpses.
Do not try to attach me with iron chains,
As I am already tied by the philosophy of equality,
By the thought of justice and freedom.
Do not try to make me beg for life in alms
As I have already embraced death
And I am immutable like the mountain
In my opposition to the class enemies,
Such as a war heroine.

Fire, corpses and chains are the weapons of the revolutionary warrior, who thus diverts the forces of coercion, denying them power over body or spirit, which have already embraced death. This process resembles a conversion to symbolic self-martyrdom, which then enables the warrior to face his or her real (or physical) demise, for it has already been embraced mentally. Death is interiorized and accepted in advance so that nothing can unsettle the warrior.

In particular, it is the experience of an alter ego's or comrade's martyrdom that facilitates this plunge into death, this substitution between the dead and the living. While expressed metaphorically in poetry, it is displayed more concretely by a mourning scarf (kaphan), which the revolutionary wears as a sign of mourning and a mark of self-sacrifice assumed at the time of recruitment. As they don it, they proclaim 'After having offered oneself in sacrifice in the

---

[41] 'Mrityulai angalisakeki chu'.

war, it is necessary to fall one day'.[42] Death is thus minimized to its furthest extent. It does not affect the individual in his or her essence; rather, it merely refers to 'the fall' (*dhalna*) of the physical body (*bhautik śarir*).

To be close to death—and to touch it, to touch the corpses—transforms one's perception of it. Death then becomes beautiful and desirable, as are the people whom one still loves in this state, as expressed by Ganga Shrestha,[43] another woman warrior.

Dear death
One might wonder how death can be dear?
How death can be beautiful?
But death can be dear, as no one can believe,
Can be beautiful as no one can imagine.
If you don't believe it
Touch and look at the death of Basu
Touch and look at the death of Icchuk
There, you'll meet the dream of Communism,
There you'll see the definition of life.

It is in the death of martyrs that the definition of life can be grasped, because it holds out a worthy promise of life for future generations. If one lives as if dead, one enters true life through death, contributing to its occurrence in the 'material world'. Consequently, all values are inverted: happiness becomes misfortune and misfortune brings happiness; life (under the present regime) is death, and death (in the People's War) means eternal life. This is the basis of the Nepalese Maoist dialectic, subsumed and inscribed within a catchphrase of Chairman Prachanda's, 'We cry while laughing, we laugh while crying', which is often cited and has inspired several texts in many modalities.

Sorrow is happiness
...Seeing happiness, I am not happy, me,
Because I wish that happiness comes from sorrow
And I do not want to see the sorrow, while enjoying happiness.

---

[42] '*Yuddhamā homiepachi ek din dhalna ta āvaśya nai ho*', in Cetan Kunwar, 'Janamukti sena yasari samarpit hundeichan mahilaharu'.
[43] 'Pyaro mrityu'.

Whatever the sorrow that it creates for us,
Our travel will be victorious,
Because sorrow leads us towards the good side.
Material happiness is dangerous for progress,
Internal sorrow shall not affect us,
Because it prevents us from reaching our goal
O friends![44]

As with an ascetic who dominates his material body through
austerities, the Maoist warrior shields his body and hardens his
mind, thereby rendering them both immune to the usual sensations.
In a significant account, Bahu[45] describes how the sensations of
tiredness, thirst, heat and fatigue are lost during a war expedition,
and taken over by feelings of subjugation and fusion—of oneself
into a huge, terrible and magnificent army collective.

SUBJUGATION

In this account, Bahu describes the attack on Ghorahi, in which
he participated. The march towards this southern location lasted
three or four days. From the outset, the revolutionaries had lost
their appetites, as well as sensations of thirst, cold and fatigue. They
walked in the sun and did not stop till they finally reached a big
pastureland, where they were allowed to sleep. Other companies
joined them there. Bahu then says that the spectacle of the People's
Army is so attractive that 'he loses [himself] in its contemplation',
and that he had the desire 'to lose [himself] in its crowd'.

This power of subjugation is expressed in Maoist poetry in such
a participatory manner that it almost resembles incantatory poetry.
It draws the reader into a tale of conflict by letting him or her share
in the emotion of death, the shock of war. It displays images that
evoke violence in its instantaneity in order to actualize the violence,
so that one participates in it through the act of reading.

Just at that time, at the time when
The old, collapsing and rotten world is on the verge of falling
And the goods of its Master are carried away by the flames

---

[44] D. Sharma, 'Dukh nai sukh ho'.
[45] Bahu, 'Mero mastishkama sajieko mansir 8 gate'.

The sanguinary killers are made insane,
They drink the blood of innocent people, they are taking their life!!
They rape our younger sisters! They are raping them!!
They empty the mothers' womb! They are emptying !!
The brothers and the fathers are in the same tomb! They are there!!
The infants will not survive! No, they won't!!
The grandmothers and grandfathers cannot sit on a wall or in a corner of the
courtyard without fear!
They are killed too, they are killed in a disgusting manner!!
A flood of blood ran and is still running!
But,
A better and golden world
A world thirsty of justice, freedom and democracy,
Gradually enflames.
Just at that time, at the time when
The assassins nostalgic of the feudal subjection
Have turned days into nights!
They are eating people alive.
They are raping our mother Nepal.
Some living corpses, having given their assent and their quiet support,
Are awaking the damned souls of the Panchayat.[46]

Through repetitive formulas expressed in the present tense and at
the very moment of action, this poem has a compelling effect. Its
density recalls a crisis that evoked panic, and entices the reader to
lend assistance.

The reader shares the revolutionary soldier's feelings at the most
intense times, and participates in the attacks by being placed on
side of the revolutionaries. He seeks refuge in a small shed, hears
the bullets from an invisible helicopter, and sees the shocking sight
of red blood against the white fog. Suddenly all the dead martyrs,
covered in blood, stand before him, brandishing their fists, enticing
him to follow their bloody path.

...

The destroying bullets drive in all directions,
Crossing the wood of the doors and shutters,
They rain like hail
On the heads and the chests of the People's warriors.
At this moment, tightening the fist, Botle, looked at the horizon,

[46] L. Bista, 'Thik yatibela'.

A sign of the end of the world,
A flash of what is love,
The brutal cut of separation...
When in the sky, black clouds were whirling,
The weak curtain of the fine fog
Wrapped me as they were looking at me,
On the white fog, a jet of blood,
A rain of blood running drop by drop...
At this moment, comrade Niru...
Comrades Hari, Govinda, Santvana and Sanjita,
Nipeksa, Renuka and Cunauti,
One after the other stand up, even if they have fallen,
Covered by blood, raising their fists...[47]

EXULTATION

Though clearly violent and bloody, the PLA's way of life is also presented as pleasant and joyful. Its goal is magnificent. It aspires not only to a local change in leaders, but to the liberation of the twenty-first century, which the PLA was to initiate with one of the smallest and poorest countries of the world as its vanguard.

I am the minstrel who strives for the liberation of the 21st century
And walks, mixing his voice to the sweet
Melody uttered by the bloody footprints of the red
Men, on their way for the Great War.[48]

Several texts even dwell on the exultation that possesses the revolutionary soldier during marches and attacks; on the grandeur and beauty experienced within the People's War, and the thought that inspires them.

How pleasant is our life in the Great War
Devoted to the liberation of the people and country
Nothing is individual any more, selfishness has been destroyed,
We walk, with widened spirit, in the tempest.
Our personal goal is to make blood flow for the liberation of the classes,
It is to build a New World after having destroyed this rotten one,
In the dialectic of laughter and tears, the history of happiness and pride.
On the way, the floods of blood strengthen the action, the will.

[47] Sangram, 'Mutthi kascha bottle ksitijma herera'.
[48] Kadam, 'Muktikami gaineko git'.

Highlighting the dream of the martyrs, we reach our goal in our spirit,
We fight as the thunderbolt, playing in the storm,
Our work is the revolution, our house is the Party.
Greater still is the Thought,
The Marxism-Leninism-Maoism and the Path of Prachanda are very beautiful.[49]

All Maoist partisans express their preference for the military branch of the movement, and speak of their impatience to be recruited into the army.

When a *Janadesh* journalist posed the question, 'What do you prefer, and why, between the organization of the party and the formation of the army?' the wounded Pushpa answered: 'It is not a question of liking the party or the army but of working where it is necessary. However, if I have the choice, I prefer to work in the formation of the army.'

The diary of Agrim, a PLA soldier who died in 2004 in the attack of Beni, bears testimony to the very mysterious pleasure felt by the self-sacrificing soldier:

Eight people of our platoon prepared for a task, we did not know for what and yet we were impatient on the way. Finally we arrived at the border of the district of Rolpa and comrades of other platoons joined us there...the walk pleased me enormously...and since I had been integrated in a formation of the army, I had the feeling of being a bird out of its cage which finally flies in the sky...
I was very happy to be in the assault group. I made a mental oath: if it is needed, I will let my blood run first to take the camp of the enemy....I looked at the expression of my comrades and in the eyes of each one, I saw a kind of glare (*camak*), in the expression of each of them I saw the anger of the revenge....I was impatient to plant the flag of liberation in the enemy's chest.[50]

Though Agrim was keen to attend a 'great meeting [that] was taking place in Dang', he and his platoon followed orders and attended a medical training session, where one exercise involved an indirect 'writing from five in the morning until midnight [till] blisters formed on our hands and they even burst'. Agrim, then, was not master of his own destiny. Indirectly, Agrim and Pushpa reveal

---

[49] Pahadi, 'Hamro jindagi'.
[50] Agrim, 'Mero dayari yasari adhurai rahyo'.

the hold the PLA leadership had over the soldiers. Obedience was
unswerving, commitment total.

LANDSCAPE IN PATHOS AND REVOLUTIONARY MODE

In their representations, the partisans' attachment to the movement
does not seem to differ radically from the interconnections between
elements in nature, as if an adherence to revolution was above all
a mystic bond between the living and the dead, between human
beings, animals and the world. Poetry underlines this adherence,
and affirms the participation of all beings in the revolution. Thus
Ghayal[51] asserts, '[T]he martyrdom of Comrade Vikalpa did not only
make the people cry, but also the villages and the forests where he
used to go.' While the landscape participates in the sorrow of defeat,
it is conversely delighted by victory, tales of which are recounted
by the mountains to the valleys, while the rivers, inflated with joy,
announce them to everyone. Bahu[52] recalls:

The stars threw their light. That night the moon also brought all its bright-
ness to us. Even the moon needed to look closely at our war for justice and
the rivers Rapti and Babai were swollen with joy and made everyone hear the
news of the victory of the great people. The sun also replenished a new light
of victory.

The elements appeared to literally participate in the attack on
Ghorahi, and many a homage to martyrs used the trope of a
mountain bowing in sadness and respect at the moment of a red
soldier's death.

On the front, in the blackberry pasture,
The three stars of the east found heroism...
By a full moon night,
Even the moon masked its face,
Mount Everest bowed its head.[53]

The motherland receives the blood of her own children and cries
bitterly. She is disfigured by the violence inflicted on the people.
Even the little birds are no longer in the mood for singing.

---

[51] 'Sahid ka. Vikalpalai gumaundako ksana'.
[52] Bahu, 'Mero mastishkama sajieko mansir 8 gate'.
[53] M. Thapa, 'Purvako tin tara'.

Today, in the river beds,
More than stones, there are
Human skulls and bones
The patches of innocent blood
Render the beautiful mountains disgusting...
In the pastures where you played,
The birds of the wood keep silent now.[54]

The revolution itself designs a universe, an imaginary world comprising an ocean of blood that the red soldiers swim across,[55] or traverse using the corpses of their comrades as a bridge. Above is the sky where all the martyrs have turned into stars that light up the revolutionary path, pointing it towards victory. Located in the east, the inaccessible mountain peak shines, surrounded by the rising sun's red horizon. The heavenly body is itself dressed in red, and spreads its rays as a sign of revolt. Through their blood and their lights, the martyrs help 'travellers' to approach the summit, almost as if the level of the ocean of blood was rising with each death, and moving towards the peak of victory. This bloodbath strengthens the revolutionaries, solidifies the soil, purifies the party, and fertilizes the revolution.

CONCLUDING REMARKS

The struggle against the old world is thus presented as an apocalypse, provoked by warriors ablaze with fury, fighters who have sworn to die and multiply till the end. If the Marxist vocabulary is set aside, this cosmogony strongly reminds one of an apocalyptic sect, whose aim is to provoke the end of the world in order to promote the advent of a better one.

The red warriors are ascetics: they renounce alcohol, seduction and material well-being. They sleep, and often live, in the forest. They practise daily corporal austerities, and they study hard. In a

---

[54] Yuvaraj Chaulagai, 'Au Yuyutsu'. This poem, entitled 'Come Yuyutsu' (a famous general in the Mahabharata who changed sides from the Kauravas to the Pandavas), is a call to the RNA soldiers.

[55] Many texts use this image. For one example, see Kulman Budha Magar, 'Nepali janayuddhama sahadat ek bharatiya Ka. Gopi'.

word, they forge iron bodies[56] of themselves—incandescent iron bodies fuelled by a terrible internal raging fury. Their goal is to kill the enemy and cleanse the motherland, and to die a 'noble death'. They are conducting a vast purification process in which they form the fire oblations.

The enemies, on the other hand, are associated with all kinds of evil forces. They are the demons fought by the gods, the wicked and powerful Kaurava pitted against the Pandava, or the demonic forces that were eliminated by the Goddess. The Goddess appears similar to the red warriors, since she too was born as a terrible red woman soldier from the anger of the assembled gods. Traditionally, the Goddess' ritual destruction of evil forces is re-enacted each year by the Hindu king (or his representative) through a sacrifice of buffaloes. This sacrifice differs radically from the Brahmanic sacrifice, since the victim does not represent the self, but the enemy's forces. This explains why this type of sacrifice is a prerogative of the ultimate tenant of power. It is therefore a kingly model, a Kshatriya modality.

Interestingly, the People's War seems to have combined the two models of sacrifice in its ideological architecture: the Brahmanic and ascetic self-sacrifice is adopted as the Maoist model, while the kingly destruction of demonic forces is one facet of their struggle against the rotten 'royal' side. In addition, the Maoists incorporate an image of their own power as one that spreads terror, for they frequently employ the idea that, like demonic power, the contact their blood makes with the earth serves to multiple their forces.

The Maoists have thus adopted the most potent sources of power in the Hindu world, and have created an asymmetry in the realm or war, a relational pattern previously unknown in Nepalese history. This asymmetry has transformed heroism into martyrdom. This construction of difference requires a strong symbolic apparatus,

[56] An image frequently used. See, for example, Balavati Sharma ('Bhalukholama shahadat prapta garnu hune mahan sahidharuprati hardik sraddhasuman'), or the following poem by Tara Nepal, 'Yuddha ho nirmam huncha' (War is cruel):

> War teaches us war,
> the forge of the conflict creates steel,
> war purifies the party.

which rests more on 'The Thought' than on social or economic factors. The 'revolutionary sacrifice' thus recalls the Brahmanic sacrifice, its complicated construction of equivalences, its abstraction and autonomy vis-à-vis the social organization. It differs from war, which involves two camps identical in nature and status, defined by the social order (which designates at birth who is to be a soldier and who not). However, although the lateralization is more developed on the revolutionary side than the royal one, the phenomena are bilateral, and the conflict presents a symmetrical asymmetry. Indeed, Maoists are also denied the noble status of warrior by being represented as terrorists, and a list of their 'atrocities' are published daily in government newspapers. While they depict themselves as heroic human weapons, the government claims that they use human shields in their attacks. In addition, both sides contain numerous, similar ideas related to martyrdom, as illustrated in this homage to the martyrs of the RNA on its website:

I regret that I have but one life to give for my country.
One crowded hour of glorious life is worth an age without a name.
Let us not mourn for the men who have died fighting,
But rather let us be glad that such heroes have lived.

The political situation is perceived as social pathology and the country is considered 'sick'. For the Maoist poet, it is a necessary evil, provoked by the red warriors of the apocalypse in order to prepare the place for the advent of 'paradise on earth', a world cleansed of tigers, vultures and wolves, whoever they may be:

From Mount Sailung at the East,
The Red People, playing the war drum
With red mourner's scarves tied on the heads,
Came on the road...
From the Cure hills, at the West
Red People blowing the trumpet of revolt and
Carrying rifles on their shoulders
Approached on the plain...
Lightening flashed across the sky
Seisms shook the earth, it was turned upside down,
The bloody ocean took away the butchers in charge of cleaning up the blood.
In the heart of a moonless night a lightening flashed
In the middle of the night the sun rose up.
Frightened, the white tiger entered the trap

Everywhere the music of revolt resounded.
In the middle of the battle, the red men started to dance, laughing,
Mount Everest placed vermillion on his head
And shook the oppressed class
Awaking them
And sent them on the battlefield for their liberation
Everest resounded with the People's music of revolution and let the red flag
fly
The white wolves
Leaving the earth started to run away,
On the earth the red men rejoiced
On the earth the red men celebrated,
The terrible rays of the sun
Reduced the man-eating vultures to ashes;
They left the places, left the villages, left the cities
left the palaces and the houses.
The earth was overturned
Rules were re-established
The government was transformed.[57]

[57] Pokhrel, 'Au hami vijayako git gaon'.

Postscript

As anachronistic as the Nepalese People's War may appear in today's context of globalization and liberalization, its scale has increased over the years and the Maoist party—CPN (M)—actually won the April 2008 elections. This led to the abolishment of the Nepalese monarchy on 28 May 2008.

Following the assassination of King Birendra Shah in June 2001, and the coronation of his brother Gyanendra, the monarch became the main political target of the CPN (M) and the abolishment of monarchy its ultimate aim.

The Kingdom of Nepal was formed at the end of the 18th century, by the military unification of around 50 independent kingdoms by the Shah dynasty of Gorkha and its army. Thus created by the sword, the country knew neither colonization, nor civil war. The People's War launched in 1996 by the CPN (M) thus appears as a movement without precedent. But this does not mean that it cannot be understood as the result of history. Indeed, it occurred during a phase of weakening of royal power, induced by the popular uprising of 1990 and the multi-party Constitution which was then promulgated. In the following years political violence flourished as governments came and went ever more rapidly.

The CPN (M) party, initially small, formed the PLA, which grew and acquired sophisticated weapons through its successive achievements versus the police first of all, then versus the RNA following its mobilization in autumn 2001, a few months after the assassination of King Birendra, Queen Aishwarya, and six other members of the royal family. Rather than putting an end to the conflict, the mobilization of the army led to its intensification. Apart from urban centres and the fertile Tarai plain in the south, the government lost control over the country to the CPN (M), which established People's Governments at village and district levels, setting in motion a cultural revolution and putting and encouraging a war economy. Because it was no longer possible to organize elections, Nepal went through a period of extreme instability, and King Gyanendra finally assumed absolute power on 1 February 2005. He suspended rights of association and expression and organised municipal elections, without consulting the political parties. This brought together the various parties around the need to revive democracy, so they boycotted the royal elections. Then, seven political parties (including the Nepali Congress [NC] and the CPN Unified Marxist-Leninist–[UML]) formed the Alliance of Seven Parties (ASP) with the Maoists (CPN [M]) in December 2005. The PLA stepped up its action during the winter of 2006 by attacking several district headquarters and by leading attacks near the capital. Soon after, in April 2006, an unprecedented popular uprising organized by the major political parties persuaded the king to hand over power, which he did in a television broadcast just before midnight on 24 April 2006.

On 18 May 2006, an interim parliament stripped the king of his powers and proclaimed Nepal a democratic secular state.

The peace agreement signed in November 2006 ended 10 years of civil war which is estimated at having caused 13,000 deaths, with thousands wounded, displaced, and missing. The United Nations monitored the PLA's soldiers and weaponry. A provisional constitution was drafted and elections for a constituent assembly organized.

In spring 2007 the interim parliament decided that the future state model would be a federal one. The ultimate decision regarding the restructuring of the state and the federal system will be carried out as determined by the Constituent Assembly.

Elections set for June and then for November 2007 were postponed until 10 April 2008 since the parties were unable to agree on the voting system for the Constituent Assembly.

No one had forecast its results.

Contrary to all expectations, the former rebel Maoists won 40 per cent of the seats, way ahead of the NC and the UML. It created havoc among the latter. After numerous episodes including the resignation of the UML general secretary (M.K. Nepal) and the leader of the Nepali Congress' (G.P. Koirala) refusal to leave his position as the prime minister, the first session of the Constituent Assembly took place on 28 May 2008. The deputies proclaimed Nepal a republic and abolished the 240-year old Nepalese monarchy.

In June 2008, the political parties agreed on the merging of the two previously opposing armies: the PLA and the former RNA, renamed the Nepal Army in spring 2006.

Although the United States still has the Maoists on its list of proscribed terrorist organizations, the CPN (M)'s two leaders (Pushpa Dahal, known as Prachanda the Terrible, and Baburam Bhattarai) have done everything possible to reassure people by declaring that they are ready to work with other parties to establish a democracy. They have stressed their commitment to a new kind of revolution: an economic revolution along modern capitalist lines.

The question of monarchy thus seems to be definitively settled, but the King's supposedly unifying role of the multi-ethnic Nepalese population has not yet found any substitute. However, the future nation will be polycentric since the next challenge for the Republic is to build a federation. The process will probably again revive ethnic feelings and demands. The creation of 'New Nepal' thus evokes a de-unification of the country by the people, 240 years after its unification by the king. However, both the people and the king are abstract figures of agency and legitimacy, embodying complex and fluctuating social and political phenomena. And, if the first of the three prepositions making up the title of this volume, Hindu Kingship, seems to be relegated to the past by the recent abolition of monarchy, it will no doubt survive in various institutions, such as patriarchy, divine sovereignty, and holy leadership of sacrificial war.

Bibliography

Acharya, Baburam, *A Brief Biography of the Great King Prithvi Narayan Shah*, 3 Vols, Kathmandu: Regmi Research Project (English translation of Sri 5 Badamaharajadhiraj Prthvinarayan Sahko Samksipta Jivani, 2024 VS/1967), 1967.

——, 'General Bhimsen Thapa and the Samar Jung Company', *Regmi Research Series* 4 (9), 1972, pp. 161-7.

——, 'Social Changes During the Early Shah Period', *Regmi Research Series* 7 (9), 1975, pp. 163-72.

Agrim, 'Mero dayari yasari adhurai rahyo' (My unfinished diary), *Janadesh*, 13 (47), 2004, www.cpnm.org.

Ajanta Standard Dictionary Nepali-English, edited by 'three authors' [sic]. Delhi: Ajanta Prakashan, n.d.

Ale Magar, K.E., 2050 VS/1993, 'Kuriti hatau, samajlai bacau' (Let Us Suppress the Bad Customs, and Save the Society), *Soni*, 2 (2): 7.

Ale Magar, Suresh, 2050 VS/1993, 'Nepal Magar Sangh: Itihasdekhi vartamansamma' (The Nepal Magar Association: past and present), *Lapha*, 1 (6): 18–19.

Anonymous, 'Magarharuka kamajoriharau ke ke hun ?' *Soro*, 1 (1), 2053 VS/1996, p. 16.

Anonymous, 'Ghaite shivirma cahalpahal' (Pleasing experiences at the medical section), *Janawaaj*, 1 (39–40), 2002, www.cpnm.org.

Anonymous, 'Sahid parivar bhanchan: Luga hoina samaj badalnuparcha' (The Family of the Martyrs says: It is Not the Clothing it is the Society that We Should Change), *Janadesh* 12 (15), 2003, www.cpnm.org.

Anonymous, 'Janayuddha balidan sangh bankeko bhela sampanna' (What are the Magars' weaknesses?) (A meeting of the People's War Sacrifice Association took place in Banke), *Janadesh*, 13 (19), 2004, www.cpnm.org.

Anonymous, 'Hatyara Gyanendra ra Parasko putla goi hani jalaiyo' (The Effigies of Criminal Gyanendra and Paras were Shot and Burnt), *Janadesh*, 13 (24), 2004, www.cpnm.org.

Anonymous, 'Interview with Comrade Parvati', *People's March, Voice of the Indian Revolution*, 5 (10), 2004, www.cpnm.org.

Anu, 'Muktiko nisvas pherne cahancha—svatantra' (It is Needed to Breathe Freely—Democracy), *Janaawaj*, 1 (39–40), 2002, www.cpnm.org.

Bahu, 'Mero mastishkama sajieko mansir 8 gate' (My Brain is Illuminated by the 8th of Mansir), *Janawaaj*, 1 (39–40), 2002, www.cpnm.org.

Baral Magar, Kesar Jang, 2050 VS/1993, *Palpa, Tanahu ra Syangjaka Magarharuko Samskrti* (The Culture of the Magars of Palpa, Tanahun and Syangja), Kathmandu: Nepal Rajakiya Pragya-Pratisthan.

Baral, L. Sharma, 'Life and Writings of Prithinarayan Shah', Ph.D. thesis, University of London, 1964.

Benveniste, Emile, *Le vocabulaire des institutions indo-européennes. 1. Economie, parenté, société*, Paris: Ed. de Minuit, 1969.

Bhagat, Satyanarayan, 'Nepalma madhesko varga-samgharsa: Ek samksipta adhyayan' (A Short Study on the Class Struggle in the Plain of Nepal), *Janaawaj*, 1 (41), December 2002, www.cpnm.org.

Bhattarai, Baburam, 'The New "Kot Massacre" should not be Accepted', 2001a, www.humanrights.de.

——, 'The Birth of a Republic', 2001b, www.insof.org.

——, 'A Communication from the Revolutionaries in Nepal on the Current (September 2002) Situation in the Civil War', *Monthly Review*, 5 September 2002.

Bhattarai, H., 2058 VS/2001, 'Kāṭṭe khane-khvaune itihas' (A History of Eating and Feeding Kāṭṭe), *Madhuparka*, 34, www.nepalnews.com.

Bista, Dor Bahadur, *Fatalism and Development. Nepal's Struggle for Modernization*, Calcutta: Orient Longman, 1991.

Bista, D.B., R. Shah, H. Budha Magar and M.S. Thapa Magar, 'Vartaman Rajako Purkha Magar Hun ya Ksatriya?' (Are the Ruling King's Ancestors Magar or Kshatriya?), *Lapha*, 4 (12–13), 1995, pp. 1–12.

Bista, K. Birtinidhi, 1975, 'The Crown and Nepal', *The Rising Nepal, Coronation Special*, 24 February, pp. 57–8.

Bista, K.B., *Le culte du Kuldevata au Népal en particulier chez certains Kshatri de la vallée de Kathmandou*, Paris: CNRS, 1972.

Bista, Lokendra, 'Thik yatibela' (Just at that time), *Janaawaj*, 1 (36), 2002, www. cpnm.org.

Bloch, Marc, *Les rois thaumaturges* (with an introduction by J. Le Goff), Paris: Gallimard, 1983.

Bouillier, Véronique, 'Du bon usage des brahmanes: les Bâhun et l'État népalais', *Journal asiatique*, 283 (2), 1995, pp. 445–68.

——, 'The Royal Gift to the Ascetics: The Case of the Caughera Yogi Monastery', *Studies in Nepali History and Society*, 3 (2), 1998, pp. 213–38.

Bourdieu, Pierre, *Esquisse d'une théorie de la pratique, précédée de trois études d'ethnologie kabyle*, Paris/Genève: Droz, 1972.

——, *La distinction, critique sociale du jugement*, Paris: ed. de Minuit, 1979.

Buda Magar, Harsha Bahadur, 2049 VS/1992, *Kirat vams ra Magarharu* (The Kirant group and the Magars), Lalitpur: U. Bohora (ed.).

——, 2054 VS/1997, *Rastraka gaurav tatha Nepalka pratham sahid Lakhan Thapa Magar (dvitiya)* (The Nation's Pride and Nepal's First Martyr Lakhan Thapa Magar [the second]), Kathmandu: P. Buda Magar ed.

Buda Magar, Harsha Bahadur (ed.), *Magar-Roman-Nepali-Limbu-English Dictionary*, Kathmandu: Lakhan Sraddhanjali Samiti, 1993.

Budha Magar, Kulman, 'Nepali janayuddhama sahadat ek bharatiya Ka. Gopi' (Gopi, an Indian Comrade Martyred in the Nepalese People's War), *Janadesh*, 13 (27), 2004, www.cpnm.org.

Budhathoki Magar, Guman Simha, 2049 VS/1993, 'Adibasi Magar ra Nepal bhumiko sambandha tatha namakaran' (The Autochthonous Magars, Their Relation with the Earth and with Toponymy), *Lapha*, 1 (3), p. 9.

Burghart, Richard, 'Gifts to the Gods: Power, Property and Ceremonial in Nepal', in *Rituals of Royalty*, D. Cannadine and S. Price (eds), Cambridge: Cambridge University Press, 1987.

Campbell, Gabriel, 'Consultations with Himalayan Gods. A Study of Oracular Religion and Alternatives Values in Hindu Jumla', Ph.D. thesis, Columbia University, 1978.

Caplan, Lionel, *Warrior Gentleman: 'Gurkhas' in the Western Imagination*, Oxford: Berghahn, 1995.

Cataut, R.D. 'prabhas', *Dotyali brihat sabdakos* (The Great Dictionary of Dotyali), Kathmandu: Belu-Bishwa Smriti Pratishthan, 2001.

Cavenagh, Captain Orfeur, *Rough Notes on the State of Nepal, its Government, Army, and Resources*, Calcutta: W. Palmer, Military Orphan Press, 1851.

Chandrasekharan, S., 'Nepal Update No. 13: Provide Political Space for the Maoists', *South Asia Analysis Group*, 2001, www.saag.org.

Chaulagai, Yuvaraj, 'Au Yuyutsu' (Come, Yuyutsu), *Janadesh*, 13 (25), 2004, www.cpnm.org.

Dabaral 'Charan', S. P., 1987, 'From the Yamuna to the Sutlej', *Regmi Research Series*, no. 4, 1987, pp. 43–54.

Dahal, Dilli R., 'The Fallout of Deviant Anthropology', *Himal*, May 1996.

——, 'Social Composition of the Population. Caste/Ethnicity and Religion in Nepal', 2003, www.cbs.gov.np.

Dandin, *Histoire des dix princes*, Translated by Marie-Claude Porcher, Paris: Gallimard, 1995.

Darlami, Niru, 'Kamared Vishal lagayatko shahadatle krantilai ajhai ucaima puryaune cha' (With the Martyrdom of Comrade Vishal, the Revolution Reached a New Height), *Janadesh*, 13 (47), 2004, www.cpnm.org.

Dekobra, 'Le Népal, royaume interdit', *L'illustration*, 3 August 1929, pp. 110–17.

Dipak, 'Rukumkot Raid: A Live Broadcasting', *Revolutionary Worker*, 11-12, July 2001, rwor.org.

Dixit, K.M. and S. Ramachandaran (eds), *State of Nepal*, Kathmandu: Himal Books, 2002.

Dollfus, P., Lecomte-Tilouine, M. and Aubriot, O., 'Les cultures à l'épreuve du temps: Esquisse d'une histoire de l'agriculture en Himalaya', in *Histoire et devenir des paysages en Himalaya*, J. Smadja (ed.), pp. 273-316, Paris: CNRS, 2003.

Dumont, Louis, *Homo hierarchicus, Le système des castes et ses implications*, Paris: Gallimard, 1966.

——, *Homo Hierarchicus: The Caste System and its Implications*, (complete revised English edition), Chicago: The University of Chicago Press, 1980.

Durkheim, Emile, *Les règles de la méthode sociologique*, Paris: PUF, 1981 [1937].

Fisher, J., *Living Martyrs*, Delhi: Oxford University Press, 1997.

Foucault, Michel, *Raymond Roussel*, Paris: Gallimard, 1963.

——, *L'ordre du discours*, Paris: Gallimard, 1970.

——, *Histoire de la sexualité 1. La volonté de savoir*, Paris: Gallimard, 1976.

——, *Dits et écrits 1, De la nature humaine, justice contre pouvoir*, Paris: Gallimard, 1994.

—— (ed.), *Moi Pierre Rivière, ayant égorgé ma mère, mon frère et ma soeur*, Paris: Gallimard, 1994.

Fuchs, Stephen, *Godmen on the Warpath: A Study of Messianic Movements in India*, New Delhi: Munshiram Manoharlal, 1992.

Gaborieau, Marc, 'Note préliminaire sur le dieu Masta', *Objets et Mondes*, IX (1), 1969, pp. 19-50.

——, 'Le partage du pouvoir entre les lignages dans une localité du Népal central', *L'Homme*, XVIII (1-2), 1978, pp. 37-67.

Fürer-Haimendorf, C. Von, 1964, *The Sherpas of Nepal : Buddhist Highlanders*, London, John Murray.

Gell, A., 'Exalting the King and Obstructing the State: A Political Interpretation of Royal Ritual in Bastar District, Central India', *Journal of the Royal Anthropological Institute*, 3 (3), 1997, pp. 433-55.

Gellner, David N., 'From Literature to Linguistics to Culture: An Interview with K. P. Malla', *European Bulletin of Himalayan Research*, 11, 1996, pp. 37-52.

—— (ed.), *Resistance and the State: Nepalese Experiences*, New Delhi: Social Science Press, 2003.

Gharti Magar, Lila Kumari, 2052 VS/1995, 'Magar samajma bhaeka kamajoriharu ra kehi ramra paksaharu' (The Weak Aspects and Some Good Aspects of the Magar Society), *Magar jagaran*, 1 (1), pp. 33-6.

Gharti Magar, Om Bahadur, 2052 VS/1995, 'Nepal Magar vidhyarthi samgha ra Magar jatiko samksipta cinari' (A Short Presentation of the Magar Student Association and of the Magar Group), *Magar jagaran*, 1 (1), pp. 1-5.

Ghayal, Batans, 'Sahid ka. Vikalpalai gumaundako ksana' (The Moment of Martyr Vikalpa's Departure), *Janawaaj*, 1, 2002, pp. 39–40, www.cpnm. org.

Giri, Gitu, 2052 VS/1995, *Pyuthan Rajyako Aitihasik Jhalak*, Pyuthan: Jilla Bikas Samiti.

Gurung, Jagaman, 2036 VS/1979, 'Alamdevi Lasargha', *Indu*, (Asar), pp. 11–16.

Gurung, Laksmi, 'Mrityulai angalisakeki chu' (I Have Embraced Death), *Janaawaj*, 1 (43), 2003, www.cpnm.org.

Gutschow, N. and Kölver, B., *Ordered Space Concepts and Functions in a Town of Nepal*, Wiesbaden: Kommissionsverlag F. Steiner GMBH, 1975.

Gyawali, Isvarcandra, 'Hami ra uniharu' (We and They), *Janaawaj*, 1 (51), 2003, www.cpnm.org.

Gyawali, S.B., 1990 VS/1933, *Sri Drabya Sahako Jivan Caritra va Gorkha Vijayako Itihas* (The Life of Drabya Shah and the History of the Victory of Gorkha), Darjeeling: Nepali Sahitya Sammelan.

Hacchhethu, Krishna, *Party Building in Nepal*, Kathmandu: Mandala Book Point, 2002.

Hamayon, Roberte, *La chasse à l'âme*, Nanterre: Société d'ethnologie, 1990.

Hamilton, Francis Buchanan, 'Some Observations on Nepal (watermark 1802), by Francis Buchanan-Hamilton', Manuscript MSS.Eur E.68 kept at the India Office, British Library, G.-B, 1802 (?).

——, *An Account of the Kingdom of Nepal*, New Delhi: Asian Educational Service, 1986 [1819].

'Hamro 10vata mag pura bhaeko chaina' (Our 10 claims were not fulfilled), *Lapha*, 2 (7), 2050 VS/1993.

Hardiman, D., 'The Bhils and Shahukars of Eastern Gujarat', in *Subaltern Studies V*, R. Guha (ed.), New Delhi: Oxford University Press, 1987.

Hasrat, B.J., *History of Nepal*, Hoshiarpur: Research Institute Press, 1970.

Heusch, Luc de, 'The Symbolic Mechanisms of Sacred Kingship: Rediscovering Frazer', *Journal of the Royal Anthropological Institute*, 3 (2), 1997, pp. 213–32.

——, *Les rois de Kongo et les monstres sacrés*, Paris: Gallimard, 2000.

Hitan Magar, Jaya Bahadur, 2043 VS/1986, 'Nepalma hami kina pachi paryau?' (Why are We Behind in Nepal?), *Kongpi*, 6 (1), pp. 5–12.

——, 2056 VS/1999, 'Adibasi mangol janajati bhanne avaj' (The Voice of the Mangol Minorities), *Konja-Marum*, 2 (5), pp. 21–23.

Hocart, A.M., *Kings and Councillors: An Essay in the Comparative Anatomy of Human Society*, Chicago: Chicago University Press, 1970.

——, 'The Basis of Caste', in *Imagination and Proof. Selected essays of A.M. Hocart*, R. Needham (ed.), pp. 95–108, Tucson: The University of Arizona Press, 1987.

Hodgson, Brian H., *Hodgson Papers*, India Office Collection, British Library, n.d.

——, *Essays on the Languages, Literature and Religion of Nepal and Tibet*, New Delhi: Manjushri Publishing House, 1972 [1874].

Höfer, Andras, *The Caste Hierarchy and the State in Nepal. A Study of the Mulukī Ain of 1854*, Innsbruck: Universitätsverlag Wagner, 1979.

Hopkins, W., *Epic Mythology*, New York: Biblo and Tannen, 1969.

Human Rights Movement in Nepal, anonymous text published by Human Rights Internet.

Hutt, Michael, 'Reading Sumnima', in *Ethnic Revival and Religious Turmoil: Identities and Representation in the Himalayas*, M. Lecomte-Tilouine and P. Dollfus (eds), pp. 23–38, New Delhi: Oxford University Press, 2003.

Hutt, Michael (ed.), *Himalayan People's War': Nepal's Maoist Rebellion*, London: Curzon, 2003.

Inden, R.B., 'Hierarchies of Kings in Early Medieval India', *Contributions to Indian Sociology*, 15 (1–2), 1981, pp. 99–125.

Jest, Corneille, 'Traditions et croyances religieuses des habitants de la vallée de Tichurong (nord-ouest du Népal)', *L'Ethnographie* 65, 1971, pp. 66–86.

Joshi, Bhuwan Lal and Leo Rose, *Democratic Innovations in Nepal*, Berkeley: University of California Press, 1966.

Joshi, G., 2022 VS/ 1965, *Vir caritra*, edited and introduced by Kamal Diksit, Lalitpur: Jagadamba Prakashan.

K.C. Prakriti, 'Feudalism: A Beginner's Interpretation', *The Kathmandu Post*, 15 March 2000.

Kadam, 'Muktikami gaineko git' (The Song of the Minstrel Acting for Liberation), *Janaawaj*, 1 (35), 2002, www.cpnm.org.

Kalpana, 'Benima jivansathi Ka. Yoddhako sahadatpachi sangalo anubhutiharu' (My Feelings After the Martyrdom of My Life Companion, Yoddha, in Beni), *Janadesh*, 13 (28), 2004, www.cpnm.org.

Kauca Magar, Balkrishna, 2055 VS/1998, 'Pratham Sahid Lakhan Thapa Magarprati apaman ki irsya' (Disobedience or Rivalry Towards the First Martyr Lakhan Thapa Magar), *Janajati manc*, 4 (1).

Kawakita, Jiro, *The Hill Magars and Their Neighbours*, Tokyo: Tokai University Press, 1974.

Khapangi Magar, Gore Bahadur, 2053 VS/1996, 'Ma bahunko haina bahunvadko virodh gardachu' (I am not Fighting against Bahuns but against Bahunism), *Kanung lam*, 2 (3), pp. 6–9.

Kirkpatrick William, *An Account of the Kingdom of Nepaul*, New Delhi: Manjushri Publishing House, 1969 [1811].

Kraemer, K.-H., 'Requiring a Social History: Must Nepali History be Re-written?', in *Nepal: Myths and Realities*, P. Thapa and J. Baaden (eds), pp. 499–520, New Delhi: Book Faith India, 2000.

Krauskopff, Gisèle, *Maîtres et possédés*, Paris: CNRS, 1989.

——, 'An "Indigenous Minority" in a Border Area', in *Resistance and the State: Nepalese Experiences*, D. Gellner (ed.), pp. 199–243, New Delhi: Social Science Press.

Krauskopff, G. and M. Lecomte-Tilouine (eds), *Célébrer le pouvoir. Dasai, une fête royale au Népal*, Paris: CNRS Éd./Éd. de la MSH, 1996.

Krauskopff, G. and P. Duel Meyer (eds), *The Kings of Nepal and the Tharu of the Tarai*, Paris: Rusca Press and CNAS, Los Angeles, Kirtipur, 2000.

Ksitij, 'Ranabhumibata sandesh' (Message from battlefield), *Janadesh* 13 (17), 2004, www.cpnm.org.

Kunwar, Cetan, 'Janamukti sena yasari samarpit hundeichan mahilaharu' (Women are Dedicated to the People's Liberation Army), *Janadesh* 12 (15), 2003, www.cpnm.org.

Lacôte, F., *L'histoire romanesque d'Udayana, roi de vatsa*, translation, introduction and notes by F. Lacôte, Paris: Ed. Bossard, 1924.

La cité d'or et autres contes, translation and introduction by L. Verschaeve, Paris: Gallimard, 1979.

Lapha Magar, Samjog, 2053 VS/1996, 'Budho dharahara ra ma' (The Old Pillar and Me), *Kanung lam*, 2 (1), p. 33.

——, 2054 VS/1997, 'Nepalko pratham sahid kaptan Lakhan Thapa Magar', (Nepal's First Martyr Captain Lakhan Thapa Magar), *Raha* 4 (3), pp. 14–15.

Lawoti, Mahendra, 'Racial Discrimination toward the Indigenous Peoples in Nepal', Non-Government Report for the Third World Conference Against Racism (WCAR)-2001, Report presented at the National Conference of the NPC in Kathmandu, 26 April 2001.

Lecomte-Tilouine, Marie, 'Hommes/divinités de la forêt. A travers le miroir au Népal central', *Etudes Rurales*, CVII-CVIII, 1987, pp. 55–69.

——, 'Pouvoir tribal et hindouisme en Himalaya. Le symbolique et ses transformations chez les Magar de Gulmi (Népal central)', Ph.D. thesis, EHESS, Paris, 1991.

——, *Les dieux du pouvoir*, Paris: CNRS, 1993a.

——, 'The Proof of the Bone. Lineage and Devali in Central Nepal', *Contributions to Indian Sociology*, 27 (1), 1993b, pp. 1–23.

——, 'About Bhume. A Misunderstanding in the Himalayas', in *Nepal. Past and Present*, G. Toffin (ed.), pp. 127–34, Pari: CNRS, 1993c.

——, 'Des dieux aux sommets', in 'Classer les dieux?', V. Bouillier and G. Toffin (eds), *Purushartha* 15, pp. 153–72, Paris: EHESS, 1993d.

——, 'Les dieux-sabres', in *Célébrer le pouvoir. Dasai, une fête royale au Népal*, G. Krauskopff and M. Lecomte-Tilouine (eds), pp. 243–82, Paris: CNRS Ed./Ed. de la MSH, 1996.

——, 'On Francis Buchanan Hamilton's Account of the Kingdom of Nepal', *European Bulletin of Himalayan Research*, 14, 1998 pp. 46–75.

——, 'The Two Kings of Musikot', in *Resunga. The Mountain of the Horned Sage*, P. Ramirez (ed.), pp. 143–70, Kathmandu: Himal Books, 2000a.

——, 'The Avatars of Varaha in the Himalayas', in *Himalaya: Past and Present*, V, M.P. Joshi, A.C. Fanger and C.W. Brown (eds), pp. 127–72, Almora: Shree Almora Book Depot, 2000b.

——, 'Ethnic Demands within Maoism. Questions of Magar Territorial Autonomy, Nationality and Class', in *Himalayan People's War*, Michael Hutt (ed.), pp. 112–35, London: Hurst & Co., 2004.

——, 'The Ruling of the Social Groups, from Species to Nation: Some Reflections on Ethnicity in Nepal', in *Ethnic Activism and Civil Society in South Asia*, David Gellner (ed.), New Delhi : Sage Publications, forthcoming.

——, (ed.), *Bards and Mediums : History, Culture and Politics in the Central Himalayan Kingdoms*, Almora: Shree Almora Book Depot, forthcoming.

Lecomte-Tilouine, M. and C. Michaud, 'From the Mine to the Fields: History of the Exploitation of the Slope in Darling (Gulmi)', in *Resunga. The Mountain of the Horned Sage*, P. Ramirez (ed.), pp. 222–64, Kathmandu: Himal Books, 2000.

Lévi, Sylvain, *Le Népal. Étude historique d'un royaume hindou*, 2 Vols, Paris: Leroux, 1905.

Licchavi Magar 2050 VS/1993, 'Ojhelma pardei sabda "Langhali"' (Langhali, a term under shadow), *Lapha*, 6, p. 12.

Lungeli Magar, Sala, 2054 VS/1997, 'Magar samajko adikavi Jit Bahadur Sijali Magar' (Jit Bahadur Sijali Magar, first poet of the Magar society), *Raha*, 4 (3), pp. 19–20.

Maharjan, Pancha, 'The Maoist Insurgency and Crisis of Governability in Nepal', in *Domestic Conflict and crisis of Governability in Nepal*, D. Kumar (ed.), pp. 163–196, Kathmandu: CNAS, 2000.

Malamoud, Charles, *Le jumeau solaire*, Paris: Seuil, 2002.

Maskarinec, Gregory, *The Rulings of the Night*, Madison: University of Wisconsin Press, 1995.

Mayer, Adrian, 'The King's Two Thrones', *Man* (n.s.) 20, 1985, pp. 205–21.

Mecidekhi Mahakali, 2031 VS/1974, 4 Vols, Kathmandu: Shri Panchko Sarkar.

Mehta, Major General Ashok K., 'Trouble in the World's Last Shangrila', 2000, www.rediff.com.

Metcalfe, C.T., *The Rajput Tribes*, New Delhi: Cosmo Pub, 1982.

Meyer, Kurt, 'Introduction', in *The Kings of Nepal and the Tharu of the Tarai*, G. Krauskopff and P. Deuel Meyer (eds), Kirtipur: CNAS, 2000.

Munamkarmi, L., 2047 VS/1990, 'Bhaktapur darbar ra 99 cok', *Nepali Samskriti* 6 (3), pp. 38–50.

Naraharinath, Yogi (ed.), 2013 VS/1956, *Itihas Prakas* Vol. 1, Part 2, Vol. 2, Part 3, Mrigasthali: Itihas Prakash Sangh.

——, 1880 Sake/1958, *Rudraksaranayamahatmyam (Kausikipradesko itihas)*, Varanasi: Yogapracarini.

——, 2016 VS/1959, *Divya Upades*, Kathmandu: Shri Bagishvara chapakhana.

——, 2021 VS/1964, *Gorkha Vamshavali*, Kasi: Aryabirsangh.

——, 2022 VS/1965, *Itihas Prakasma Sandhipatra Samgraha*, Varanasi: Kalpana Press.

Naraharinath, Yogi and Krishnabahadur Gurung, 2020 VS/1963, *Srigurung Magar Vamsavali*.

Nepal, Gyanamani, 2040 VS/1983, 'Siddha autariko rajain garne utkantha' (The Human Reincarnation's Desire to Reign), *Pragya*, 12 (2, 44), pp. 40–6.

Nepal, Tara, 'Yuddha ho nirmam huncha' (War is Cruel), *Janaawaj*, 1 (35), 2002, www.cpnm.org.

'Nepalko itihas rajbhogmala' (The Rulers of Nepal History), *Ancient Nepal*, (7), 1969, pp. 1–24; (8), 1969, pp. 1–24; (9), 1969, pp. 1–24; (11), 1970, pp. 1–17.

Ojha, G., 'King's "Sacrifice" Needed for Political Stability: Experts', *The Kathmandu Post*, 2 June 2003.

Onesto, Li, 'Red Flag Flying on the Roof of the World, Inside the Revolution in Nepal: Interview with Comrade Prachanda', *Revolutionary Worker*, 1043, 20 February 2000, www.revcom.us.

Oppitz, Michael, 'The Wild Boar and the Plough', *Kailash*, X (1), 1983, pp. 187–226.

——, 'Die Trommel und das Buch', in *Formen kulturellen Wandels und andere Beiträge zur Erforschung des Himalaya*, B. Kölver and S. Liehnard (eds), pp. 53–126, Sankt-Augustin, VGH-Wissenschaftverlag, 1986.

——, *Frau für Fron, Die Dreierallianz bei den Magar West-Nepals*, Frankfurt: Suhrkamp, 1988.

Pahadi, Satya, 'Hamro jindagi' (Our Life), *Janadesh*, 12 (18), 2003, www.cpnm.org.

Panjiar, Tej Narayan, 'In My Own Words', in *The Kings of Nepal and the Tharu of the Tarai*, G. Krauskopff and P. Deuel Meyer (eds), pp. 49–55, Kirtipur: CNAS, 2000.

Pant, Divyadeva, 1992 VS/1935, *Shahavamsha-caritam*, Kashi: R.M. Pallasule ed.

Pant, Mahes Raj and Dines Raj Pant, 'King Mukunda Sen's Invasion of Kathmandu Valley', *Regmi Research Series*, 13 (12), 1981, pp. 182–4; 14 (1/2), 1982, pp. 5–17, 14 (3/4), pp. 43–9, 14 (5), pp. 69–72, 14 (6), pp. 90–6, 14 (7), pp. 100–2, 14 (8), pp. 113–19, 14 (9), pp. 129–33.

Pasang, 2060 VS/2003, 'Yuddhako ek tippani' (Notes on War), in *Janakranti*, 7 (4), www.cpnm.org.

Paudel, N. (ed.), 2020 VS/1963, *Bhasha vamshavali*, 2 Vols, Kathmandu: Puratatva Bibhag.

Pignède, Bernard, *Les Gurungs: Une population himalayenne du Népal*, Paris: Mouton, 1966.

Pfaff-Czarnecka, J., 'A Battle of Meanings', *Kailash*, 18 (3–4), 1996, pp. 57–92.

Pokharel, Dhaneshvar, 'Au hami vijayako git gaon' (Come, Let Us Too Sing the Song of Victory), *Janadesh*, 14 (23), 2005.

Pokharel, Sanjeev, 'Maoist War: Violence Between Hope and Sorrow', Paper presented at the meeting of the Norway-Nepal Association, Oslo, 29 October 2002.

Poudyal, R.R., 'The Coronation—Some Interesting Rituals', *The Rising Nepal, Coronation Special*, Kathmandu, 24 February 1975.

Prachanda, 'On the Massacre of the Royal Family in Nepal', 11 June 2001, www.insof.org.

Pradhan, Kumar, *A History of Nepali Literature*, New Delhi: Sahitya Akademi, 1984.

Prachanda and 'Other Leaders of the CPN (Maoist)', *Problems & Prospects of Revolution in Nepal*, A Collection of Articles by Com. Prachanda and Other Leaders of the CPN (Maoist), www.insof.org.

Pulami Magar, Thakur, 2052 VS/1995, 'Im'ko dhoka kholi herda' (Opening the Door of *Im* [=house in Magar] to see), *Im*, 1 (1), p. 3.

Pun, Tek Bahadur, 2060 VS/2003, 'Magar jatiko jatiya apaman "silanyas" natak', (The Play *Silanyas* Derogatory Towards the Magar Group), Kathmandu.

Punmagar, Dan Bahadur, 2050 VS/1993, *Magar Pujari ra Devasthalharu. Ek Adhyayan* (Magar Priests and Temples. A Research), Butwal: C. Sinjalimagar and M. Srismagar.

Quigley, Declan, 'Scapegoats: The Killing of Kings and Ordinary People', *Journal of the Royal Anthropological Institute*, 6 (2), 2000, pp. 237–54.

Rajesh, 'Melagairile punah tesro patak ragat bagaundako kshan' (When Blood Runs for the Third Time), *Janaawaj*, 1 (41), 2002, www.cpnm.org.

Rajvamshi, S. (ed.), 2020 VS/1963, *Sen Vamshavali* (The Sen Genealogy), Kathmandu: Rastriya Abhilekhalaya.

Ramirez, Philippe, 'Luttes d'influence dans l'empire de la Déesse', in *Célébrer le pouvoir*, G. Krauskopff and M. Lecomte-Tilouine (eds), pp. 209–42, Paris: CNRS/MSH, 1996.

——, 'Pour une anthropologie religieuse du maoïsme népalais', *Archives de sciences sociales des religions*, 99, 1997, pp. 47–68.

——, *De la disparition des chefs: Une anthropologie politique népalaise*, Paris: CNRS, 2000.

Ramjhan, 'The Hanuman Dhoka Royal Palace: A Brief Introduction', in *The Rising Nepal, Coronation Special*, Kathmandu, 24 February 1975, pp. 9–15.

Rana, Pudma Jung Bahadur, *Life of Maharaja Sir Jung Bahadur of Nepal*, Kathmandu: Ratna Pustak Bhandar, 1974 (1909).

Ranamagar, B.K., 2054 VS/1997, *Gorkha Magaraharu* (The Magars of Gorkha), Kathmandu: R. Ranamagar ed.

——, 'Maoist Insurgency from Magar Perspective', *The Kathmandu Post*, 29 March 2001.

Rana Magar, G.J., 2050 VS/1993, 'Samskarle thagieka Magar jati', (The Magar Group Cheated by the Life Cycle Rituals), *Gyāvāṭ*, Baisakh, pp. 21–4.

Rana Magar, Dol Bahadur, 2052 VS/1995, 'Nepal Magar samghko aitihasik ruparekha' (The Stages of the Nepal Magar Sangh History), *Magar Jagaran*, 1 (1), pp. 24–7.

Rana Magar, Tek Bahadur, 2052 VS/1995, 'Jatiya utthanko lagi "Nepal Magar samgha" ko sthapana' (The Creation of the Nepal Magar Sangh for the Promotion of the Group), *Magar Jagaran*, 1 (1), p. 45.

Ranabir, 'Jivan' (Life), *Janadesh*, 13 (47), 2004, www.cpnm.org.

Regmi, D.R., *Medieval Nepal, Part I*, Calcutta: Firma Mukhopadhyay, 1965.

——, *Medieval Nepal, Part II. A History of the Three Kingdoms 1520 A.D. to 1768 A.D.*, Calcutta: Firma Mukhopadhyay, 1966.

——, *Inscriptions of Ancient Nepal*, Vol. II, New Delhi: Abhinav Publications, 1983.

Regmi, M.C., *Land Tenure and Taxation in Nepal. IV: Religious and Charitable Land Endowments: Guthi tenure*, Berkeley, IIS: University of California, 1968.

——, 'Preliminary Notes on the Nature of the Gorkhali State and Administration', *Regmi Research Series*, 10 (11), 1978, pp. 171–4.

——, 'The Lakhan Thapa Affair', *Regmi Research Series*, 12 (5), 1980, pp. 72–5.

Regmi, Sudha, 'Bir sahid Ka. Ayamlai samjhada' (Remembering the Heroic Martyr, Comrade Ayam), *Janadesh*, 12 (15), 2003, www.cpnm.org.

Ricoeur, Paul, *L'idéologie et l'utopie*, Paris: Seuil, 1997.

Rima, 'Mero manaspatalma Ka. Rejina' (In the Deepest of My Mind, Comrade Rejina), *Janadesh*, 13 (47), 2004, www.cpnm.org.

Roka Magar, Jhum Bahadur, 2056 VS/1999, 'Pratham sahid Lakhan Thapa Magarko Mulyankan Ojhelma' (The Evaluation of the First Martyr Lakhan Thapa Kept Under Shade), *Sang*, 1 (1), pp. 7–10.

Sagant, Philippe, *Le paysan Limbu, sa maison et ses champs*, Paris: Mouton, 1976.

——, 'Traditions enfantines: l'apprentissage des techniques au Népal oriental', in *De la voûte céleste au terroir, du jardin au foyer*, B. Koechlin et al. (eds), pp. 629–35, Paris: EHESS, 1987.

——, 'Le double pouvoir chez les Yakhthumba', in *Célébrer le pouvoir. Dasai, une fête royale au Népal*, G. Krauskopff and M. Lecomte-Tilouine (eds), pp. 283–314, Paris: MSH/CNRS, 1996.

Said, Edward W., *Orientalism*, New York: Random House, 1979.

Sales, Anne de, 'Actes et paroles dans les rituels chamaniques des Kham-Magar', Ph.D. thesis, Université Paris X, Nanterre, 1985.

——, *Je suis né de vos jeux de tambours*, Nanterre: Société d'ethnologie, 1991.

——, 'The Kham Magar Country: Between Ethnic Claims and Maoism', *European Bulletin of Himalayan Research*, 19, 2000, pp. 41–72.

——, 'Remarks on Revolutionary Songs and Iconography', *European Bulletin of Himalayan Research*, 24, 2003, pp. 5–24.

Sampang, Bhumi, 'Janakrantidekhi janayuddhasamma' (From the People's Revolution to the People's War), *Sainik avaj*, (10) 11, 2002, pp. 13–14.

Sangkalpa, Untitled Song, *Janadesh*, 13 (47), 2004, www.cpnm.org.

Sangram, Jivan, 'Mutthi kascha bottle ksitijma herera' (Tightening the fist, Botle Looked at the Horizon), *Janadesh*, 12 (18), 2003, www.cpnm.org.

Sartre, Jean-Paul, *L'être et le néant*, Paris: Gallimard, 1943.

Sharma 'Dhakal', Nilahari, 2020 VS/1963, *Jutho sutak nirnaya* (Rules of Impurity), Varanasi.

Sharma, Balavati, 'Bhalukholama shahadat prapta garnu hune mahan sahidharuprati hardik sraddhasuman', (Homage to the Great Martyrs Martyred at Bhalukhola), *Janadesh*, 13 (27), 2004, www.cpnm.org.

Sharma, Deva, 'Dukh nai sukh ho' (Sorrow is Happiness), *Janaawaj*, 1 (43), 2003, www.cpnm.org.

Sharma, J.P. 'Coronation: The Indigenous Way to Ideal Government', in *The Rising Nepal, Coronation Special*, pp. 97–100, *The Kathmandu*, 24 February 1975.

Sharma, Janakalal, 2020 VS/1963, *Josmani santa parampara ra sahitya* (The Josmani Santa Tradition and its Literature), Kathmandu: Royal Nepal Academy.

Sharma, P.R., *Preliminary Study of the Art and Architecture of the Karnali Basin, West Nepal*, Paris: CNRS, 1972.

Sharma, Simana, Untitled Poem, *Janaawaj*, 1 (43), 2003, www.cpnm.org.

Shrestha-Schipper, Satya, 'Religion et pouvoir chez les Indo-Népalais de l'ouest du Népal', PhD thesis, Nanterre: Université Paris X, 2003.

Shrestha, Ganga, 'Pyaro mrityu' (Dear Death), *Janaawaj*, 1 (43), 2003, www.cpnm.org.

Shrestha, Kesar Lall, unpublished document, *Speaking Stones.*

Shrestha, C.B., 'Religious Aspects of the Auspicious Coronation', *The Rising Nepal, Coronation Special*, 24 February 1975, Kathmandu, pp. 33–5.

Singh, R.C.P., *Kingship in Northern India*, New Delhi: Motilal Banarsidass, 1968.

Sinha, B.C., *Hinduism and Symbol Worship*, New Delhi: Agam Ala Prakashan, 1983.

Sitalkumar, 'Dhvans ra nirmanko dvandvatmak visleshana' (A Dialectic Analysis of Destruction and Creation), *Janawaaj*, 1 (39–40), 2002, www.cpnm.org.

Sris Magar, Dharma Prasad, 2052VS/1995, '"Magar" jat nam kasari utpati bhayo ta?' (How Was Born the Name of *jat* 'Magar'?), *Im*, 1 (1), pp. 4–5.

Steinmann, Brigitte (ed.), *Le Maoïsme au Népal. Lectures d'une révolution*, Paris: CNRS éditions, 2006.

Stiller, Father L.F., 'A Letter of Fr. Guiseppe da Rovata (Dec. 29, 1769)', *Journal of the Tribhuvan University*, 5 (1), 1970, pp. 6–20.

——, *The Rise of the House of Gorkha: A Study of the Unification of Nepal, 1768–1816*, New Delhi: Manjusri Publishing House, 1973.

'Strategy and Tactics of Armed Struggle in Nepal', Text adopted by the Central Committee of the Maoist Party of Nepal, March 1995, www.cpnm.org.

Subedi, Chavi, 'Tera lashmathi gumne...' (Walking on your Corpse...), *Janaawaj*, 42, 2003, www.cpnm.org. Reprinted in *Janadesh*, 14 (11), February 2005.

Sushanta, 'Sahid Krishna Sen! Lalsalam!!' (Martyr Krishna Sen! Red Salute!!), *Janadesh* 13 (47), 2004, www.cpnm.org.

Svalok, 'Yad gar Narayanhiti' (Remember, Narayanhiti), *Janaawaj*, 1 (46), 2003, www.cpnm.org.

Tamang, Niresh, 'The Brahmin Stranglehold over Nepal', *Dalitstan Journal*, 1 (2), October 1999, online edition.

Tamang, Seira, 'Legitimating Marginalized Voices', *The Kathmandu Post Review of Books*, 3 (23), 28 March 1999, online edition.

Tawa-Lama, Stéphanie, 'Political Participation of Women in Nepal', in *State Leadership and Politics in Nepal*, D. Kumar (ed.), pp. 171–84, Kathmandu: CNAS, 1995.

Thapa, Deepak (ed.), *Understanding the Maoist Movement of Nepal*, Kathmandu: Martin Chautari, 2003).

Thapa, Dharmaraj, 2041 VS/1984, *Lok samskritiko gherama Lamjung* (Lamjung's Folk culture), Kathmandu: Sajha Prakashan.

——, 2050 VS/1993, *Citavan-darpan* (The Mirror of Citwan), Kamaladi: Nepal Rajakiya Pragya-Pratisthan.

Thapa 'Guruchan' Magar, Shivalal, 2047 VS/1990, *Magar Gurung vamsavali ra vartaman sadarbhama janajatiko samasya* (The Magar Gurung Genealogy and the Problem of Nationalities in the Present Context), I. Thapa Magar and S. Thapa Magar (eds), Damauli.

——, 2052 VS a/1996a, *Ojhelma pareka magarharu* (The Magars Kept Under Shade), I. Thapa Guruchan Magar and S. Thapa Guruchan Magar (eds), Tanahun.

——, 2052 VS b/1996b, 'Pratham Sahid Lakhan Thapamagar (dvitiya)' (The First Martyr Lakhan Thapamagar [the second]), *Soni* 4 (4), pp. 3–7.

Thapa Magar, Hira, 2052 VS/1995, 'Magar jatima hindukaranko asar' (The Influence of Hinduization on the Magar Group), *Magar jagaran*, 1 (1), pp. 7–8.

Thapa Magar, M.S., 2049 VS/1992a, *Pracin Magar ra Akkha lipi* (Ancient Magar and the Akkha Alphabet), Lalitpur: Vrji Prakashan.

——, 'Pratham Sahid Lakhan Thapa Magar', The First Martyr, Lakhan Thapa Magar, *Kairan*, January–February, 1992b, pp. 10–11.

——, 2052 VS/1995a, 'Dasai Tihar Magarharuko cadaparva ho ki hoina?' (Are Dasai and Tihar Magar festivals or not?), *Im*, 1 (1), pp. 9–10.

——, 2052 VS/1995b, 'Ke Dasai Tihar Magarharuko cadparva ho' (Are Dasai and Tihar Magar festivals?), *Kanung lam*, 1 (2), pp. 3–4.

Thapa, Mani, 'Purvako tin tara' (Three Stars of the East), *Janadesh*, 13 (28), 2004, www.cpnm.org.

Thapa, Pandava, 'Agoka muslobat umrieka kavitaharu. Dui' (The Poems Born from the Ignited Torch. Part II), *Janadesh*, 13 (27), 2004, www.cpnm. org.

Thapa, Ram Bahadur (Badal), 'Hami cunautiharuko mukabila garna jastosukai mulya cukauna pani tayar chaun' (We are Ready to Finish the Affront of the Challenges by All Means), *Janaawaj*, 1 (50–51), 2003, www.cpnm. org.

Thapa Magar, Sagar, 2057 VS/2000, 'Ahvan' ('The Waking Up'), *Kanung lam*, 6 (2), 2003, p. 18.

Thapa, Sushri Shiva, 2050 VS/1993, 'Gorkhali', *Gyāvat*, Baisakh, p. 51.

Thapar, Romila, *From Lineage to State*, New Delhi: Oxford University Press, 1984.

Timsina, N.N., 'Ridiculing Brahmanism', *The Kathmandu Post*, 21 June 2001, www.nepalnews.com.

Tod, James, *Annals and Antiquities of Rajasthan*, 3 Vols, New Delhi: Motilal Banarsidass, 1987 (1920).

Todorov, Tzvetan, *Poétique de la prose* (Paris: Seuil, 1978).

Toussaint, F., 'Mort et crémation du roi', 'Rites funèbres pour le roi', unpublished reports from the French Ambassador in Nepal to the French Foreign Minister, 1972.

Tower, Sargent L. and R. Schaer (eds), *Utopie, la quête de la société idéale en occident*, Paris: Bibliothèque Nationale de France/Fayard, 2000.

Tucci, Giuseppe, *Nepal. The Discovery of the Malla*, New York: Dutton, 1962.

Unbescheid, G., 'Blood and Milk or the Manifestation of the Goddess Manakamana', *Journal of the Nepal Research Centre*, 8, 1985, pp. 95–130.

Vajracarya, G., 2033 VS/1976, *Hanuman Dhoka rajdarbar* (The Royal Palace of Hanuman Dhoka), Kirtipur: CNAS.

Vajracharya, Dhanvajra, 2028 VS/1971, 'Karnali Pradesko Aitihasik Ruprekha' (Historical Sketch of the Karnali Region), in *Karnali Prades. Ek bito Adhyayan*, pp. 11–62, Jumla: Bhim Prasad Shrestha.

Vansittart, Eden, *Notes on Nepal*, New Delhi: Asian Ed. Services, 1982 (1896).

Vernant, Jean-Pierre, *L'univers, les dieux, les hommes*, Paris: Seuil, 1999.

Verschaene, *La cité d'or et antres contes*, Paris: Gallimard, 1979.

Vikas, 'Pyara pyara kamaredharuko samjhanama' (Remembering the Very Dear Friends), *Janadesh*, 13 (25), 2004, www.cpnm.org.

Vivash Yatri, 'Marne chaina kadapi jantako astha', (The People's Support will Never End), *Janadesh*, 12 (14), 2003, www.cpnm.org.

Whelpton, John, *Kings, Soldiers and Priests: Nepalese Politics 1830–1857*, New Delhi: Manohar, 1991.

Witzel, Michael, 'The Coronation Rituals of Nepal, with Special Reference to the Coronation of King Birendra (1975)', in *Heritage of the Kathmandu Valley*, N. Gutschow and A. Michaels (eds), pp. 415-67, Sankt Augustin: VGH Wissenschaftsverlag, 1987.

Wright, Daniel (ed.), *History of Nepal*, Delhi: Cosmo Publications, 1970 (1877).

Yami, Hisila, 2054 VS/1997, 'Sthaniya sattako avadharana' (A Reflection on Local Power), *Nava cetana*, 3 (1), pp. 31–40.

Index